# Indian Women Writing in English

## A Feminist Study

*Edited by*

**Sunita Sinha**

ATLANTIC

PUBLISHERS & DISTRIBUTORS (P) LTD

ATLANTIC
PUBLISHERS & DISTRIBUTORS (P) LTD

7/22, Ansari Road, Darya Ganj, New Delhi
Tel.: +91-11-4077 5252, 2327 3880
E-mail: orders@atlanticbooks.com
Web: www.atlanticbooks.com

Reprint 2018, 2026

Published by Atlantic Publishers & Distributors (P) Ltd.



Printed & bound in India by Atlantic Print Services

***A paean to L'ecriture feminine***

Dedicated to the pioneering coterie of profound women writers and poets the world over who evolved a rich literary legacy advocating education for women, freedom of expression, and egalitarian values which wields immense significance today.

# Contents

# Introduction

The emergence of feminism has been a matter of great enthusiasm to feminists and non-feminists alike since the earliest development of feminism as a concept. One decade into the twenty-first century, we have begun to speak of "feminisms" in the plural and affirm the amalgamation of various types of feminism with other fields of study, indicating a developing evolution of what feminism embraces.

Not too far from today, the rage at male domination or gender equality was all that was required to make one a feminist. In this context, Bell Hooks' definition of feminism in *Feminist Theory: From Margin to Centre* seems quite an eye opener—"Feminism is a movement to end sexism, sexist exploitation and oppression." This definition shatters the myth that feminism is all about "a bunch of angry women who want to be like men". It strongly underlines the notion that feminism is not a movement that is essentially an anti-male one, rather it is one, which creates fully self-actualized females and males to "live together, realizing our dreams of freedom and justice, living the truth that we are all created equal". The focus has shifted considerably from feminism being an anti-male campaign to feminism as a quest for gender justice. The time has come for all of us to realize that feminism requires a clearer definition and more strong efforts to end sexist oppression.

Feminism, as a novel way of life and as a rising aspect, came into being in India with the feminine psyche attempting to redefine woman's role in the society. Recent writers depict both the diversity of women and the diversity within each woman, rather than limiting the lives of women to one ideal. The novels emerging in the twenty-first century furnish examples of a whole range of attitudes towards the imposition of tradition, some offering an analysis of the family structure and the caste system as the key elements of patriarchal social organization. They also re-interpret mythology by using new symbols and subverting the canonic versions.

In the contemporary scenario there are many women writers who have been concerned with the complete absence or rather negative portrayal of women in literature. Therefore they seek to re-read patriarchal myths and in the process, they not only represent women from women's point of view, but also tend to rewrite the literary canon. From Toru Dutt to Kamala Das, Sarojini Naidu to Suniti Namjoshi, Arundhati Roy to Shashi Deshpande, and many more, the gamut of Indian women writers relate in an astonishing variety of themes that focus on woman and her predicament. Each writer, in their own way,. has tried to convey their thoughts in a distinct personal voice, yet they have been successful in forming a part of the chorus, a collective tone emphasizing the sovereignty of women. The female protagonists in their writings evince sufficient vigour and courage to question the oppressive role of society, religion, and culture, but yet they refrain from taking the paths suggested by the western feminists. They rather seek to find their own paths. These women writers have given literary work in India an unmistakable edge. They are able to sensitively portray a world that has in it women rich in substance. Their women are real flesh-and-blood protagonists who make us look at them with awe in respect of their relationships to their surroundings, their society, their men, their children, their families, their mental make-ups, and themselves. Our women writers have grappled with complex issues such as sensuality, servility, subjugation, and society. However, they have handled these complexities with a sense of balance, never disregarding our Indian traditions, yet discovering that there is more in the offing.

It is certain, therefore, that if Feminism is to have a future, feminist writing must be able to exhibit that feminism has much wise and useful things to say to women who struggle to cope with everyday problems. We need to manifest that good feminist writing can make most sense when it comes to understanding love and relationships, for example, and make a real difference to those who take it seriously. That is what Beauvoir's *The Second Sex* strove for in 1949. Now, we need new feminist voices to speak out because though it is true that Beauvoir's insights are central to contemporary feminism, it is also true that we need newer ways of analysis having a genuinely global range, illuminating everyday life and developing truly new ideas about what women's oppression today consists in, so that it can point the way towards every field of life.

In the present study on *Indian Women Writing in English*, an attempt is made to compare the textual representations of gender and gender roles by the select postmodern women writers. Each of the nineteen articles interprets the concept of feminism in various ways, and by probing the relationship of the feminist paradigm to fields like humanism, literature, and psychology, they exhibit that the future of feminism is not fractured, but all-encompassing.

The metaphor of silence assumes immense significance in the novels of Anita Desai because she delves deeply into the chasm of the inner lives of her characters. Anita Myles in her paper, "The Metaphor of Silence in the Novels of Anita Desai", attempts to signify that oriental silence is in reality a resistance against gender specific discrimination. As Myles points out, "She [Anita Desai] uses the motif of Silence and Death to question and resist the gender-specific exclusion. Thus, in the writings of Desai the reader encounters the compelled silence as well as sound silence or the silence of language."

In his comprehensive paper, "Narrativizing the Feminine Margins in the Masculine Centre-Space of Indian Ethos: A Study of Shashi Deshpande's *The Dark Holds No Terrors* and Arundhati Roy's *The God of Small Things*", Gulrez Roshan Rahman studies both the printed works as typical gynotexts where the author's chief concern is about women discovering "a world of their own", to use Showalter's phrase, which, in turn has reinforced the attitudes and aspirations of their female readers and ultimately, their literary successors.

Nishi Pulugurtha's "Gendered Space and Diasporic Identity: A Reading of *Brick Lane*," focuses on the processes of "unhoming", "dislocation", and "identities" as they proceed and emerge within the diasporic space and also presents women and their gendered spaces as evocative symbols of a new, inspirational, and a more just and fairly ordered society.

With Kamala Das, we come across a new kind of woman's writings which is bold, daring, tantalising, and self-assertive. From the beginning Kamala Das demonstrates a continuity of theme and expression concerning central division of the self. Her work is a compelling account of the presence of this schism. Deepshikha, in her paper, "The Split-Self and Self-Assertion in Kamala Das's Poetry" offers a detailed analysis of Kamala Das's novels that speaks out her heart and redefines as well as liberates herself both as a woman and a poet.

Gauri Shankar Jha, in his scholarly paper, "Anita Desai in Search of Alternatives" analyses the feminist slants in Anita Desai's writings. However, he opines that, "To me, feminism is a romantic concept which could not establish itself on any soil of the globe, whether the East or the West, as an alternative for the 'other'. Yet the search continues." He further remarks that, "Anita Desai is also indulged in the same pursuit and the present paper aims to trace her journey of the quest, which proves futile in its final leg."

In her paper, "A Comparative Study between Kamala Das and Taslima Nasrin in the Light of 'Feminism and Sex'", Babli Mallick portrays the two authors as "the two atomic forces who try to destroy the claustrophobic embrace of fixed belief about women in their seemingly decorated, well-protected society under the invisible chain of patriarchal authority."

Srutimala Duara's paper, "*The Dark Holds No Terrors*: Quest for Identity" critically examines *The Dark Holds No Terror* as a feminist text which explores the quest of a woman to visualise herself as a human being, independent of her traditional role as daughter, wife, and mother, and effectively brings out Shashi Deshpande's concern for the woman's struggle to secure self-respect and self-identity.

Garima Gupta's paper, "Assaulting the Darkness: A Feminist Critique of Kiran Desai's *The Inheritance of Loss*," discusses in detail the women characters in the novel and remarks that, "The women in Desai's novels are all pegs in the same social wheel. They may be educated, westernized or illiterate; however, their gender guarantees them only one thing and that is a second place to men in their lives."

Era Tyagi's paper, "Exploring Man-Woman Relationship in the Novels of Anita Desai and Bharati Mukherjee," focuses on "the personal struggles of middle-class woman in contemporary India as they attempt to overcome the social limitations imposed by tradition bound patriarchal culture" as dealt by the two great women writers in Feminist Indian Fiction.

Madhu Shalini's paper, "Reinvesting the Self: A Gynocentric Approach to Manju Kapur's *The Immigrant*", shows women's reaction against similar social pressures. "Her women characters" says Madhu Shalini, "like Virmati, Aastha refuse to conform to the image of the effeminate, docile, and long suffering woman, a picture nurtured through a male oriented culture. Since education has opened new vistas for them, the new woman is talented, skilled, and one who indulges in deep self-analysis and introspection. A meek acceptance, thus, has given way to interrogation which helps these female characters of present-day novels to seek bolder alternatives and better pastures."

In her paper, "Feminist Slants in the Short Stories of Shashi Deshpande, Anita Desai and Jhumpa Lahiri," Reena Mitra presents Anita Desai, Shashi Deshpande, and Jhumpa Lahiri as eminent Indian English women writers and explores the feminist interpretations and inferences that may be traced in their short stories. She poignantly remarks, "These writers, in the main, portray the world of women who are beset with circumstantial pressures and struggle hard against the antagonistic contemporary social structure that pushes them to the utmost point in the periphery and prevents them from emerging as individuals with identities of their own."

Mahasweta Devi is a renowned Bengali author who has been acclaimed internationally for her literary works. She has many of her novels and short stories translated into other Indian and foreign languages. In her paper, "Goddesses and Mythological Female Figures in Mahasweta Devi's *Statue*," Elisa Armellino analyses the English translation of the short story 'Statue' made by Gayatri Spivak from the Bengali language. The author presents Dulali, the protagonist as a positive female character enduring social injustices without surrendering to them and preserving her dignity and critical skills despite cultural and social biases.

"Integrity or Deceit: A Critical Study of Shashi Deshpande's Novel, *In the Country of Deceit*" by Vinita Jha depicts Deshpande's concern for women's emancipation and their search for identity in the hostile world of male chauvinism. As Jha says, "*In the Country of Deceit* deals not only with the theme of adult love leading to the path of deceit and adultery, but also with that of sin and redemption. Devayani seems to be a well-developed character because at last she proves her integrated character by being honest to her own self."

In her explorative paper, "The Narrative Voices and Female History in Ashapurna Devi's *Subarnalata*", Arpa Ghosh offers "a vivid portrayal of the tough, determined heroine engaged in sole combat against smaller, meaner, collective social forces, and gives the text a timeless and a tragic dimension."

Kamala Das is one of the best-known contemporary Indian women writers whose works have evinced contradictory responses in the Indian academia. Some laud her boldness, compelling sincerity and striking originality, while others dismiss her work as sensationalist, limited in scope, and unsophisticated. "Kamala Das's Poetry: Issues of Intertextuality and Feminisms" by Purnendu Chatterjee is definitely an interesting read. Talking about the issues of intertextuality, Purnendu remarks, "The concept of intertextuality may be applied to those poems where the poetic persona and the autobiographical self are different. However, in poems where Das's autobiographical self and her poetic self merge, the tools of intertextuality will throw up erroneous configurations, for in these poems the author is not dead, she is alive, pulsating, and vital". Further, exploring the feminist stances in her poetry, the author elaborates, "Das's feminist stances never indulge in mindless imitations of Western agendas..., Das's feminisms weave out patterns of evolving forms till it dissolves in her feminine sensibility that finally transforms into a grand melioristic vision."

Anju Bala Agrawal's "A Study of Male Chauvinism in Anita Desai's *In Custody*" focuses on the emotional turbulence and mental chaos of Deven, the protagonist in Desai's novel, *In Custody*. The paper interestingly explores the male psyche and shows Desai successfully departing from her earlier obsessive interior landscapes of hypersensitive and neurotic women.

Shashi Deshpande's forte has been the Indian woman, her conflicts and predicaments against the background of contemporary India. In her article, "Feminist Slants in Shashi Deshpande's Fiction," Baby Kumari makes an in-depth analysis of the feminist concerns in Deshpande's novels.

From Christine de Pizan to the present, women have looked at Joan of Arc and Meerabai as a positive example of a brave and active female. Joyashri Choudhury in her paper, "Self-portrait and Self-narrative of Meerabai and Joan of Arc", shows how the self-determination enabled Joan of Arc and Meerabai to construct their own self-portraits and self-narratives which is very much akin to the feminist voice theory.

Deepali Sharma's article, "The Act of Defiance in Shashi Deshpande's *The Dark Holds No Terrors* and *Roots and Shadows*," discusses woman's experiences and her dilemmas as she goes through an uneasy transitional phase through which Indian society is re-defining itself in keeping with the changing times. "Thus, perhaps the writer has tried to convey to the society that the need of the time, in this transitional phase, is not a total revolt but a gradual change in the society for which everyone has to put some effort to bridge the gap between the old and the new generation," says Sharma.

I wish to express my gratitude to the contributors in this editorial venture, who enthusiastically contributed to this project and enriched the anthology with their perceptive papers. I especially wish to thank Dr. K.R. Gupta, Chairman, Atlantic Publishers and Distributors (P) Ltd. for the confidence evinced in me and for seeing the book through the press.

**Sunita Sinha**

# Contributors

**Anita Myles.** Professor, Department of English, D.D.U. Gorakhpur University, Gorakhpur, Uttar Pradesh.

**Gulrez Roshan Rahman.** Associate Professor, Department of English, Marwari College, Kishanganj, B.N. Mandal University, Madhepura, Bihar.

**Nishi Pulugurtha.** Ph.D., Assistant Professor, Department of English, Brahmananda Keshab Chandra College, Kolkata, West Bengal.

**Deepshikha.** M.A. Ph.D., LNMU, Darbhanga, Bihar.

**Gauri Shankar Jha.** Head, Department of English, I.G. Govt. College, Arunachal Pradesh.

**Babli Mallick.** Department of English, Vasanta College for Women, Rajghat, Varanasi, Uttar Pradesh.

**Srutimala Duara.** Associate Professor, Department of English, Handique Girl's College, Guwahati, Assam.

**Garima Gupta.** Assistant Professor, Department of English, University of Jammu, Jammu.

**Era Tyagi.** Research Scholar, Dayalbagh Educational Institute, Agra, Uttar Pradesh.

**Madhu Shalini.** Associate Professor, University Department of English, B.R.A. Bihar University, Muzaffarpur.

**Reena Mitra.** Professor of English in Amity School of Languages, Amity University, Lucknow, Uttar Pradesh.

**Elisa Armellino.** Dipartimento di Scienze del Linguaggio, Universita delgi Studi di Torino, via Verdi, 10, 10121 Torino, Italy.

**Vinita Jha.** Reader in English, MDDM College, BRA Bihar University, Muzaffarpur.

**Arpa Ghosh.** Head and Associate Professor of English, Vivekananda College for Women, Kolkata, West Bengal.

**Purnendu Chatterjee.** Member, Expert Committee on School Education; Assistant Master, Hooghly Collegiate School, Kolkata, West Bengal.

**Anju Bala Agrawal.** Associate Professor and Head, Deptt. of English, R.C.A. Girls' P.G. College, Mathura, Uttar Pradesh.

**Baby Kumari.** M.A., Ph.D., LNMU, Darbhanga, Bihar.

**Joyashri Choudhury.** Associate Professor, Head of Department of English, Khagarijan College, Assam.

**Deepali Sharma.** Assistant Professor, AIESR, 'D' Block, Amity University, Noida, Uttar Pradesh.

# 1

# The Metaphor of Silence in the Novels of Anita Desai

*Anita Myles*

*Silence is a true friend that never betrays.*

Confucius

Paradoxically enough silence is not the arrant refusal to express oneself; in fact it serves as indirect articulation which in turn is extremely ambiguous so far as implications are concerned. Silence has been defined in multifarious modes, one of the most pertinent connotations being that it is the inner limit of discourse and interaction. If silence is dependent on speech, the latter is equally beholden to the former. Factually inferring silence is as articulate as verbal expression and though may signify nothing in isolation but in a particular context and in a specific situation it becomes extremely potent and suggestive. Silence, therefore, pertains to both the presence as well as the absence of language, the difference being rarely cognitive. Silence is an essential device for expressiveness because a speech not interspersed by silence tends to be monotonous, incoherent, meaningless and unanalyzable. Even though Silence is the essence of the cogent word yet it is not easy either to hear it or to know its implication hence the language of silence takes a universal shape.

Silence is not merely a simple phenomenon but contains different cognitions taking various forms: viz., the silence of inner suffering when words fail to express the deep emotions, the meditative silence (*Mauna*) to which ascetics, saints and religiously inclined people resort which may be termed as the silence of enlightened personalities signifying bliss, calm, joy, tranquility and inner contentment. For such personalities silence leads to the exposition of truth. Rabindranath Tagore recognized the significance of gesture as he spoke in the language of dance and pictures which for him were not abstractions rather they were unique signals attempting to convey something beyond the surface. Silence, therefore, has diverse amplitudes of relativity corresponding to states of mind emerging as a complex phenomenon that tends to embody and enfold variegated concepts.

The pens of litterateaurs manifest 'silence' through sound that reverberates in the world of letters. Critics have highlighted the employment of silence in drama but silence is equally articulate in fiction—specially the fiction that deals with the agony of the soul. It is interesting to note that quantatively more women writers than male have harnessed silence in their transcriptions whose resonances vibrate meaningfully in their creative writings for their cry is loaded with disgust and repulsion against the existing social patterns, norms and prejudicial structures. The modulation of silence varies from woman to woman, nation to nation, race to race, class to class and economic status to economic status. Hence the same silence appropriates contradistinct connotations in different contexts. These female writers are incessantly conscious of the fact that truth lies beyond the bounds of language and that language, in fact, discriminates and corrupts the truth. A significant and undeniable fact remains obvious that verbal language has its limitations due to regional restrictions whereas the language of silence is universal and proves its effectiveness in situations when speech fails to communicate or to be understood due to myriad unavoidable reasons.

Anita Desai applies the metaphor of silence to denote resistance against gender discrimination. Approximately in all her novels she has nonchalantly acknowledged that women lead marginal lives in a male-dominated periphery. The oriental silence of these women is a peculiar trait of their traditional upbringing and it is an agonizing fact that the women in her novels embark upon experiencing the suppression of desires enforced upon them by various restrictions such as religious, social and conventional, ultimate outcome being that these women instinctively tend to shrink into their shells leading a life of solitude, exile and neglect. Thus, the expulsion and seclusion of the Indian woman borders upon gender exile; which surprisingly is hailed as a virtue in the Indian social context. It is this type of silence verging upon a life of alienation and self banishment that Anita Desai, a novelist of mixed descent discloses in her novels also observing that in most cases this attitude of reticence culminates in death. She uses the motif of Silence and Death to question and resist the gender-specific exclusion. Thus in the writings of Desai the reader encounters the compelled silence as well as sound silence or the silence of language. Paradoxically inferring, the pursuit of silence is in reality the opposition to silence.

The metaphor of silence becomes of paramount significance in the novels of Anita Desai because she delves profoundly into the chasm of the inner lives of her characters. Her forte as a novelist is in reality, the exploration of sensibility—the particular Indian sensibility. She resorts to a style that smoothly unfurls the inner dilemma and fragmentation of the consciousness of her characters. However, it is not imperative that the inner contention of these characters is denoted in language, syntax and imagery and it is at such moments that silence becomes a potent instrument for communication. The same silence reflects the extreme conflict between environmental forces and the mental flux within: one external and the other internal. The Indian woman was always considered as the epitome of silence, withdrawal and regression but the multiculturalism that crept into the Indian system with the coming of the British affected the psyche of the Indian women in multifarious ways while she silently set out on the task of defining herself as against the social backdrop and hence we find that the women in Desai's novels were preparing themselves silently for the onset of the new age. The novels of Anita Desai narrate this saga though the progress is a gradual process beginning from negativity to positivism. Her range is wide enough for she delineates the woman in all her roles—as a mother, a daughter, a wife, a sister, a harlot, an in-law in a basically patriarchal, patrilineal setup.

Maya in *Cry, The Peacock* (1963) is a hypersensitive, obsessive young girl married to Gautam, a lawyer leading a lonely life, apprehensive of death because once an astrologer had predicted that in the fourth year of her marriage either she or her husband would die. She hesitates to share this anxiety with her husband, suffers in silence almost becoming neurotic though trying her level best to be the submissive, patient, tolerant, compromising, traditional and understanding wife that Gautam wanted her to be. But she failed to come up to his standards due to the inherent apprehension which compelled her to be an easy prey to silence and seclusion. Failing to comprehend her behaviour, Gautam hastily concludes that she was a 'neurotic', 'mad woman'. The entire novel traces her disturbed psyche, the guilt of pushing Gautam to his death, the permanent state of acute shock and ultimately her own violent death. *Cry The Peacock* is the epic of destructive love where mistrust, misunderstanding and uncompromising attitude lead to marital discord. Gautam's nonchalant attitude turns Maya into a self-centered, overdemanding, possessive woman. She continues to retreat within the self, becomes more of an introvert. Anita Desai has contrasted Maya with two other women in the novel: her mother-in-law and Nila, her sister-in-law who is bold enough to maneouvre her divorce and lead an independent life.

In many ways Monisha in *Voices in the City* (1965) is quite like Maya. She too suffered, thought of ending her life to escape the problems confronting her but later looses control over everything and sets herself ablaze thus meeting her gory death. In both the novels Anita Desai has brought to the forefront the impact of stressful urban life on young couples. Monisha's younger sister Amla takes a leaf out of her life. She had learnt much from Monisha's experiences and was wary enough to compromise, to surrender for the sake of peace and love. If Monisha's silent sufferings lead to her untimely death women like Amla, Nirode's mother, Aunt Lila exhibit the courage to be vocal, to have their way and ultimately to live life on their own terms.

Sarah, in *Bye-Bye Blackbird* (1971) is of English origin and has been richly contrasted with native women like Mala, Bala, Ratna, etc., essentially demonstrating the disparity between the East and the West. Belonging to a progressive cultural background, Sarah becomes quite oriental in her ways after marrying an Indian immigrant Adit Sen. As a foreigner she stands apart from the other women characters of Anita Desai though she also suffers silently from a sense of alienation and nostalgia but her self-determination and courage help her to overpower her dilemmas, "like a silent volcano, not dead, yet not bursting". *Bye-Bye Blackbird* is rooted in Mrs. Desai's experience of a mixed marriage where she makes proper use of self-introspection, self-discovery and finally compromise.

Sita and Raman escape the gratifications of mutual love and understanding between husband and wife in *Where Shall We Go This Summer?* (1975). A mother of four children, Sita was herself dispossessed of a mother as a child, had an uncaring father and found out to her consternation that Rekha was not her real sister. All these factors added to her emotional instability, she became more of an introvert, resorting to nostalgic moments of silence and despair. Then to spend more time in silence and self-introspection she goes for a brief holiday to Manori all alone where she discovers herself as never before. There is a new awareness and a fresh realization that she must accept things as they are. She is both determined as well as courageous enough to cultivate the art of survival in a world beset with immense problems.

The women characters depicted so far live dual lives, unsure, uncertain and hence silent sufferers; for some silence leads to death, for others to self-introspection followed by an inclination for reconciliation with the world at large. Nanda Kaul in *Fire on the Mountain* (1977) is different from this point of view as she has an invigorated personality, capable of subsisting and nourishing not only herself but also others even while she endures the trauma of an unfaithful husband. She silently undergoes separation with her grown up children and later death of her husband. Then she forgets her woes as she begins to stoically sustain her daughter Tara (a victim of a broken marriage) and her granddaughter Raka. Illa Das another sufferer gives strength and moral support to Nanda.

If in the case of Maya and Monisha silence ends in physical death, in the case of Sarah, Sita, Nanda, Tara, Raka, Illa it is silence accompanied by the death of personality. Just as the title *Fire on the Mountain* suggests a wasteland; bare and barren due to frequent forest fires and failure of rain, the lives of these women experience a fleeting death of personality. But nature has its own ways of rejuvenation. Life begins afresh even on barren soil, so it happens in the lives of these women. Their silence ameliorates persuading them to ruminate over the past through a state of self-introspection, locate their faults and weaknesses if any, self-discovery ensues and inadvertently the latent courage to rise above the storm surfaces and rescues them well in time. They pull themselves out of the mire: the death of the personality is momentary, rejuvenation occurs making them stronger than before. From hence forth the women in the novels of Anita Desai muster up the courage to stand on their principles right from the outset. Weak women like Maya or Monisha are substituted in later novels by stronger and more courageous women.

Bim in *Clear Light of Day* (1980) is one such strong woman character of Anita Desai whose inner vitality assists her in sustaining a family of seven including three incapacitated members. Her sister Tara shirks her responsibilities but later in life succumbs to guilt consciousness. Bim's responsibilities make her an introvert, her silence leads to aggressiveness culminating in frequent violent outbursts. Nevertheless, as time passes she gradually transforms—the old self dies and a new Bim is in the making—calm, loving, affectionate, forgiving and tolerating. She has achieved all this through silent self-introspection, self-discovery and self-transformation for she soon realized that life is too short to be wasted thus.

Though Sarla's description in *In Custody* (1984) is sketchy yet it defines to the core Anita Desai's metaphor of silence well. While Deven, her husband is busy appreciating the poetry of Nur, Sarla, has sufficient reason to be frustrated, dissatisfied and disillusioned with life. As the title of the novel suggests she is 'in custody' of loneliness, alienation and isolation making her intensely belligerent while unable to endure it for long she goes back to her parents' home only to realize that she missed her 'cage'. She is an undecided, shattered woman with an inner craving to go back to her husband's home. She begins instantaneously to set her inner world in order. The return brings her immense contentment—a sort of triumph over her life of neglect and degradation.

Sufia Begum compromised when her husband, Nur got married a second time to Imtiaz Begum, a prostitute by profession. Sufia surrendered silently realizing the fact that intellectually she was no match for Nur. Perhaps Imtiaz would nurture this aspect of his personality better. Shackled to ancient Indian traditions Sufia derives satisfaction rather than resentment from this sacrifice on her part.

The characters delineated in *Baumgartner's Bombay* (1988) are quite different from those found in Desai's earlier novels. Hugo Baumgartner, a German living in Bombay accidentally meets Lotte, an acquaintance from Germany, now living in Calcutta. Lotte is a cabaret dancer when Hugo meets her. His delight knows no bounds for he shares with Lotte his deep sense of isolation and alienation as a foreigner living in Bombay. Lotte, too has undergone similar traumatic experiences in a foreign land yet she keeps her sorrows at bay to comfort Hugo. The novel brings out not only the dilemma of people trying to adjusting in an alien country but also the invincibility of love and affection in giving succour to others.

As they share their past with each other Lotte narrates that she married Kanti Sethia for the sake of security and companionship. Not being accepted by the family she was turned out of the house soon after the death of Kanti. She sustains her husband as a long as he is alive, then supports Hugo but like a true woman of strength camouflages her own desolation and emotional upheaval in adopting a philanthropic attitude towards others. Perhaps this is a common point that Lotte shares with some other women characters of Anita Desai—they are all strong women who may be under a short spell of dismay and distraction but soon they push it aside for the vibrant side of their personality strengthens them. The undeniable capacity for forbearance and sustenance in times of adversity remains the same whether the woman is an Indian or of foreign origin.

This idea captivated Anita Desai for quite sometime for in her next novel *Journey to Ithaca* (1995) the central characters are two foreign ladies, Sophie and Laila. Whila Laila's silent suffering is due to betrayal in love Sophie's is more due to domestic reasons. She alienates herself from her parents and children, tours around the world, comes to India only to bolster her husband, Matteo's ego who has embarked on a spiritual quest. They meet Laila, henceforth addressed as the 'Mother' because she is the head of an *Ashram* in Bihar. Matteo is impressed by the Mother for she teaches no religion except the main tenets of love, sacrifice and tolerance which are the actual need of the hour. Sophie finds out all about the past of the Mother and then drifts away. For quite sometime she moves away emotionally from Matteo as well. However, in the moments of isolation she indulges in self-introspection discovering her immense inner strength. She even goes back to her children after loosing the youngest one deciding to bring the family together in spite of all obstacles. Thus she is able to shun the emotional void within her. Sophie fits well in the description of Helen Deutche who says that

> Only exceptionally talented girls can carry a surface intellect without injuring their affective lives for women's intellect, her capacity for objectively understanding life, thrives at the expense of her subjective emotional qualities. (124)

It's the portrayal of the mind of the protagonist who though silent tends to herald a new morality which is not confined to physical chastity alone but demands self-fulfillment.

In delineating Sophie Anita Desai's perspective broadens extensively when she admits that even in the contemporary society women suffer because they silently develop a tenacious will power to control the adverse situation as best as possible. Sophie keeps a firm balance when she cares for both husband and children simultaneously; if she is physically away, she is emotionally close by. Sophie's reconciliation is therefore, different for it helps resolve her own dilemmas. In the delineation of Laila, the Mother Desai accentuates the concavity of spiritual life specially which cuts one off from the down to earth mundane realities. Laila comprehends much later that her unhappiness is due to inefficaciousness in coordinating the physical and the spiritual—two sides of life which are equally important. Her silent sufferings lead her nowhere. Neither is she able to give solace to Matteo nor to Sophie. In many ways Sophie is more "enlightened" than the Mother for she creates a fine balance amongst her variegated roles as a woman.

The traumatic experiences of Uma in *Fasting, Feasting* (2000) throw ample light on the women of postcolonial India. In this novel too, Anita Desai dwells at length upon the silent sufferings encountered by women (married, unmarried or widowed) who utilize the same silence to invigorate themselves. This novel also reveals a metaphorical death of the old personality; the physical and the spiritual have been conjoined at least in the characters of Uma and Mira masi to create a new personality which though silent faces chivalrously the onslaughts of fate. Their meditative silence rejuvenates them in the end to live and accept life as it comes.

After her unsuccessful marriage Uma is a shattered person, condemned by one and all as ill-fated, doomed to lead a life of sorrow and isolation with weakening faith in the joint family system. She was almost an outcaste, confined to her room, with no one to comfort her. Afflicted by an acute sense of failure Uma resorts to silence and stoicism to heal the deeply inflicted wounds on her psyche. She emerges victorious with the help of Mira masi, an old widow relative who too, once was condemned to a life of isolation and silence. But Mira masi mustered up her courage to survive in spite of difficult odds, went on pilgrimages and forgot the world in the love of God. However, hers is not a selfish love for she trains Uma in a similar manner. Thus, she is an excellent example of the merging of the physical and the spiritual.

Descriptions of Aruna, Anamika, Mrs. Patton and Melanie are woven in the same pattern. The latter two are foreigners by depicting whom Desai stretches the metaphor of silence which exists not only on Indian soil but also in America. In their own way each of these characters is a victim of silent sufferings living in a claustrophobic environment and craving for inner strength to overcome the crises, perhaps projecting a silent reaction against the set norms of society whether it is of traditional India or modern America where there is plenty of social freedom. Psychologically a woman is a woman whether Indian or American; the problems may be varied, the scenario may be different but the silent suffering within is still the same, the urge to overcome and conquer is equally the same.

*The Zig Zag Way* (2004) is a male dominated novel where the character of Betty Jennings is sketchy yet here too, we observe her intense struggle to compromise with life as she skillfully steers her way from innocence, wonder, discovery and sorrow. The locale too, shifts from India to Mexico, a land that fascinated the novelist since long.

Thus, it is quite noticeable that the metaphor of silence has been explicated on a vast canvas by Anita Desai for she writes of pure housewives, working women, concubines, social workers, and sex-workers on the one hand and of mothers, sisters, daughters, wives, daughters-in-law, sisters-in-law and aunts on the other. Sometimes the women in her novels mutely juggle with variegated roles all at once. Yet the common point in each character is the metaphor of silence—a silence which begins in agony, helps in self-discovery and ultimately provides inner strength for encountering the onslaughts of destiny. In Anita Desai's universe silent suffering is not worthwhile because life is too short and too precious to be wasted. Woman has been endowed with the innate capacity to extricate herself from this mire. Silence encourages an awakening of the woman's consciousness and then imparts the capability of conquering the bastion of male domination. Silently then, they tread on the path of self-fulfillment dethroning the age-old myths of feminity, motherhood and marriage.

The brief psycho-analysis of the women characters of Anita Desai confirms and reiterates the fact that they live marginal lives according to the Indian lifestyle. Their oriental silence is in reality a resistance against gender specific discrimination. It is heart rending to see her women characters emotionally subdued owing to various kinds of restrictions and pressures from religion, society and conventions. Having no alternative they resort to a life of silence—a silence which can be explained variously as psycholinguistic, socio-cultural and expressive or interactive. The situation compels them to retreat into a life of solitude, exile and neglect. Strangely enough this kind of silence has been upheld as a virtue among traditional Indian women but on the contrary perhaps no heed has been registered to the silent suffering within. After reading her novels the silence inflicted by the self or by external factors becomes an audible silence for it has the unique power to urge the reader to think. In the early novels the metaphor of silence is associated with physical death; in the later novels it takes the form of death of personality and in the last phase of her writings the silence becomes religious and meditative in nature (Sophie, Laila, Mira Masi, and Uma). In this sense one observes a well marked progression and evolution in the metaphor of silence as used by Anita Desai—the movement is from negativity to positivism and later to compromise and adjustment. Silence is a word which connotatively denotes 'nothing' but in reality silence 'silently' performs innumerable functions helping to link and bond people together. It helps to heal a wound and even vice versa, to wound a person. Silence may be a tool of self-exploration at the same time it hides information from others. Silence can also be judgmental for it may signal either assent or favour/ dissent or disfavour. It may trigger off deep thoughtfulness or contrarily complete mental inactivity. Hence, in spite of being an ambiguous subject, silence assumes a vast function as it is interdisciplinary—linguistic, discoursal, literary, social, cultural, spiritual, a sort of metacommunicative term.

## WORK CITED

Deutsch, Helene. *Psychology of Women: Psychoanalytical Interpretation*, Vol. 1. "Girlhood". New York: Bantam, 1973.

# 2

# Narrativizing the Feminine Margins in the Masculine Centre-Space of Indian Ethos: A Study of Shashi Deshpande's *The Dark Holds No Terrors* and Arundhati Roy's *The God of Small Things*

*Gulrez Roshan Rahman*

Gynotext and diasporic women writers on women are so closely related that *écriture féminine* seems to be solely concerned about the marginalization of women in the patriarchal mainstream set-up. In this regard 'gynotext' is nothing but *gynocriticism* in velvet gloves. Like Julia Kristeva, other leading French feminist critics also associated with feminine writing with the female body. Helen Cixous, for example, posited an essential connection between women's bodies, whose sexual pleasure has been repressed, and women's writing. "Write yourself. Your body must be heard", Cixous urged in an essay entitled "The Laugh of the Medusa" (1976). Cixous believed that recognizing this connection would enable women not only to realize their sexuality but to enter history and move toward a future based on 'feminine' economy of giving rather than the 'masculine' economy of hoarding. Luce Irigaray focused on women's sexual pleasure (*jouissance*), arguing that it could not be expressed by the dominant masculine language. Irigaray explored the connection between women's sexuality and women's language through the following analogy in a book entitled *Ce Sexe qui n'en est pas un* (*This Sex Which is not One*, 1977): just as women's *jouissance* is more multiple than men's unitary, phallic pleasure, so 'feminine' language is more diffusive than its 'masculine' counterpart.

This emphasis on feminine writing as an expression of the female body drew criticism from almost all the quarters—the French feminists, the North American feminists and others. The group of North American feminist critics, including Sandra Gilbert, Susan Gubar, Patricia Meyer Spacks, and Elaine Showalter, created a different model, which Showalter herself dubbed *gynocriticism*. In *A Literature of Their Own,* Showalter outlines such a tradition by providing a comprehensive overview on women's writing through three of its phases. She defined these as the "Feminine, Feminist, and Female" phases, phases during which women imitated a masculine tradition (1840-1880), protested against its standards and values (1880-1920), and advocated their own autonomous, female perspective (1920-present). In this context, prominent writers like Kamala Das, Anita Desai, Nayantara Sahgal, Shobha De, Shashi Deshpande, Manju Kapoor, Jhumpa Lahiri, and above all, Arundhati Roy have emerged as the most significant voices against the feminine marginalization. Especially, Arundhati Roy's *The God of Small Things* represents, in my humble view, layers of voices of marginality with a garb of creative *gynotext* that forms a class in itself.

A land of lush green backwaters, deceptively beautiful, "Past butterflies drifting through the air like happy messages. Huge forms/ A Chameleon/ A startling shoeflower/ The scurry of gray jungle fowl running for cover" (305) and across the unpredictable, wild Meenanchal river to the Ayemenem house presents three generations—the descendants of the venerable Rev. E. John Ipe and Aleyooty Ammachi—who broke the rules, crossed into forbidden territory, tampered with the laws that lay down who should be loved and how and how much and conjured up "a time when the unthinkable became thinkable and the impossible really happened" (31).

In *The God of Small Things*, Roy unfolds an excruciatingly beautiful tale in cinematographical style, of the disintegration of a family set in postcolonial milieu focusing on Kottayam district where Syrian Christians were dominant in a community that naturally adapted to the English language and culture. The atrocities and horrors that flash by in fragments—of crushed innocents, of conflicting marriages, of police custodial deaths, of cruel casteism, of masculine hegemony—all victims of irrational societal norms project one face of postcolonial India "a picture of the uncivilized, brutal and almost a tribal society that India appears to the western world" (Vimala Rama Rao, et al. 46). Yet within that dark face of India, plural voices emerge from the margins, shouting to be heard; and in a sense, that is what the novel is all about. The scope of this paper, therefore, is to identify those voices, especially the voice of the author raised in protest against rank oppressive forces, a critical voice that "eventually becomes the voice of your conscience" (Customer Comments, *Online Review*).

"The voice of children", avers Maria Calivis, "is very important because they come out with truths about themselves that sometimes adults overlook" (*The Hindu*, 2001). Significantly, the novel is recalling life as seen through the eyes of the seven-year-old twins, of the traumatic experiences that led to loss of childhood, of powerlessness in an oppressive adult world that reduce their lives to nothingness. The dominant theme of the novel is "the intrusion of the violent and ugly adult world into the innocence, purity, fragility and make believe of childhood" (Vimala Rao, et al.). The story centres around Estha and Rahel and the arrival of their cousin Sophie Mol and her mother, Margaret, from England. As a U.S. reader observes:

> Roy captures the essence of growing up in the postcolonial third world. It depicts the loss of identity that one feels trying to belong to a colonizer's culture...one sees how even tiny people know 'their place'. How 'brown feet in Bata sandals' know where they stand in relation to white Sophie Mol. (Maria Calivis)

Estha and Rahel's existence in the Ayemenem house is shaky right from the beginning: to their grand aunt, Baby Kochamma, they are half-Hindus without a father, therefore 'little monsters and always suspect' even to the servant Kochu Maria, Sophie Mol is "sundarikutty, a little angel" and, the twins 'little demons'; for their beautiful, blind grandmother, Mammachi, the blindness extends to the soul in her blatant partiality to her white-skinned, blue grey blue-eyed granddaughter. With Sophie Mol in the limelight, the sense of insecurity deepens for the twins.

Little snatches of information and events underscore the single identity of the twins. They are described as dizygotic two-egg twins, Estha older by eighteen minutes. Although there was no confusion identifying them as usually happens with identical twins, the author explains that "the confusion lay in a deeper, more secret place" (2) for "Esthappen and Rahel thought of themselves together as me, separately, individually, as we or us. As though they were a rare breed of Siamese twins, physically separate, but with joint identities" (2). This is shown tangibly, as when Rahel feels the taste of the sandwich Estha eats in the train when he is 'returned' or when Rahel wakes up one night giggling at Estha's funny dream. After twenty-three years of separation, when the twins meet again, memories are the only bridge that reunites them as they cross into forbidden territory in an amorphous relationship that defies definition, very much like Ammachi's banana jam that was neither jam proper nor jelly.

For the twins who are "Hansel and Gretel in a ghastly fairy tale" (293) there are precious few happy childhood memories. They share the childish habit of playfully reading words backwards—'Pots' for 'Stop', 'Naidni Yub, Naidni Eb' for Be Indian Buy Indian—being precocious with their reading, which game is read as perversity and interpreted by Miss Mittins as 'Satan in their eyes'. On the way to Abilash Theatre in Cochin, they are surrounded by some party men in the communist procession. One of them opens the car door on Rahel's side, speaks kindly to her asking if she is feeling hot, then jokingly adds, "Ask your daddy to buy you an Air Condition!" (79). Rahel feels happy, pleased to have Chacko, her uncle, mistaken for her father, "Like a normal family" (79). The children enjoy playing with Velutha, greedy for love, even if it could come only from one, who to the adults is an 'untouchable'. Above all, they cling tenaciously to the affection of their mother and fear rejection, however mild it may be. Rahel, therefore, punishes herself by not having supper in the Lodge to make amends for having hurt Ammu earlier at the Theatre. She does this to regain the loss of her mother—"A little less her Ammu loved her" (112). When Sophie Mol appears on the scene, Rahel watches "hawk-eyed to try and gauge how much Ammu loved Sophie Mol, but couldn't" (143). The culmination of the fear of loss of love occurs when Ammu shouts at the twins that they are two milestones and that she suffers because of them; careless words spilled in desperation, but also the oppressive language of a mother to children powerless to oppose. The harsh words drive the children to undertake measures that cause the tragedy of Sophie Mol's death inseparably affecting their own lives in the process.

Sophie Mol occupies centre-stage of the play the family enacts, with Ammu and her children at the margins:

> Rahel looked around her and saw that she was in a play.
>
> But she had only a small part.
>
> She was just a landscape. A flower perhaps. Or a tree.
>
> A face in the crowd. A townspeople.
>
> Nobody said hello to Rahel. Not even the Blue Army in the greenheat. (172-73)

The adulation and special treatment accorded to Margaret and Sophie Mol drives Ammu off stage from where they watch the high drama with disgust verging on rebellion. She begins to hope it had been Velutha at the procession after all, an insidious fatal attraction for Velutha growing within her as she identifies with his "living breathing anger against the smug, ordered world" (176) that she so raged against. It set off the "rage of the suicide bomber" (144) that leads her to eventually "love the man her children loved by day" (44).

Velutha makes up for the loss of love and recognition of the twins and becomes "the god of small things". The term 'untouchable' is rendered-a-misnomer by Estha and Rahel effortlessly and she lands in his arms. He carries them on his back and treats them like a prince and princess. Velutha is privileged with the twins in a way Sophie Mol is not and they avoid her like poison. However, she manages to, persuade them to take her with them across the river, consequently letting loose terror. She herself ends up with death by water, a mere-child with red-brown hair floating down the Meenachal with fish-nibbled eyes.

Things change in a day for them. They wake up near the History House and bear silent witness to Velutha being crushed to death under the heels of policeman. More terror follows in the police station. Baby Kochamma heaps guilt on the children. She glibly calls them 'murderers' and tells them "what matters is whether you want to go to jail and make Ammu go to jail because of you" (318). She tricks them into complying with her suggestion that Estha should just say 'Yes' to identify Velutha in the lock-up:

> The Inspector asked his question. Estha's mouth said 'yes'
>
> Childhood tiptoed out.
>
> Silence slid like a bolt.
>
> Estha returns to Rahel and whispers in her ear:
>
> You were right. It wasn't him. It was Urumban.
>
> Thank god, Rahel whispered back
>
> Where d'you think he is?
>
> Escaped to Africa. (320)

They float on this fiction, this make-believe as a temporary safety value saving them from mental breakdown. However, the guilt remains. They reply the scene as children, as teenagers, as adults unable to resolve the extent of their role in the deaths of Ammu, Velutha and Sophie Mol. They are victims of adult exploitation. Instead of having them exorcise their memories that haunted them, they wind up feeling. They are sinners, not the sinned, perpetrators and not the victims.

Twenty-three years later, when the twins meet again, they are "A pair of actors trapped in a recondite play with no hint of plot or narrative. Stumbling, through their parts, nursing someone else's sorrow. Grieving someone else's grief" (191). Estha had "terrible pictures in his head" (32) that got lodged deeply within him, like "mango hair between molars Rahel drifted through childhood, drifted in and out of marriages, with empty eyes reflecting the quietness in Estha's soul. The lessons learnt from History too early in life had driven one insane and the other insecure for life. Destroyed childhood is a global crisis." As Leela Menon observes, "the reports of gun-toting school children in the U.S. killing and injuring of classmates testify to increasing psychological trauma and social alienation. In contrast, Indian children are more victims than offenders." Roy takes the smallest of the small, and shows how the sweet rose of innocence fades when they become victims of adult aggressiveness and cruelty.

A strong voice is raised against the system of patriarchal oppression operating in the Indian system. *The God of Small Things* presents complex relationships that are doomed one way or the other. It becomes the fertile ground for the study of various postcolonial issues of marginality such as gender bias, domestic violence, Anglophilia and dowry evil in a country where "various kinds of despair competed for primacy" (19), and where between "the terror of war and the horror of peace" terrible things kept happening.

The lives of Mammachi and Pappachi involve an interesting study of domestic violence and anglophilia rolled into one. As Chacko avers, they are as a whole, a family of 'anglophiles' with an inclination for anything English-Chacko has an English wife, their obsession for watching "The Sound of Music" Ammu's fad for instilling love for the English language in the twins, Pappachi's unshakable good opinion of the covetous Mr. Hollick and of course, Pappachi's lifestyles, especially his manner of dressing "coasting down importantly down the narrow road in his wide car, looking outwardly elegant but sweating freely inside his woolen suits" (48). Roy pokes fun subtly at the ridiculous lengths anglophilia runs in the family, making them prisoners of a war won and lost, making them "adore our conquerors and despise ourselves" (53). The westernization stops with the externals. Inside, they are tradition-bound to the core.

Domestic violence begins with Pappachi's disappointment in not having been named after the moth he had discovered. "Pappachi's Moth was held responsible for his black moods and sudden bouts of temper. Its pernicious ghost...tormented him and his children and his children's children" (49) though Roy would have us believe that in reality he had been ill-tempered long before he discovered the moth. The disappointment becomes an excuse to legitimize his violence on wife and daughter. Ammu remembers the Father Bear Mother Bear stories she was given to read and how it really registers in her mind; in her version, "Father Bear beat Mother Bear with a brass vase. Mother Bear suffered those beatings with mute resignations" (180). As Ammu grows older, she develops "a lofty sense of injustice and the mulish, reckless streak that develops in someone small who has been bullied all their lives by someone Big" (181-82). Chacko puts an end to Pappachi's beating Mammachi when he comes home for holidays. He had grown up and was strong. Pappachi never touched Mammachi thereafter, but he never spoke to her either as long as he lived. He brought out his favourite rocking chair and smashed it to pieces to vent out his frustration. He was jealous of his wife and the attention she was getting with her pickle factory and would not help her though she was almost blind. His Nirmala C. Prakash sees it, in the Mammachi-Pappachi relationship, they remain as islands and "fail to shape up as continents because their relationship lacks mutual love, understanding and adjustment" (36).

Double standard becomes the norm of this family. Pappachi is used to very gentle and decent behaviour with outsiders but terrorizes his own family:

> He donated money to orphanages and leprosy clinics. He worked hard on his public profile as a sophisticated, generous, moral man. But alone with his wife and children he turned into a monstrous, suspicious bully, with a streak of vicious cunning. They were beaten, humiliated and then made to suffer the envy of friends and relations for having such a wonderful husband and father. (180)

Chacko who saves his mother from the violence of his father mercilessly chases his sister out of 'his' house. Mammachi is no exception: to her Sophie Mol is "loved from the beginning" (137) whereas the twins are neglected. She subscribes to gender bias by recognizing Chacko's "men needs" and has a side door leading to her son's room for the worker women to enter, while the same failing in her daughter, Ammu's relationship with Velutha, creates an uproar.

Tragedy strikes the family with the arrival of Sophie Mol; but that is only one way of looking at things. Basically, the family members suffer because of their distorted approach to Love Laws—the love laws that were made "long before Christianity arrived in a boat and seeped-into Kerala like tea from a tea bag" (33), the laws that lay down "who should be loved and how. And how much" (33). At twenty-seven Ammu's life had already been lived. She had married the first man who proposed to her because her father did not have the suitable dowry for her. Baby Kochamma, who "lived her life backwards" in her old age, had, remained a spinster for the same reason. She also shared the common view that a married daughter had no position in her parents' home:

> As for a divorced daughter—according to Baby Kochamma, she had no position anywhere at all. And as for a divorced daughter from a love marriage, well, words could not describe Baby Kochamma's outrage. As for a divorced daughter from an intercommunity love marriage—Baby Kochamma chose to remain quiveringly silent on the subject. (45-46)

Marginalized thus, by both society and family (Chacko's my factory, my house, my wife, etc., whereas Ammu and children have no "Locus Standi") she flouts at society and its rigid ethical codes in rebellion, breaking Love Laws and destroying the twins she had tried so hard to protect. Ammu is a tragic victim, struggling against terribly tyrannical forces. In Indira Bhatt's view, "It is the helplessness of the powerless against the powerful ones" (Bhatt, 47).

The domination of men stifles, the voices of women as they fight against cruel patriarchy at different levels: Mr. Hollick, the English estate manager bequeathing on tea-pickers a number of ragged, fight-skinned children on the estate, Pappachi's rages and brutal attacks on wife and daughter, Father Mulligan's subtle emotional exploitation of ex-nun Baby Kochamma, and Chacko who enjoys the profits of the pickle factory run by Mammachi but would not lift a finger to defend the defenceless children of his own sister. On the other hand, the victims themselves become victimizers: "Mammachi provided the passion. Baby Kochamma the plan. Kocku Maria was their midget lieutenant" (258). It was Baby Kochamma's idea that Estha be returned to his father; this bitter, spiteful woman who deflects her hatred for Velutha on the children and Ammu. Goaded on by Baby Kochamma, Ammachi loses control for the first time in her life and becomes the cause for Ammu's suffering.

Throughout the novel there is a reference to Conrad's *Heart of Darkness*; Roy subverts the theme, for in her work, Kunz is not the oppressor but the oppressed, the native with his heart of darkness. Casteism is one of the cantankerous social evils that eats at the heart of the nation, tearing its people apart in a social divide of touchable and untouchable. Roy brings the marginal to the centre in her novel by making Velutha the "god of small things" drawing him in such vibrant colours that every other character pales in comparison. Kuttappan, his physically handicapped brother and "a safe Paravan" is a foil to Velutha, "a Paravan with a future" (119), the progressive, talented Dalit at loggerheads with a society that withholds his identity from him and would destroy him if he crossed the limits.

Mammachi concedes—"with Touchable logic"—that if Velutha had not been a Paravan, he would have become an engineer. Like a magician he could make intricate toys with wood—tiny boats, rattles, windmills—that earns him the title. He is ambitious, strives to overcome social hurdles through politics by becoming a communist card-holder. Velutha strives against forces that are too strong for him, fortresses that are centuries old and cannot be pulled down in a day. However, like Ammu, he defies a hypocritically smug society, in his case, a caste-ridden society that treats people like him as lesser than mortals having absolutely no human rights either to life, liberty or love.

Mammachi recalls the time when Paravans were outcastes, and "were expected to crawl backwards with a broom, sweeping away their footprints" (73). Conversion to Christianity during the British rule could not help them escape from the scourge of *casteism*. They suffered marginalization spiritually, being segregated in separate churches, end economically, being denied government benefits since officially they had become casteless, or non-existent. In Roy's words, they were not "allowed to leave footprints at all" (740). Velutha's life is summed up in the definition given to the word 'dalit'. 'Dalit' means "burst, split, scattered, dispersed, broken, torn asunder, destroyed or crushed" (Selvaraj 10).

Velutha becomes a victim of the police atrocity to which he succumbs in its custody. In life, he fares no better. Exploited by his employers, he is paid less than touchable workers; exploited by his party, he is betrayed for personal gain; exploited by Ammu in a fragile spider-web relationship they know cannot survive; and finally exploited by Baby Kochamma who transfers her hatred for the communists on to Velutha. The twins alone love him for what he is and miss him so much when he dies, "He left behind a hole in the universe through which darkness poured like liquid tar" (191). The *Heart of Darkness* is shown at its worst when the touchable policemen mash him up under their boots and then step back to assess their work at an aesthetic distance: "Their work, abandoned by God and History, by Marx, by Man, by Woman and (in the hours to come) by Children, lay folded on the floor" (310).

Was Velutha's death needless, or contrived? Roy, the realist reveals her anger at such forces of oppression by her deadly controlled irony in relating the hounding of Velutha by the police. This is very much part of the India she portrays in the novel, corrupt and horribly violent, indifferent to atrocities that happen in real life. Like lynching dalits for skinning a dead cow. Kancha Ilaiah in his "Social Equality: Lessons from the U.S." draws parallels between India (the dalit bias) and the U.S. (the Black bias) and wishes India could learn from the U.S. example allowing Afro-Americans to maintain their black identity with dignity and self-respect. He says "such spiritual and social democratic values are responsible for advancement of blacks in all walks of life". When will India's intellectual class think not only creatively but also sensitively and positively and thus accord dignity of labour and socio-spiritual to its masses, irrespective of any kind of divide like caste, class of gender? Mari Marcel Thekaekara, while examining this issue of casteism states the dalit plea is: "In the last century we got rid of slavery and apartheid. Let this century be the one to annihilate casteism."

To conclude, the title *The God of Small Things* is significant because it celebrates the life that is filled with "small things", "small lives", "small people" and "small events". In themselves "small" but leading to far-reaching consequences. Roy has written literature "that dares to dare", touching on a variety of ideas and ideologies, and in her words, tries to "explain complicated things in simple language" (*Frontline* 14). Her treatment of women is a little disheartening since they are all negative and destructive, whereas writers like Anita Desai and Shashi Deshpande have moved to creating a new and empowered female selfhood. However, the novel is perhaps only her own past 'exorcised' while her present social concerns prove amply her self-actualization as a *pro-active* citizen fighting for the cause of the marginalized tribals over the Narmada Project. Meanwhile, "little events, ordinary things, smashed and reconstituted, imbued with new meaning" (32) will be what *The God of Small Things* is all about. "And there will be no more dreams." Thus, the diasporic women writers of gynotext have devised special framework within which to examine and evaluate all varieties, formal and informal, of female-authored works ranging from diaries to novels to poems. These focus on the feminine gender in its relationships with the mainstream society, both of which exist along a continuum of attitudes towards sex, sexuality, gender, identity and language. Like the typical gynotext Roy's *The God of Small Things* endeavours to discover "a world of their own", to use Showalter's phrase, which, in turn has reinforced the attitudes and aspirations of their female readers and ultimately, their literary successors. The male world too gains an insight into the feminine world by proxy perhaps.

Thus, the present paper humbly attempts to discuss the feminist perspectives as studies in marginality in the same way as we unjustifiably use the label 'North-East' amorphously for the people and culture of the land of seven sisters. Just as Indian mainland runs concurrent to the patriarchal set-up, so the Northeast India willy-nilly becomes the substitute of the feminine margins. Marginality, of course, implies exclusion from the Centre, and it creates a luminal space where the marginalized are voiceless subalterns dispossessed of history and identity. And the context for the aforesaid study has been Arundhati Roy's *The God of Small Things* and Shashi Deshpande *The Dark Holds No Terrors* which are unanimously regarded as seminal narratives of gender and marginality.

As Simone de Beauvoir says: "One is not born, but rather becomes a woman" (Beauvoir 1974: 295). This notion of 'becoming' a gender and not being one does not mean a movement from disembodied freedom to cultural embodiment, but rather a move from a 'natural' to a 'biological' state.

Shashi Deshpande has endeavoured to show through her novel *The Dark Holds No Terrors* that insensitivity toward a blooming daughter Saru sows the seeds of frustration and emptiness in her heart. The nefarious behaviours of Saru's mother and patriarchal attitudes of the Indians that prefer a male child instead of a female one cause to generate a sense of relative deprivation in Saru *vis-à-vis* her brother, or for that matter, any male child. After Dhruva's death, she is left with no child accept a female one. Instead of giving her daughter a careful and healthy upbringing she constantly craves for her dead son and leaves Saru with unbearable pangs of rejection and vacuity. She becomes a representative voice of the mainstream Indian patriarchal social set-up which eulogises a male child as a symbol of power and an agent of carrying forward one's progeny. Her rejection of Saru itself paves the way for her subaltern revolt. Recalling her adolescent days, Saru used to stand before the looking glass to have an idea about herself, and her mother's reaction used to be the dirtiest one:

> I was an ugly girl. At least, my mother told me so. I can remember her eying me dispassionately saying—you will never be good looking. (*The Dark* 61)

But the readers fail to appreciate such obnoxious treatment that Saru receives from her mother. Generally speaking, the women's body, sex and gender are the fundamentals on which all types of gender discriminations are committed, and sought to be legitimized. Death of a child, whether male or female should normally be a matter of equal sorrow and grief for the family. But the way Saru's mother blames her for the death of her brother Dhruva:

> Why didn't you die?
>
> Why are you alive when he is dead? (*The Dark* 29-30)

With such heart rending events and statements Saru's psyche is bruised. She recalls one such exchange of dialogues with her mother:

> "I don't want to get married."
>
> "Will you live with us all your life?"
>
> "Why not?"
>
> "Why can't?"
>
> "And Dhruva?"
>
> "He is different. He is a boy." (*The Dark* 40)

Saru's mother is a shameful manifestation of the patriarchal tendencies of such orthodox society as ours. The very coming to an age of maturity of a woman should be according to her, a matter of shame, humiliation and subjugation for her. So, her remark about Saru who has grown up young and beautiful is highly reprehensible, just as it is offending to Saru:

> You are growing up; she would say and there was something unpleasant in the way she looked at me.... And it became something shameful, this growing up so that you had to be ashamed at yourself. (*The Dark* 55)

And understanding of the term 'gender' in all its ramifications will facilitate around standing around gendered consciousness and possible subversion of self-affirmation. Gender is a social and cultural construct rather than a biological one. Further, it also suggests that the movement from sex to gender involves an individual's participations. Thus the process of 'becoming' one's gender is invested with an emancipatory potential and attests to what butler calls 'the essential freedom at the origin of gender'.

Adrienne Rich defines patriarchy as 'the power of the fathers; a familial, social, ideological, political system in which man by force, direct pressure or through ritual, tradition, law and language, customs...determine what part women shall not play and in which the female is everywhere subsumed under the male'.

The sociologist, today, use the term *subaltern* not in the Gramscian sense but for women who have no voice in a patriarchal regime like India. What renders them subaltern and pushes them to the margins are factor outside their control like race, class, sex-categorization, region, gender, etc. Ammu in Arundhati Roy's *The God of Small Things* is denied higher education, whereas her brother receives it, because her father curiously thought that higher education may spoil a girl. Moreover, he considers it a waste of money. Even Saru's mother in *The Dark Holds No Terrors*, though unsuccessful, tries to dissuade the father from sending Saru to study medicine. Marriage subjugates and enslaves women. In a patriarchal setup a woman is recognized only by the name of her husband. Pappachi, an imperial Entomologist under the British use to beat his wife Mammachi with a brass flower-vase every night—all because of his frustration arising from empty retired life and also because Mammachi was a successful violinist and popular in the pickle-making business.

Ammu also speaks, through her revolt in her love for Velutha. But while Saru reconciles when her husband turns-up, Ammu and Velutha careless of life and the lives of others.

Thus, Indian diasporic literature in English problematizes concepts such as of nation, religion, gender, identity, space, marginalization, assimilation and acculturation in exploring the diasporic experiences of life. Focusing on experience of woman with distinct ethnic communities, sexual politics, etc., it brings out the realities of woman's lives. While as the male sensibility looks back with nostalgia at the culture left behind, women welcome new found liberty in the newly emerged postmodern social milieu which is free from constraints and restraints of phallocentric taboos prevalent back home.

## WORKS CITED

Bhatt, Indira. "Victims and Victimizers." *Critical Practice,* Vol. VI, No. I, Jan. 1999.

Calivis, Maria. "Towards A Better World." *The Hindu*, Sept. 16, 2001.

Customer Comments. *Online Review.*

Deshpande, Shashi. *The Dark Holds No Terrors.* New Delhi: Vikas Publishers, 1990.

Ilaiah, Kancha. "Social Equality: Lessons from the U.S." *The Hindu*, Dec. 5, 2002.

Menon, Leela. "Desroyed Childhood." *The Hindu*, June 17, 2001.

Rain, N. "Scimitars in the Sun." *Frontline*, Jan. 19, 2001.

Rama Rao, Vimala, J. Sindhu and Nirmala C. Prakash. "Arundhati Roy's *The God of Small Things:* A Spectrum of Responses." *The Journal of Indian Writings in English.* Vol. 26, No. 2, July 1998.

Roy, Arundhati. *The God of Small Things.* India Ink Publishing Co. Pvt. Ltd., New Delhi, 1997.

Selvaraj, A. *Christianity and Social Transformation: The Kerala Story.* ICRO, Trivandrum, 2002.

Thekaekara, Marcel Mari. "Annihilating Caste." *The Hindu*, June 10, 2001.

# 3

# Gendered Space and Diasporic Identity: A Reading of *Brick Lane*

*Nishi Pulugurtha*

Bangladeshi immigration to London is related to Britain's colonial expansion and trade. The very first immigrants from Bangladesh arrived as early as the eighteenth century chiefly as hands on ships. Many of them stayed back in London, thereby forming the first Bengali settlement in London. During the World Wars, the increase in labour saw the arrival of many more immigrants from Bangladesh. John Eade notes—"Tower Hamlets emerged as the political and cultural dynamo of this rapidly expanding British Bengali population."[1] Today the area around Brick Lane is the place that has become synonymous with the Bengali community and Monica Ali's novel *Brick Lane* (2004) takes its title from this street in the East End of London. Writing about this location in his review of the novel, Sukhdev Sandhu says,

> Brick Lane has always been a holding area, a temporary interzone for immigrants who have not yet settled; whose lives are defined by the past—their own or that of their parents—but who wish to seize the future; who wish to become the consumers rather than hunch-backed toilers. It's a slow and incomplete journey as far as many Bangladeshis are concerned. The canny ones, those with contacts or who strike it lucky with property or businesses, move away.... The others aren't going anywhere fast, no matter how gentrified the area.[2]

Sandhu suggests that the geographical locale, the street represents a kind of cultural condition that seems to arise from a particular historical moment.

Migration is a very unsettling experience and results in insecurity caused by uprooting and marginality. Immigrants redefine their identities and beliefs as an adaptive strategy. Monica Ali's *Brick Lane* is an example of the answer to the perennial question of how the individual can both remain constant and change. Marriage brings Nazneen to England. Relocated among an alien land and people, Nazneen's character undergoes a gradual change, one that supposes possibilities of new cultural affiliations and opportunities which takes place due to the external influences of the new environ she is in. This also involves a rejection of much of the past and an assimilation of new values.

Monica Ali's *Brick Lane* is written in the third-person narrative that privileges Nazneen's view of herself as living a life governed by religion and fate. The novel begins with the story of her difficult birth and how, when left to her fate, she survives. One of the major concerns of the novel is the notion of cultural differences and addresses gender relations within the Bangladeshi community in London, social isolation, the role of religion, and economic and emotional relationships with people and places "back home" in Bangladesh. Further issues include class, repression, attitudes to mainstream British life, and participation in the workforce. *Brick Lane* also refers to the ideas of education, conflicts caused by the very diversity of experiences, and aspirations of second generation immigrant children who attend British schools and the responses to racism within the community. Most importantly, the novel emphasizes the loneliness and disappointment that result from displacement and migration.

In *Brick Lane*, Nazneen transgresses boundaries fixed on her by her gender, culture and economic status. Her new life in London causes her to come out of the traditional space as she renegotiates the space she now inhabits. England, for Nazneen, becomes the place where she can exercise her power to choose.

This paper is a study of the gendered space that the diasporic subject inhabits. It examines the evolution of the new identity of Nazneen and the way she positions herself in the new socio-cultural environ she is in and how that contributes to her identity.

*Brick Lane* tells the story of Nazneen who immigrates to London from Bangladesh as an eighteen-year-old following her marriage to Chanu, many years older than her and an immigrant from Bangladesh. Nazneen has two daughters, Shahana and Bibi and a son Raqib who dies in infancy. Her character serves to highlight the position of women in the diaspora. She lives in England but then within her home it is a totally different world as she is completely alienated from the host country. The novel reveals the way in which migration brings about a change in the lives of the women who have undergone immigration. Nazneen has almost no contact with the world around her in London during the first decade of her life there. Her only link with London is her husband, she does not socialize in her new environment as her husband disapproves of it. Her space is limited to the apartment where she lives and the Bangladeshi women in the community that surrounds her in Brick Lane.

Nazneen was given up for dead at birth and her survival was nothing short of a miracle. Her mother always attributed this to her good fate. It is a lesson that she passed on to her daughter that everything in life was predestined. Though it was something she did question once, she was also grateful to her mother for her stoicism and courage. It is from her mother that Nazneen got the principle that "ruled her life"—"What could not be changed must be borne. And since nothing could be changed, everything had to be borne" (*Brick Lane* 16).[3] However, what is interesting about Nazneen's character is that inspite of such a belief she is nevertheless able to take things up in her hands and make an independent decision when she decides not to go to Bangladesh along with her husband Chanu towards the end of the novel. This is an extremely important decision, more so because it is something that she had been longing for. It is in taking this decision that she, for once, rejects what had been the principle of her life.

> It was mantra, fettle and challenge. So that when, at the age of thirty-four, after she had been given three children and had one taken away, when she had a futile husband and had been fated a young and demanding lover, when for the first time she could not wait for the future to be revealed but had to make it for herself, she was as startled by her own agency as an infant who waves a clenched fist and strikes itself upon the eye. (*Brick Lane* 16)

Avtar Brah notes that "Identity...is simultaneously subjective and social, and is constituted in and through culture. Indeed, culture and identity are inextricably linked concepts."[4] Brah further says that "...identity is not a singular but rather a multifaceted and context-specific construct."[5] This is evident in the development of Nazneen's character. Her character and personality have been clearly constituted by what she had been taught in her formative years in rural Bangladesh. The diasporic experience does bring into contention existing ideas about identity and femininity within the traditional discourse.

Marriage to Chanu, a Bangladeshi immigrant to England thrusts her into an alien land. Throughout the novel memories of the home that she had left behind remain with Nazneen. These memories are poignantly described by Ali.

> Nazneen fell asleep on the sofa. She looked out across the jade-green rice fields and swam in the cool dark lake. She walked arm in arm to school with Hasina, and skipped part of the way and fell and they dusted their knees with their hands. And the mynah birds called from the trees, and the goats fretted by, and the big sad water buffaloes passed like a funeral. And heaven, which was above, was wide and empty and the land stretched out ahead and she could see to the very end of it, where the earth smudged the sky in a dark blue line. (*Brick Lane* 21)

Unlike her sister, Hasina, who elopes, Nazneen marries the man chosen for her by her father. Chanu did not beat her and seemed to be a kind man. When Nazneen first sees him, he seems to be completely integrated within the cultural ethos of London, the city where he is located. He speaks perfect English and has a cell phone, which, for Nazneen is a symbol for the modern. It is much later that she realizes that the cell phone is used primarily to remind him of prayer times. A week after her marriage she overhears him telling someone on the phone about his newly wedded wife. The conversation lays bare many of the notions that she had as to why Chanu had chosen to marry her. It actually put things in the right perspective.

> A blind uncle is better than no uncle. Her husband had a proverb for everything. Any wife is better than no wife. Something is better than nothing. What had she imagined? That he was in love with her? That he was grateful because she, young and graceful, had accepted him? That in sacrificing herself to him, she was owed something?... She realized in a stinging rush she had imagined all these things. Such a foolish girl. (*Brick Lane* 23)

Chanu, is, as he himself puts it, an educated man. He has a degree from Dhaka University and also collection of certificates and diplomas acquired in Britain gracing his wall. He is immensely proud of his language and culture and loves to quote from Bengali. He also quotes from English texts, thereby showing his status as an educated man, and some of what he says do make some sense. He is ambitious and has great hopes for himself. When the novel begins he is a council clerk eagerly expecting promotion, however, the promotion never materializes and he if forced to become a mini-cab driver. His countless projects, ventures and ambitions lead to nothing.

Used to the open spaces and vast fields, relatives and friends at home, life in the confined space of her London home seems stifling to Nazneen. There is hence a great sense of longing for social contact.

> What she missed most was people. Not any people in particular...but just people. If she put her ear to the wall she could hear sounds.... In all her eighteen years, she could scarcely remember a moment that she had spent alone. Until she married. And came to London to sit day after day in this large box with the furniture to dust, and the muffled sound of private lives sealed away above, below and around her. (*Brick Lane* 24)

It is this that causes her to often reminiscence about her home in Bangladesh.

> And she drifted off to where she wanted to be, in Gouripur tracing letters in the dirt with a stick while Hasina danced round her on her six-year-old feet. In Gouripur, in her dreams, she was always a girl and Hasina was always six.... When she woke she thought *I know what I would wish* but by now she knew that where she wanted to go was not a different place but a different time. She was free to wish it but it would never be. (*Brick Lane* 45)

Avtar Brah in *Cartographies of Diaspora* defines the idea of home in two ways:

> On the one hand, 'home' is a mythic place of desire in the diasporic imagination. In this sense it is a place of no return, even if it is possible to visit the geographical territory that is seen as the place of 'origin'. On the other hand, home is also the lived experience of a locality.[6]

In the case of Nazneen, there is a deep sense of longing which causes her to slip off into recollections of her distant homeland. The letters her sister, Hasina, writes are another close link with Bangladesh. There is a possibility of return towards the end of the novel when Chanu decides that he would go back to Bangladesh with his family. However, by then things have changed and her children do not want to go back. Moreover, Nazneen, herself has changed. The idea of the country that he has left behind, Bangladesh, that Chanu tries to preserve and safeguard in his home are a contrast to the picture of the state of affairs in that country that Hasina's letters reveal. Hasina's letters to Nazneen speak of women being beaten, raped, and exploited and disfigured by their husbands with acid. As Francoise Karl notes,

> In the case of Chanu, the idealized Bangladesh he has kept intact in the corner of his mind and to which he will eventually return, comforts him in the illusion that his stay in the UK is only temporary and that it is merely a form of inverted colonization—"when the English went to our country, they did not go to stay. They went to make

> money, and the money they made, they took it out of the country. They never left home. Mentally."[7]

This desire to preserve the past in a time warp is a mode of preserving one's identity. Nazneen's relation with her husband is such that she does not argue or retort to anything he says. "She never said anything to this" is the only reaction we get when Chanu does not want her to venture out (*Brick Lane* 45). He believes that since he provides her with everything that she needs there is no need for her to go out. Nazneen's reaction to this is passive and she goes about her chores in a routine manner. The only person with whom she could connect to was Razia, who often came over to her place. Nazneen looked forward to Razia's visits and the stories that she told. Moreover, she was the one person who took her mind off from Hasina and her troubled state in distant Bangladesh.

Nazneen is also keen to learn English, something that Chanu feels there is no need for her to do so. During her first pregnancy when she ventures out and needs to relieve herself, it is the first time she speaks whatever little English she knows. She feels extremely happy at this and that too at a point when she is away from Brick Lane.

> And in spite of the rain, and the wind which whipped it into her face, and in spite of the pain in her ankle and arm, and her bladder, and in spite of the fact that she was lost and cold and stupid, she began to feel a little pleased. She had spoken, in English, to a stranger, and she had been understood and acknowledged. It was very little. But it was something. (*Brick Lane* 61)

The novel offers a striking description of the way Nazneen feels about Chanu:

> Every particle of skin on her body prickled with something more than physical loathing. It was the same feeling she had when she used to swim in the pond and came up with a leech stuck to her leg or her stomach. (*Brick Lane* 61)

In spite of an inherent passivity in the way she interacts with and reacts to her husband and his ideas, Nazneen does show her anger and revulsion for Chanu:

> Nazneen dropped the promotion from her prayers. The next day she chopped two fiery red chillies and placed them, like hand grenades, in Chanu's sandwich. Unwashed socks were paired and put back in his drawer. The razor slipped when she cut his corns. His files got mixed up when she tidied. All her chores, peasants in his princely kingdom, rebelled in turn. Small insurrections, designed to destroy the state from within. (*Brick Lane* 63)

In the case of first generation immigrants, the nature of contact with non-Bangladeshi people and social relations follow a gender pattern. Men intermingle with other people outside their community while the women socialize only within their family network since they are dependent on the will of their husbands. Second generation characters such as Nazneen's teenage daughters Shahana and Bibi and Razia's children Tariq and Shefali present different levels of assimilation to British culture. The nature of their identity struggles is different from those of their parents. They do not try to fit into the culture but rather work to find their own space by drawing on the culture, they have been brought up in often rejecting the culture of their parents. This, of course, brings about conflicts between first and second generation immigrants in the novel. Nazneen's teenager daughters Shahana and Bibi are integrated into British society. Their identity is constructed according to British cultural norms and they have no sense of belonging to Bangladesh. The conflict arises when Chanu forces them to maintain a link with his native culture. This seems meaningless to the girls, who are unable to relate to a place and a culture they have never known. Chanu insists on his daughters' learning Bengali and reciting Tagore:

> Shahana did not want to listen to Bengali classical music. Her written Bengali was shocking. She wanted to wear jeans. She hated her kameez and spoiled her entire wardrobe by pouring paint on them. If she had to choose between baked beans and dal it was no contest. When Bangladesh was mentioned she pulled a face. She did not know and would not learn that Tagore was more than poet and Nobel laureate, and no less than the true father

> of her nation. Shahana did not care, Shahana did not want to go back home. (*Brick Lane* 180)

Chanu is angered and frustrated by his daughters' rejection of what he thinks are their true roots. He wants them to adhere to a way of life that they are unaware of. As Hewinson says,

> The impulse to preserve the past is part of the impulse to preserve the self.... The past is the foundation of individual and collective identity, objects from the past are the source of significance as cultural symbols.[8]

In *Brick Lane*, the characters never get to see the real England. They spend a lifetime confined to Brick Lane and seldom venture away from it. As Chanu says, "All this time I have been struggling and struggling, and I barely had time to lift my head and look around" (*Brick Lane* 289). After living for thirty-two years in London, Chanu takes his family out to see London. Ironically enough, this trip to the sights of London makes him feel more like an outsider. Clad in a brand new outfit he has bought specially for the excursion, Chanu looks like a perfect tourist. He has loaded his "numerous pockets with a compass, guidebooks, binoculars, bottled water, maps, and two types of disposable camera", so much so that people end up taking pictures of him and his family (*Brick Lane* 289). When Chanu begins to pack things to go back home to Bangladesh, Nazneen stares at a picture of a country house on a mug. The picture of a cottage with a mouse leaning on a gate on a cracked mug is the picture of England with which Nazneen is not familiar with. Having never ventured out, an idea comes upon her that this is the England she would visit. This is because she never left the space of her home and her world is limited to Brick Lane. Chanu lives in a world that seems to have frozen in space. It is rather ironic since it is Chanu who brings home a computer and rants about the internet.

Nazneen suffers an undeniable diasporic experience as she undergoes a physical dislocation when she leaves Bangladesh to come to Britain. However, the experience is different in the case of her daughters, Shahana and Bibi who belong to the second generation and have been born and raised in London. But they too inhabit a border space, a hybrid space, a third space[9] and are also situated in what Avtar Brah calls 'diaspora space' which can be defined as "multi-locationality across geographical, cultural and psychic boundaries".[10] Brah goes on to define diaspora space as distinct from diaspora. Diaspora space:

> marks the intersectionality of contemporary conditions of transmigrancy of people, capital, commodities and culture. It addresses the realm where economic, cultural and political effects of crossing/transgressing different 'borders' are experienced; where contemporary forms of transcultural identities are constituted; and where belonging and otherness is appropriated and contested... *diaspora space*, as distinct from diaspora foregrounds what I have called the '*entanglement of the genealogies of dispersal*' with those of 'staying put'.[11]

What Brah says here is applicable to the second generation characters in *Brick Lane*. It is also applicable to the way Nazneen takes the one decision in her life when she refuses to return to Bangladesh with Chanu, instead she decides to stay on in London. Nazneen's daughter tells her that she could do anything here as this is England.

In Ali's novel, Nazneen was initially chosen by Chanu because she was a country girl and, as such, would make a good cook and a good mother. The reason why Karim chooses her is similar as she represents a certain idea of the Bangladeshi woman—"the real thing" (*Brick Lane* 385). Nazneen's affair with Karim clearly originates in her fascination for a world to which she does not have access because she is a woman. It is for the first time that she does what she wants to.

> She had submitted to her father and married her husband; she had submitted to her husband. And now she gave herself up to a power greater than these two, and she felt herself helpless before it.... How could such a weak woman unleash a force so strong? She gave in to fate and not to herself. (*Brick Lane* 299-300)

Nazneen's affair with Karim brings about a change in her and also in her relation with her daughters and husband. Most of all it makes her "feel good"—"It was as if the conflagration of her bouts with Karim had cast a special light on everything, a dawn light after a life lived in twilight. It was as if she had been born deficient and only now had been gifted the missing sense" (*Brick Lane* 301). Karim represents a new direction for Nazneen, a vent to look beyond the confines of the stifling atmosphere of domestic life. As a middle man, Karim acts as an intermediary between her and the garment factory, but on another level, he is also her link with the outside world. Nazneen is attracted to him Karim seemed very different from Chanu. He was more sure of himself and had strong stands. Even the way he dressed and carried himself was so very different. His certainty, dress, and language are signs that he belongs in the Western world—a characteristic towards which Nazneen feels strongly attracted. After they have become lovers, we see Nazneen ruminates that what she and Haṣina and Chanu sought but could not find was something that came to Karim very easily. He knew and had a place in the world. He does not stand out as different in the London setting and even when he displays religious affinities, they are sort of a hybrid kind, for instance he receives Salat alerts on his mobile phone. She finds his very act of praying erotic. Karim seems to stand for a very Western way of life for Nazneen. Unlike her husband, Chanu, who never listens to her, Karim often, makes her feel as if what she says is important. He, therefore, represents a space for her, a space which she never had. She begins to feel that she too is an individual and has some kind of an identity of her own. The reason why Karim likes her is that she offers a different image of womanhood.

> There's your westernized girl, wears what she likes, all the make-up going on, short skirts and that soon as she's out of her father's sight. She's into going out, getting good jobs, having a laugh. Then there's your religious girl, wears the scarf or even the burkha. You'd think, right, they'd be good wife material. But they ain't. Because all they want to do is *argue*. And they always think they know best because they've been off to all these summer camps for Muslim sisters. (*Brick Lane* 384-85)

He likes her since she is, as he puts it, "the real thing" (*Brick Lane* 385). This is because his notion of the "real" is bound by constructions of gender and culture.

Nazneen's slow awakening parallels a movement from inside to outside, a gradual emancipation which takes her from the confines of her house to that of her neighbourhood, then to the rest of the city. It is paralleled by a series of other, more profound changes. Against her husband's advice, she finally learns to speak English and the novel ends on a slightly humorous but touching image, that of Nazneen in her sari, ice-skating with her two daughters while her friend Razia tells her: "This is England,... you can do whatever you like" (*Brick Lane* 491):

> She looked at the ice and slowly it revealed itself. The criss-cross patterns of a thousand surface scars, the colours that shifted and changed in the lights, the unchanging nature of what lay beneath. A woman swooped by on one leg. No sequins, no short skirt. She wore jeans.... She said, "but you can't skate in a sari". Razia was already lacing her boots. "This is England," she said. "You can do whatever you like." (*Brick Lane* 491)

This scene represents Nazneen's emancipation and the beginning of a new life, the image of the ice and its scars can be seen as a metaphor for immigration.

Though she misses Bangladesh and all that it is for her, Nazneen's experience of life in London brings her face to face with a totally different world. Once she begins to work, she acquires a certain financial independence that allows her to stay in England when Chanu goes back to Bangladesh at the end of the novel. Chanu overcomes the trauma of his successive failures by purchasing a ticket to fly back to Bangladesh and make a fresh start. The situation would be very different in the case of exiles or migrants who do not have this choice. The letters exchanged by Nazneen and Hasina are a reminder that there are several categories of migrants and that migrants are lucky enough to have fled a place of oppression. Whenever he is faced with a new challenge or a new difficulty, he escapes into dreams, into a fantasized homeland which sharply contrasts with the more realistic picture of Bangladesh as revealed by Hasina in her letters in which she tells her sister, Nazneen, about deprivation and hunger, about rape and prostitution. The improved means of communication and transport have brought about a change in the way distances are envisaged. They have also, as Francoise Karl notes, caused a sense of destabilization "creating the de facto possibility of being in between places and in between worlds, of being one day at the centre of hypermodernity and the next to be locked up in an Indian house without air conditioning or modern facilities...."[12]

Monica Ali's novel also provides an analysis of the way religion comes to influence identity by playing an important role in that it links the diasporic subject to a larger imaginary community. As Vijay Mishra says "When not available in any 'real' sense, homeland exists as an absence that acquires surplus meaning by the *fact* of diaspora, so that Sikhs in Vancouver and Sri Lankan Tamils in Toronto clamour for a homeland (Khalistan or Tamil Eelam) or, in some quarters, Muslims seek a pan-Islamic utopia in the European heartland."[13]

The final chapters not only unveil the characters' real motivations but also present local political life in the suburbs of London in a very bleak light. The Bengal Tigers, who spend their time arguing over the choice of an official name and an official language, cause people to turn away from them and lose interest in political meetings. Ali's depiction stresses the fact that local political life is used by some to express their yearning for identity and their need for recognition. Hence, it does not have a lasting influence and dissipates slowly. The final chapters of *Brick Lane* tell of the struggle between Muslims and non-Muslims around Brick Lane and the problems of children and teenagers, violence and drugs. Interestingly, because they are rooted in the local, female characters seem somehow more likely to act against the breaking up of the local fabric, while their husbands, like Chanu, have turned their backs on the local.

The motivation and support to move on and change is provided by Nazneen's love for her daughters and by the experience of sexual awakening in the arms of her lover Karim.

She becomes more confident, happy, and evolves an identity of her own. Nazneen's feelings as an immigrant are quite different from that of Chanu. Being always in an inferior position in patriarchal society, Nazneen does not care for social status as Chanu does. Rather her feeling of deprivation comes mainly from the sense of bondage, lack of space in both the literal and metaphoric sense. Once she comes to know her power to choose her own destiny, she just cannot leave a country, which gives her the opportunity to do so. Thus for Nazneen, England is not just a place to earn money or a degree, it is a place where she can exercise her power to choose her own destiny. As a woman, Nazneen's metamorphosis supposes possibilities of new cultural affiliations and therefore new opportunities.

In *Brick Lane*, Ali shapes a woman character who transgresses boundaries fixed on her by her gender, culture, caste and economic status. Nazneen is determined by strategies of resistance, escaping from traditional space, using her sexuality in order to move beyond restrictions imposed on her and thus renegotiating the space in which she lives. The gendered space underlines the idea of home which remains problematic.

## NOTES

1. "Keeping the Options Open: Bangladeshis in a Global City." *London, the promised land? The immigration experience in a capital city* ed. Anne J. Kershen. Aldershot: Avebury, 91-105.
2. "Come hungry, leave edgy". *London Review of Books*. 9 October 2003.
3. All quotations from the novel are from *Brick Lane*. Black Swan, London, 2003.
4. Avtar Brah, *Cartographies of Desire*, 21.
5. *Ibid.*, 47.
6. *Ibid.*, 192.
7. *Critical Identities in Contemporary Anglophone Diasporic Literature*, Palgrave Macmillan, 2009: 81.
8. *The Heritage Industry*, London: Methuen Books, 1989: 86.
9. Bhabha, 164.

10. Brah, 194.
11. *Ibid.*, 242.
12. Francoise Karl, *Critical Identities in Contemporary Anglophone Diasporic Literatures*, Palgrave, London, 2009: 39.
13. Mishra, 2.

## WORKS CITED

Ali, Monica. *Brick Lane*. Black Swan, London, 2003.

Bhabha, Homi. *The Location of Culture*, Routledge, London, 1994.

Brah, Avtar. *Cartographies of Diaspora: Contesting Identities*. Routledge, London, 1996.

Eade, John. "Keeping the Options Open: Bangladeshis in a Global City." *London, the promised land? The immigration experience in a capital city* ed. Anne J. Kershen. Aldershot: Avebury, 91-105.

Hewinson, Robert. *The Heritage Industry*, London, Methuen Books, 1989 [1987]: 86.

Karl, Francoise. *Critical Identities in Contemporary Anglophone Diasporic Literature*, Palgrave Macmillan, 2009.

Mishra, Vijay. *The Literature of the Indian Diaspora: Theorizing the Diasporic Imaginary*. Routledge, London and New York, 2007.

Sandhu, Sukhdev. "Come hungry, leave edgy". *London Review of Books*. 9 October 2003.

# 4

# The Split-Self and Self-Assertion in Kamala Das's Poetry

*Deepshikha*

Most luminous among the Indian writers of English, to whom English is as natural a medium of expression in both prose and poetry, Kamala Das (1934-2009) has made enormous contribution to the growth of Indian poetry in English. Bold, free, frank and unconventional in expression and resentment and protest, she has made poetry the very instrument with which much could be achieved. Poetry to her was a tool to work towards freedom. Most Indian poets in English do not have the candour of Kamala Das in creatively analysing and evaluating their experience. Just as the American confessional poets such as Sylvia Plath and Anne Sexton she exploits the confessional mode in order to discover the images that evoke the joy and frustration of achieved womanhood. Sandra Gilbert and Susan Gubar have included her name as the only representative from Asia in their Norton Anthology of Literature for women.

With Kamala Das, we come across a new kind of woman's writings which is bold, daring, tantalising and self-assertive. Here is a woman conscious of her femininity but determined to vindicate it against male supremacy. Candid, daring and controversial in life and literature, Kamala Das, made enormous contribution to the growth of Indian poetry in English. Writing in two Indian languages, English and Malayalam, Das is the author of many autobiographical works and novels in both languages, many highly prestigious anthologies of poetry in English, various collections of short stories, as well as essays on a wide range of topics. Her work in English has been widely anthologized in the Indian subcontinent, Australia, and the West; and she has won numerous awards for her writing, including the Sahitya Akademi Award (the highest Indian literary/cultural honor) in 1985 and the nomination for the Nobel Prize in literature in 1984. From the 1970s when her career was at its peak, to the late 1990s, India-based, English-language literary critics have written extensively on Kamala Das.

Thus, of all the women poets of the present in India, Kamala Das projects herself as a fervent feminist poetic voice always exacting for a dignified place of hour, a respect for the naturalistic freedoms and choices. Her poetry contributes for the strong reactions and justifications for the most needful awakening of woman as a living entity in being-in-the world. Women's social unrest in respect of education and career, sexual desire and frustration, suffocation of a caged loveless marriage, numerous affairs, the futility of lust, the shame and sorrow of not finding love after repeated attempts, the loneliness and neurosis that stalks women especially and such other things which were not spoken of candidly are powerfully dealt with for the first time in her poetry. Those who say that theme in the poetry of Kamala Das is love and for Kamala Das love hardly goes beyond sex and lust do not do justice to her as they tend to neglect the seriousness of purpose in her poetry. Kamala Das protests against the marginalization of women and social injustices and communicates a powerful female sensibility in her poetry.

In their 'Introduction to a collection of Feminist' essays published in 1987 Gail Chester and Sigrid Nielson declare: "Writing plays a vital part in forming our perceptions of our lives as women, in working out our feminist views and in communicating them to others."[1]

Only by writing an expression could the woman writer succeed in breaking down existing social power structures and create a place for herself in the world of masculine hierarchies. The woman writer could thereby alter her existing marginalized position and accept her rightful role as a significant part of society. By writing the self, the woman writer could challenge accepted notions of the female and redraft general opinion on the feminine mystique. This exaggerated role of the woman writer is emphasized by another feminist writer Rosalind Brackenbury:

> Nobody writes in a vacuum, away from the political and social structures in which we live. We breathe the air of today's thought, we digest it in everything we read and consider; also, we create it. This is largely the role of women today: to create, present and consider a new world.[2]

Women's body is the main site of oppression and therefore they should write their body without censoring it, "Censor the body and you censor your breadth", writes Cixous in her seminal essay, "The Laugh of the Medusa" on *l'écriture feminine*. Writing should be more from the body than from the brain implying that women should write without rationalizing their feelings, they should write with the force of the unconscious which is a "reservoir" of tremendous energy. Kamala Das's method in her poems is quite similar to that of Cixous's method. Her poems sing the unfulfilled desire of women; the pain and suffering they bear as sexual objects; and the way they give up themselves despite their unwillingness. The women in Das's poetry sing their abyss which is very much what Cixous urges them to do. She writes poetry as only a woman can write. She celebrates femininity, woman's body to be more specific, and in the process proves herself to be a feminist of the most radical kind. Her celebration of woman's body has not been taken kindly to by the conservative circles. However with growing sensitivity to the feelings of women and increasing stress being laid on the integrity of woman's body, in the intellectual, literary and social spheres in recent years, her poetry has come to be seen in an entirely different light.

Kamala Das writes about the plight of womanhood in Indian society with amazing candour. As in her poem, "The Suicide" she writes:

I must pose,
I must pretend,
I must act the role
Of happy woman
Happy wife
I must keep right distance
Between me and the low
And I must keep right distance
Between me and the high. ("The Suicide")

Life is no bed of roses for an Indian woman. Her path is strewn with thorns in the form of innumerable do's and don'ts! Womanhood is a curse under the Indian skies. This is most tersely and poignantly expressed in the line "the weight of my breasts and womb crushed me" (*An Introduction*).

Her poem "The Old Playhouse" is a vehement indictment of patriarchy. A girl comes to the house of her husband with great expectations of love and happiness. Alas! Her new home soon proves to be the graveyard of her dreams. Kamala Das gives expression to a woman's indignation when her husband systematically reduces her to the position of a sex-slave:

You planned to tame a swallow, to hold her
In the long summer of your lust so that she would forget
Not the raw seasons alone and the home left behind her
Also her nature, the urge to fly.

These lines describe the fate of every girl who gets trapped into marriage. Her desire to grow, to have self-knowledge and self-realization is crushed. She is reduced to the position of a helpless hanger-on on her husband. She is nothing more than a sex-object:

You dribbled spittle into my mouth, you poured
Yourself into every nook and cranny. You embalmed
My poor lust with your bitter-sweet juices
You called me wife.

In the suffocating atmosphere of her new home the woman "loses her will and reason". The room is filled with the oppressive smell of "male breath". Even the cut flowers in the vase smell of human sweat. She feels herself to be a dwarf cowering beneath the "monstrous ego" of her husband. Kamala Das's feminism differs from that of Western feminists like Kate Millet, Elaine Showalter and Virginia Woolf. She is not opposed to male domination. Her feminism is rooted in love as love is what a woman needs most. Without it she will wither away like a flower plucked from its stalk. As she says:

> I want to be loved
>
> And
>
> if love is not to be had
>
> I want to be dead.

Kamala Das's feminism matured over the years into an existentialist view of things. One can notice certain ambivalence in her feminism. In her later poems, she does not regard her breasts and womb as symbols of subjugation. On the contrary, she exults in them. They are the symbols of her power and glory. Her poem "Jaisurya" is a celebration of motherhood. A woman needs a man to attain this moment of ecstasy which she gets when she hears the cry of her new-born baby. A woman's life would be lustreless without a man whose touch alone can make her "gleam like burnished brass" ("The Looking Glass").

The poetry of Kamala Das must be viewed in the light of her feminine consciousness. She acquired this consciousness under hostile circumstances dependent upon the society of her childhood days. Repressive attributes caused fragmentation of her self. As a poet, she is conscious of her creative faculties and tries to break chains and restraints. She indulges in self-awareness, self-exposure and self-introspection in order to define herself poetically. The aim of the poet is not self-exposure; but self-discovery and self-examination. She structures self-exploration in order to search her lost identity as a woman and as a poet. In a crowded world of men and women, she finds herself utterly alone. In poems like "The Freaks", "My Grandmother's House", "A Hot Noon in Malabar", "The Sunday Cat", "The

Invitation" and "The Looking Glass", she describes an ache growing inside her and disturbing her.

In her poetry, Kamala Das challenged the phallocentric idea of society. Her poetry seeks to declare through her writings that for a woman writing what she had written was not something totally unexpected. Her writing necessitates a feminist reading. Her ability to depict, not as a male but as a female, the situations, characters and dilemmas straight out of every day dogmatic life, particularly her own, needs to be recognized.

At the age of 15, she got married to Mr. Das who was an officer in the Reserve Bank of India, Bombay. Dwivedi records that her life became miserable in the company of her nonchalant, lustful husband whose sexual escapades with maidservants made "his contact with his wife usually cruel and brutal". The extract from her autobiography *My Story* is quite vivid and clear in this regard:

> She grew revengeful towards him, and reacted in a non-traditional fashion in lovemaking, offering herself to any handsome and resourceful man who came across her, and forgiving even her rapists. Her husband had no soothing words for her, no time to spare for her and was even busy sorting out his files and affecting signature on them. And as a traditional wife, she was expected to discharge her domestic duties well and look to the needs and comforts of her husband. This eroded her own distinct personality and dwarfed her forever.[3]

The above context rather interestingly asks if Das at all could in reality have considered her husband a friend. It is to be noted that in September 1971, Kamala Das published a short prose-piece in *The Illustrated Weekly of India's* "Love and Friendship" series. Eunice de Souza records that the piece titled "I Studied All Men—I Had To" is an account of Kamala Das's early marriage, her husband's admiring talk about easy women, sluts and nymphomaniacs. Kamala Das narrates as follows:

> Last week the Editor of a Kerala Weekly, a well-known capitalist, offered in return for my autobiography, a month's holiday at the most expensive hotel.... I was

> thrilled. My husband said: "Why not take K. along with you as diversion? You seem to find him attractive. After working hard, I shall not, grudge you a bit of relaxation." This is what I mean by friendship. It is hard to find a friend as good as my husband. In view of the tradition and conventionality of Indian women, this confession of Kamala Das may appear to be too permissive to be accepted.[4]

Das once said, "I always wanted love, and if you don't get it within your home, you stray a little."[5] Though some might label Das as "a feminist" for her candour in dealing with women's needs and desires, Das "has never tried to identify herself with any particular version of feminist activism".[6] Das's views can be characterized as "a gut response", a reaction that, like her poetry, is unfettered by other's notions of right and wrong.[7] Nonetheless, poet Eunice de Souza claims that Das has "mapped out the terrain for post-colonial women in social and linguistic terms".[8] Das has ventured into areas unclaimed by society and provided a point of reference for her colleagues. She has transcended the role of a poet and simply embraced the role of a very honest woman.

An analysis of her poems reveal that the woman personas of her poems represent her own mutilated self-tormented by both past and present and resulting in deep sense of crisis. She feels exploited and cheated by the civilization of which she is a part. Her community, family and civilization expect her to perform the role of a temptress, the goddess, the child and the mother. She has no respect for the culture which has made use of her. She examines her private life because that is the authentic life for her.

The 'Suicide' is a long poem which throws light on the poet's problem of identity. She is disturbed to see the erosion of her personality.

> But
>
> I must pose
>
> I must pretend
>
> I must act the role

Of happy woman
Happy wife I must keep the right distance
Between me and high
I must keep the distance
between me and the low
o sea, I am fed up
I want to be simple
I want to be loved
And
If love is not be had
I want to be dead....

She finds herself condemned to play the part of the "other". She is not allowed to choose her lot. It is some male who compels her to choose her roles. She is forced to act either as slave or idol. It was never she who chose her lot. She is fed up, grows nostalgic and goes back to the days of her Malabar house.

Kamala Das seems to find no way out of her tormented inner world and knows that there can be no easy solution. Her sense of identity is so fragile that she thinks there are many 'Is' residing within her every thought and impulse, claiming its own identity. In "*An Introduction*" she proclaims:

...I am the Sinner
I am a Saint, I am the beloved and the Betrayed,
I have no joys which are not yours, no
Aches which are not yours.
I too call myself I.

The painful assertion "I too call myself I" ensues from the typical predicament of being a woman. It is perhaps "the only way to retain her sense of personal worth in the world in categories". It has been rightly pointed out that one poem "Introduction" focuses on "pertinent questions relating to a woman's...identity...".[9]

The portrait of the woman persona that emerges out her poems is a complex one. It is so partly because Kamala Das reveals her feminine sensibility in diverse role such as a wife, beloved, daughter, sister, granddaughter, mother, mistress and even nymphomaniac. "Kamala Das has more to say about the pathos of a woman emerging from a passive role to the point of discovering and asserting her individual freedom and identity...."[10]

"The Conflagration" belongs to the group of poems that give voice to the woman's spirit of rebellion against male domination and ego. There is a desire to extricate from this "Soul Killing" subjugation:

> Woman, is this happiness,
> this lying buried
> Beneath a man? It's time again to come alive.
> The world extends a lot beyond his six foot frame.

"The Old Play House" also voices her protest against the male domination and the consequent dwarfing of the feminine identity:

> Cowering
> Beneath your monstrous ego, I ate the magic loaf and
> Became a dwarf. I lost my will and reason to all
> Questions I mumbled incoherent replies.

Kamala Das caricatures the feminine role to emphasize the plight of being a woman in this world. Her quest for self-knowledge only leads her to the painful realization that is an "Old Playhouse with all its light put out".

The "conflict between passivity and rebellion against the male-oriented universe" is a theme which preoccupies her most. Poems such as "The Proud One", "Captive", "Substitute", "The Conflagration" enable us to witness the transition from passivity to rebellion. In her poems she examines "the psychic disintegration which results, when self-rejects established norms". The psychological trauma, frustrations and the resultant quest for identity and wholeness is a result of the revolt against male dominated world and society. Kamala Das's poetry underlines the predicament of contemporary woman beset by the crisis of divided selves. Her aims as a poet are to bring about harmony out of her existence.

In "The Freaks" from the collection *Summer in Calcutta* (1965) she talks about the woman who is physically near her partner but whose presence is only darkness suggested by his dark mouth and "sun-stained cheeks". The woman has long suffered from this deprivation. There cannot be anyone to help as the man cannot unleash anything even if willing. This is the major cause of deprivation in the woman:

.... The Heart
An empty cistern, waiting
Through long hours, fills itself
With coiling snakes of silence

The need of love for a woman has been stretched out from mythological figures in the poems of Das. "The Maggots" is one such poem appearing in her collection *The Descendants* (1967) which highlights the passionate love between Radha-Krishna in the same tone as can be found in the mythology. Radha craves for the love of Krishna in spite of the fact that she is married. Radha has been loved by Krishna for the last time and on the same night she is being loved by her husband:

That night in her husband's arms,
Radha felt
So dead that he asked, what is wrong,
Do you mind my kisses, love?

Das brings in the compromising self of the woman who has always given herself. This poem brings in the contradictory selves of the woman in Radha which is common to most women in the world. Radha's body is facing the crucial moment of colonization, in a way; it is also implicative of self-exploitation which the woman cannot evade. "The Looking Glass" in the same collection as above begins with the line:

Getting a man to love you is easy

Which sets the tone how a woman can objectify the man if she desires him in her way. This is a very deconstructive attitude applied by Das but for this she should have to be honest about her "wants as a/ Woman". The woman stands equally with the man never hesitating about the gaze that would otherwise reduce her to an object. Symbolically, she stands equal to the phallus without fear, without the slightest thought of being inferior:

.... Stand nude before the glass with him
So that he sees himself the stronger one
And believes it so, and you much more
Softer, younger, lovelier....
Admit your Admiration.

Hidden in these lines is the politics by which she can bring the man to the way she wants her. It is suggestive of the subversion of the power of Symbolic order. Das does not blur the differences which distinguish a man from a woman but uses the same difference to fulfill the woman's desire:

.... Gift him all,
Gift him what makes you woman, the scent of
Long hair, the musk sweat between the breast,
The warm shock of menstrual blood, and all your
Endless female hungers.

Thus, we can conclude that Kamala Das's poems summarizes the thwarted desires, the frustration of living in a male-dominated world, the bafflement of the modern Indian woman who attempts to liberate herself, physically and emotionally, from the role of thraldom imposed by the past.

## NOTES

1. Gail Chester and Sigrid Nielson (eds.), *In Other Worlds: Writing as a Feminist*. London: Hutchinson, 1989.
2. Rosalind Brackenbury, "Women and Fiction: How We Present Ourselves and Others", *In Other Words: Writing as a Feminist*, Chester Gail and Sigrid Nielson (eds.). London: Hutchinson, 1989: 56.
3. Kamala Das, *My Story*. New Delhi: Sterling Publisher, 1988.

4. Qtd. in Eunice de Souza, "Kamala Das" *Osmania Journal of English Studies*, 1977 (De Souza, Eunice. "Kamala Das" *Osmania Journal of English Studies*, Spl. No. Contemporary Indian Poetry in English, Dept. of English, Osmania University; 1977: 1927).
5. Shobha Warrier, Interview. Rediff on the Net. Online. Available: http://www.rediff.com/news/1996/3107adas.htm
6. P.P. Raveedran, "Text as History, History as Text: A Reading of Kamala Das's Anamalai Poems." *Journal of Commonwealth Literature* 29, 2 (1994): 52.
7. Eunice De Souza, Ed., *Nine Indian Women Poets*. Delhi: Oxford University Press, 1997: 8.
8. P.P. Raveendran, *op. cit.*
9. Devendra Kohli, *Kamala Das* (New Delhi: Arnold-Heinemann, 1975): 188.
10. *Ibid.*, 29.

# 5

# Anita Desai in Search of Alternatives

*Gauri Shankar Jha*

The sway of feminism has plagued many a writer; Anita Desai is one of them. To me, feminism is a romantic concept which could not establish itself on any soil of the globe, whether the East or the West, as an alternative for the 'other'. Yet the search continues. Anita Desai is also indulged in the same pursuit and the present paper aims to trace her journey of the quest, which proves futile in its final leg.

A host of critics acclaim Anita Desai to be a feminist and in her writings, she behaves so. In the Indian context, the Hindu scriptures provide the highest berth to a woman, almost adorable in her all forms: as a daughter, a wife, a mother, a sister, etc. Still we have some unsaid and unwritten regulations to discipline the institutions of family, society, and community as a whole that becomes a part of culture and civilization—call it traditional, orthodox, or anything else. It is here that we encounter certain junctures, which prove suffocating, and uneasy; finally, leading to the perception that they are being dehumanized and forced to buckle down under the tormenting forces of the system. It is from here that the search for alternatives begins, progresses but culminates in the void—that is what we have to establish in this paper.

Reasoning and rationality have brought devastating effect to our thinking pattern and we are bound to suffer in such a trap. Women have been made women because they think so; the moment they start enjoying their status they will prevail upon their mail counterpart. Nevertheless, the anxiety remains unresolved: how to stop the influence of the West where women have turned into a commodity and exploited thereof. Anita Desai incorporates existential dilemma, psychological strains, philosophical queries, and cultural etiquettes in the premises of personal relationships. Women are silent and introvert activists who go on contemplating without yielding and thus become an object of study and research, a theory to be experimented and a specimen to be dissected and disseminated. Anita Desai's works prostrate to such conjectures. In all her works, she has observed human life and human relationships closely and keenly. She travels within an individual—the interior world and thus becomes, basically, an incisive curator with sharp psychological tools. Our present study concentrates on her seminal work *Fire on the Mountain* where solitude has been celebrated as a possible alternative and solution to the feminine existential problem, but finally dissolves into nothingness. Prof. Jasbir Jain puts it as below:

> Solitude is necessary for an inward questioning. It is necessary for a while to live with images, so that they can cohere and emerge. Privacy, she feels, needs to be fiercely protected, for all else is linked to it: contemplation, intuition, visionary sense, and finally, critical faculty. (1987: 6)

Solitude asks for withdrawal and the society asks for involvement: the choice is ours: and the turmoil continues for the whole life; it is all about detachment and attachment; the *Ramayana* and the *Bhagwad Gita*, the East and the West, the present and the past; the tradition and the modernity; the being and the becoming; the pervading and the possibility. Such an oscillation is, simply, to discover a meaning, a pattern and a substance in life; Nanda Kaul goes for it: her frantic desire is to divorce her vicinity and surroundings in all their forms of noise and action; isolation is her option; nihility is her desire; non-entity is her liking; periphery is her yen; that is why, she substantiates her inner desire:

> I want no more. I want nothing. Can I be not left with nothing?

Once she gets into Carignano she feels safe, sound and content. However, the world does not end here; she cannot be spared; Raka and Ila break in and puts an end to her dream world. Prof. Jasbir Jain elaborates it further:

> Withdrawal, which does not come naturally to her, takes her nowhere and involvement is equally meaningless. Both are destructive forces: there is no centre of equilibrium, no centre of harmony. It is difficult to be like Buddha and to meditate amidst suffering.... The impulse of the average human being is very different, it is an impulse of aggression...and sets the forest on fire. (31)

In fact, Nanda's movement towards withdrawal is an urge for freedom to liberate her from the enslavement of involvement, from the absurdity of life, to escape from the existential dilemma of life and to establish her own romantic world. It is the outcome of the tussle between the reason and unreason, conviction and self-knowledge, theory and practice, rituals and pragmatism—and it constitutes the paradox of human life.

Now the question is: how to define the human life, how to outline its objectives and how to make it meaningful. Nanda's movement from the mainstream to a corner point at Kasauli is almost without substantial reason, a rebellion's step, so is the desire of her granddaughter Raka and such a domain of unreason has the element of fantasy and unreality, of make-believe and of hallucination or imagination (37). This is the quest for alternatives, which Anita Desai wants to establish in all her works. For this purpose, she employs the tool of fantasy and the juxtaposition—that of the two worlds of real and unreal. Three worlds move simultaneously; that of Nanda, Raka and Ila and the seat of Kasauli is the epicentre of all these turmoils. Anita Desai makes a deliberate attempt to legitimise all the three worlds. By a different parameter, the world of Nanda Kaul is a conscious and self-grafted world, that of Raka is an unconscious contraption as the ulterior desire of an abandoned teenager and that of Ila is created out of compulsions of economic deprivation and the ideology of social reformation. Ram Lal's drive into the world of supernatural and superstition serves the intention of flawless relief from the suffocating constraints of worldly orders. That is why their associations are strange and uncomfortable. The companionship of Nanda and Raka is a forced one; Nanda feels ignored by Raka whereas Raka feels drifted towards Ram Lal for no reason at all. Raka is not faithful to anyone; she appears to be a rebel in search of absolute freedom. This is an unusual world, where all characters live as strangers, indifferent to all ongoing. Anita Desai brings the past and the present together and makes the characters play their roles. Nanda has spent all her life in consolidating the social sanctum and delivering the best for the contentment of this fabric, though it was all against her inner world's dictates; in her withdrawal, she has created the world of make-believe. On the other hand, Raka, with her immature mind evaluates every individual, every incident and every quarter; her inference is both tantalizing and horrifying. Both Nanda and Raka have fabricated an artificial world by negating and questioning the past, which is both fatal and suicidal. The world at Kasauli is an escape from the harsh reality of the world and the visit of Raka and Ila disturbs it; in such a case, the dream world is bound to be shattered.

The uncomfortable junctures in the novel are mostly out of unhappy conjugal life, for instance, the inconsiderate husband of Nanda and strange human relationships as that of Ila Das's brother's extravagant nature ruining the economy of the family and the sisters. It is a commonplace in Anita Desai's novels to portray the pictures of incompatible marriages; it can be felt in *Where Shall We Go This Summer* (between Sita and Raman), in *Clear Light of the Day* (between Bim's parents) and in *In Custody* (between Sarla and Devan)—these relationships are unfulfilled and unfulfilling. Most of the time the tyrannical husband/father are reluctant to forego the possession of the women that later on develops into the roots of violence and of psychological inhibitions. These inhibitions can be noticed in the discontent of other sorts of human relationships: Raka is a product of such a discontent that is why she is tempted towards the forces of destruction and not towards the glooming of civilization, and finally sets the forest on fire:

> the hill with its one destroyed house and unbuilt one... appealed to Raka with the strength of a strong sea-current pulling, dragging. There was something about it, illegitimate, uncompromising and lawless—that made her tingle. The sense of devastation and failure, somehow drew her, inspired her. (9)

Such a thinking pattern or situation is horrific, hostile and unexplainable, so is the incident of chasing of Ila Das by the young boys. Vulnerability invites violence and Prof. Jasbir Jain argues:

> Violence envelops everything, life and death, activity and passive acceptance, the conscious and the unconscious. It inhibits the world of mind, and the dreams and nightmares; it invades the streets in the form of riots in *Clear Light of the Day* and sprawls over the countryside in *Fire on the Mountain.* (80)

Such vulnerability confirms the attack on dignity and being of individuals, justifies the need of protection and independence in one's life, and brings the element of fear and insecurity. We also trace the two prominent characteristics, that of, involvement and withdrawal as a common trait of womanhood. The calamity is invited in the world of contrasts and contradictions. Anita Desai shifts the attention of the readers from the external world of wild nature to the internal world of turmoil, surmounted by the strained human relationships; that is why, Raka drifts away from the human civilization and is attracted towards the burnt houses, the demented birds and the lawless jackals. Whether her desire is legitimate or not, is a matter of contemplation. However, one fact is clear that her desire for solitude is the desire for freedom from the clutches of family, society and the norms of the world. Desai elaborates her desire:

> It was the ravaged, destroyed and barren spaces in Kasauli that frew her: the ravine where yellow snakes slept under grey rocks and agaves growing out of the dust and rubble,

> the skeletal pines that rattled in the wind, the wind-labelled hill tops and the seared remains of the safe, cosy, civilised world in which Raka had no part and to which she owed no attachment. (91)

All the three prominent characters of the novel respond differently to the world of Kasauli, and their responses determine their constitution: Nanda wants to merge with the nature and disown all the possible claims (4); Raka wants freedom from 'the seared remains of the safe, cosy, civilized world' (91); and Ila Das, 'like wandering lost in Chinese landscape' (141) who fails to withstand 'the heat or the chill and droop away'. The world created at Kasauli is a flawed one as Anita Desai wants to create it as a refuge for the loners, as an alternative space, as the forbidden paradise, knowledgeable and yet ignorant (a pseudo one), as an island well inhabited but inhospitable to the outsiders, fit for the singular insider and unfit for the others—away from the hustle-bustle of the external world—yet this world is not congenial, not habitable, signifying neither the hollowness of the past nor the barrenness of the present. What is the implication and utility of such a paradise, which stands as a meaningless alternative? Nanda Kaul has spent her whole life in learning the art of living: in her married life by sacrificing herself to the expectations of others, and now at Kasauli, by rejecting everything—yearning for a life of peace and tranquillity which she could never have—the intruders are there as uninvited beings: Raka and Ila Das; and, in the end, death and fire that brings an end to everything—the alternative world, the paradise, the dream land, the world of make-believe and the world of escape: it is, simply, a romantic world, an imaginary construct—all unpragmatic. Like Shakespeare's *As You Like It* Anita Desai's world is bound to collapse and so it fails to check the notion of ageing, barrenness, loneliness, decay and death, and what we have, is a shelter of all negatives.

Nanda has close affinity with nature because she has also resorted to drift away from the common ground of civilization and culture. Her ulterior wish is:

> Everything she wanted was here, at Carignano, in Kasauli. Here on the ridge of the mountain, in his quiet house. It

> was the place, and the time of life, that she had wanted and prepared for all her life—as she realised on the first day at Carignano, with a great, cool flowering of relief and at last she had it. She wanted no one and nothing else. Whatever else came, or happened here would be unwelcome intrusion and distraction. (3)

Vasant A. Shahane is of the view that:

> Nanda Kaul had reached such a stage in her life—old age, infirmity, resignation, loneliness, withdrawal, non-involvement—that she felt much closer to the trees than to any human being. (122)

In fact, Nanda Kaul has been exploited at different levels: as a wife by her husband with extra-marital relationship, by her children as mother and finally by the grandchild Raka in her solitude. She has no option but to submit to all these adverse forces revealing her handicapped entity—and here lies the intention of the novelist to project the pathetic picture of Indian woman.

Interestingly, even a lifeless mute letter becomes an intruder in her well-nourished privacy. She pretends to be completely detached from her past and the present to have a secure future that would be of her and her only; but the memory of the past irks her, the compulsions of the present irritates her—whatever it may be—in the name of duty, social obligations or the wild expectations of human relationships. So, Raka's arrival is an invasion on her solitude though she, herself, is another appendage—as another solitary figure to that island: "solitude never disturbed her" (80). Nanda compares her with 'uninvited mouse' and 'cricket', and she in her spirit belongs to the place:

> Certainly it belonged to no one else, had no meaning for anyone else. Raka alone understood Carignano, knew what Carignano stood for—she alone valued that, Nanda Kaul knew. (80)

Subsequently, there comes a time when the statue of the Buddha stood as the 'sole survivor' before these queer beings: Nanda and Raka, 'human portents of isolation' with 'intense desire for love', yet having 'mutual barriers of communications'.

Ila Das stands in contrast to Nanda, fascinating and repelling, a committed social worker with acute financial crisis, posted ads a welfare officer; her brutal rape and murder by Preet Singh is an act of utter vengeance.

Anita Desai has been able to create an unkind world: unkind to all its inhabitants—this way or that way. Now this unkind and unjust world is to be destroyed with a hope of a new and better world. Therefore, the fire is essential to emancipate and purify; it will devour everything and will allow regenerating a new pattern of civilization, a new identity in the world of self-exile. O.P. Budholia opines:

> The writer writes the subtleties of varied groups of human relations in this novel. The novel displays deftly the unconscious eagerness, curiosity for pursuing the unfulfilled ideals, search for belongingness and feminine sensibility—Carignano too exists like a living entity in this novel.

After all, her endeavour to preserve her identity and dignity, her quietude and solitude disturbs her and she has to trade back to her past foe solace and respite. Apparently, all characters are wrestling against odds of life and times, more particularly for the feminine cause and prove to be altruistic hedonist largely. However, Nanda has withdrawn, Raka is unaware and Ila is seriously indulged in the exploration which could not bring an end to the social disparities, evil practices and prevalent injustices, rather an end to the whistle blowers.

Obviously, Desai voices the multifacet of humanity and the intricacies of human relationships. There is a distinct metamorphosis of characters; at least Nanda has undergone so. In addition, Ila is engrossed in the elevation of ideal illusionary world of social reformation:

> I do believe the woman would listen to me if it weren't for that impossible priest. It's so much harder to teach a man anything. Nanda—The women are willing, poor dears, to try and change their dreadful lives by an effort but do you think their men will let them? Noo, not one bit. (129)

Carignano turns into a site for self-discovery. The female characters are haunted by the sense of insecurity, unfulfillment and inhospitality at several junctures. Therefore, the 'barrenness' and 'starkness' of Kasauli suits them. Nanda's psychic depth can be fathomed by her linear thought: "All she wanted was to be alone, to Carignano to herself, in this period of her life when stillness and calm were all that she wished to entertain" (17). Interestingly, Ila represents her past and Raka the present as well as the future. Carignano stands as a hub of penance and laboratory for experimentation for change for all the three characters who seek refuge to transform their lives: as an alternative to the chequered pattern of the society, culture and the world.

Perhaps, Anita Desai wishes to raise the issue of gender inequality that came up with the postcolonial resistance to patriarchal and colonial structures; definitely, it is a recent construct to focus on the discordance of race, gender and culture. It talks of 'the third world women', who have been victim of 'double colonisation' under imperial ideology of 'native and foreign patriarchies'. Yet this 'third world woman' could attract the attention of the mass as being marginalised and with the primary duty to serve the canter. Leela Gandhi maintains:

> ...the representation of the average third world woman as 'ignorant, poor, uneducated, tradition bound, domesticated, family oriented', victimised' facilitates and privileges the representation of the Western woman as educated, modern, as having control over their own bodies and 'sexualities' and the 'freedom' to make their own decisions...the 'third world woman' can thus be seen as yet another object of Western knowledge simultaneously knowable and unknowing. (86)

The 'third world women' is contrasted against 'native women' and Spivak terms it as 'gendered subaltern'. Spivak in her essay "Can the Subaltern Speak" writes:

> Between patriarchy and imperialism subject constitution and object formation, the figure of the woman disappears, not into a pristine nothingness, but a violent shuttling

> which is the displaced figuration of the 'third world women' caught between tradition and modernisation. (Spivak 1988: 306)

Thus, the women are a 'gendered subaltern' who either disappears or is silenced and the society never speaks about herself. Leela Gandhi finds her:

> She is simply the medium through which competing discourses represent their claims; a palimpsest written over with the text of other desires, other meanings. (90)

It must be noted that the feminist battle for individual rights was considerably mere successful in the colonies than 'at home'. They profess the activities of wife and mother-in-exile, housekeeper and hostess. The question of emancipation is both feminist and cultural. Leela Gandhi quotes Kirsten Holst Petersen as saying: "Which is the more important, which comes first, the fight for female equality or the fight against western cultural imperialism?" (93).

Ultimately, such anxieties about the 'women question' dichotomise the claims of 'feminism' and 'anti-colonialism'. Katherine Mayo in his book *Mother India* prohibits Indian women to copy the Western women; he says:

> It would be an evil day for India if Indian women indiscriminately copy and imitate Western women. Our women will progress in their own way—we are by no means prepared to think that the Western woman of today is a model to be copied. What has often been termed in the west as the emancipation of women is only glorified name for the disintegration of the family. (163)

Leela Gandhi quotes Partha Chatterjee saying that while it was deemed necessary to cultivate and imitate the material accomplishments of Western civilization, it was compulsory to simultaneously preserve and police the spiritual properties of national culture, he says:

> The home in its essence must remain unaffected by the profane activities of the material world—and women in its representation—westernised women was fond of

useless luxury and created little for the well-being of the home. (1920-22)

Throughout the novel, Anita Desai is trying to create an alternative female identity, which is divorced from the confinement of domestic life or away from the legitimacy of social dictates. These characters succeed in finding a new location, which is both, secluded, marginalised, and can be aptly termed as the world of wish-fulfilment. However, the mission fails and the artificial world proves to be a hub of wild illusions, of utter failure and uninvited death. To bring in the poetic justice and judicious catastrophe 'fire' is inducted to bring about a sort of annihilation and the possible regeneration of a Utopian world. Here culminates the search for the alternatives in sheer nothingness.

## WORKS CITED

Budholia, O.P. (2001). *Anita Desai: Vision and Technique in Her Novels*. B.R. Publisher, Delhi.

Desai, Anita (2013). *Fire on the Mountain*. Random House India, Noida.

Gandhi, Leela (2010). *Postcolonial Theory: A Critical Introduction*. O.U.P., New Delhi.

Jain, Jasbir (1987). *Stairs to the Attic: The Novels of Anita Desai*. Printwell Pub., Jaipur.

Kohli, D. and Just, M.M. (2008). *Critical Perspectives*. Pencraft International, New Delhi.

Mayo, Katherine (1986). *Mother India*. Indian edition, Anmol Pub., Delhi.

Spivak, G. (1988). *Can the Subaltern Speak* in *Marxist Interpretations of Culture*. ed. Cary Nelson and L. Grossberg. Macmillan Education, Basingstoke.

# 6

# A Comparative Study between Kamala Das and Taslima Nasrin in the Light of 'Feminism and Sex'

*Babli Mallick*

Kamala Das and Taslima Nasrin are the two most distinguished women writers who have considerably influenced the minds of high intellectuals as well as the lower middle class by celebrating their 'essential feminity'. They are like two atomic forces who try to destroy the claustrophobic embrace of fixed belief about women in their seemingly decorated, well-protected society under the invisible chain of patriarchal authority. However, now these writers by their torch of pain illuminate the buried darkness and bring the black and white picture of women predicament in modern society. They are like the 'New Women' who try to tear the mask of hypocrisy without caring a rap about their position as a beautiful, well-decorated nodding doll—with no complains and demands but only a scapegoat in the name of ideal daughter, sister, wife or mother. So, Kamala Das and Taslima Nasrin, after being reared up in a very conservative family under an all powerful father or husband revolt against it to free themselves from 'do' and 'do not's' cage and to fly free by confessing their literal self in the pages which is an appeal to the society to transcend from narrowness of restriction on women to the liberal state awareness.

While telescoping the features of Kamala Das's poetry and analysing her personal self, M.K. Naik in *A History of Indian English Literature*, observes:

> The most outstanding work expressive of the bitter service of womanhood by Kamala Das. The most obvious colourful feature of Kamala Das's poetry is the uninhibited frankness with which she talks about sex.... (But) Her persona is no nymphomaniac; she is simply every woman who seeks love, she is the beloved and betrayed expressing her endless female hunger, the eternal eve proudly celebrating her essential feminity.

So, Kamala Das's poetry can be termed as revolutionary poetry. This revolution come along with Kamala Das when she shattered all the chains of colonial and nationalist themes and allowed her literal self to breathe a fresh air for getting the individual or self-identity of Indian English poetry. She has brought this movement of change not only by indianising the English but also as a daring persona who, for the first time, had the guts to tell frankly about sex and the muted whisper at the core of womanhood and their intolerable pain as well as suppressed condition in the patriarchal society. In this context, Bruce King observes:

> Das's themes go beyond stereotyped longings and disappointments...are part of a larger than life personality, obsessive in its awareness of its self, yet creating a drama of selfhood.

In a Rediff Interview (dated 9 March, 2007), an interviewer asks her,

> Didn't you feel loved when you were young.

Das's reply to this echoes the core thoughts of her writings:

> Not enough really. That's why I leapt into several relationships which were not very correct, probably hoping to be loved. Because there was this capacity in me to love, to envelop something with love, and there wasn't anyone strong enough to reciprocate adequately.

So, we can say that her poetry is mostly informed by this intense desire to be loved. For Das's poetry certainly can be read without any knowledge of her personal life, for her concerns are universal, transcending the limits of the private. Das is very often marked as a feminist writer: as Dwivedi observes:

> Her poetry and prose reflects her restlessness as a sensitive woman moving in a male-dominated society and in them she appears to be a champion of woman's cause.

But rather than labelling Das as a feminist author, it is far more respectful to look upon her as someone who voices the discontents and disappointments of a human being deprived of the basic human necessities. Das's predicament as a daughter, a wife or a lover equates her with those who feel victimized in relationships, for most relationships are power equations in which the powerful/powerless division is constructed, almost by default. Das deserves, as Kaustav Bakshi observes in his book: *Indian Poetry in English* because she shows the courage to revolt against constructed notions of relationships and gender or social roles in her own way:

> Yet I was thinking, lying beside him,
>
> That I loved and was much loved.
>
> It is physical thing, he said suddenly
>
> End it I cried, end it, and let us be free.
>
> This freedom was our last strange toy.
>
> ['The Substitute']

*My Story* relates how she was denied love and treated as a sex object by her husband who was involved in other relationship. Das writes,

> I was a victim of a young man's carnal hunger and perhaps out of our union, there would be born a few children.

She felt that she was losing her identity as an individual for she was degenerating into a puppet expected to perform in tune with her husband's demands:

> You called me wife,
>
> I was taught to break saccharine into your tea and cowering
>
> To offer at the right moment the vitamins

Beneath your monstrous ego I ate the magic leaf
I lost my will and reason, to all and your
Questions I mumbled incoherent replies.
["The Old Playhouse"]

These very lines echo the eternal pain of the women in our society how they become a nodding doll first in the hands of parents than in the hands of husband. As it is clear from such lines in the poem "Next to Indira Gandhi" addressed to her father,

You choose my clothes for me
My tutors, my hobbies, my friends.
And at fifteen with my first
Saree you picked me a husband.

She feels no less incarcerated after marriage than she felt at her father's place. Gloria Steinem says,

> Women of every race are the only discriminated group with no territory, no country of their own, not even a neighbourhood. In a patriarchy, a poor man's house may be his castle, but even a rich woman's body is not her own.

Thus, Das's poems embody an intense search for a room of her own. She revolts against the social roles. She is compelled to play, only because she is a woman. In "Of Calcutta" she writes,

I was sent away to protect my family
Honour, to save a few cowards to defend some
Abstractions, sent to another city to be
A relative's wife, a house free from his home and
A mother for his sons, yet another nodding
Doll for his parlour, a walkie talkie one to worm his bed.

The male domestic violence is a recent issue, but the torture and suppression of women is an eternal problem. And Das exposes these drawbacks in a very startling way by mingling it with naked reality.

As already pointed out, Das's poetry is predominantly informed by an urge to be loved. So, after having failed in gaining actual love, she desperately turns to other men. Her husband hardly had any objection to her having sexual liaisons with them. Thus, in turn was a further below to her ego. She writes her poem "Composition"—

> When I got married
> My husband said,
> You may have freedom,
> As much as you want.
> My soul balked at this diet of ash.
> Freedom became my dancing shoe,
> How well I danced,
> And danced without rest,
> Until the shoes turn grimy on my feet
> And I began to have doubts.

Das continues to move from one relationship to the other. Her quest for love, however, does not end. In "The Substitute", she writes, rather contemptuously;

> After that love become a swivel door when one went out another come in.

She also boldly presents the sexual themes in her poem, such in "The Looking Glass":

> Notice the perfection
> Of his limbs, his eyes reddening under
> Shower, the shy walk across the bathroom floor
> Dropping towels and the jerky way he
> Urinates. All the fond details that make
> Him male and your only man, gift him all,
> Gift him what makes you woman, the secret of
> Long hair, the musk of sweat between the breasts
> The warm shock of menstrual blood and all you
> Endless female hungers. Oh yes, getting
> A man to love is easy, but living

Without him afterward may have to be

Faced....

Rather than a poet of free love, she expresses the disappointments of sexuality. She describes a void to be failed with others or with alternative passions. In "The Freaks" she laments a lack of deep sexual passions of the kind that go with love, there is mere appetite without feelings of intimacy. Das's notion of a woman's complete absorption in lovemaking is corroborated by Simone de Beauvoir:

> The act of love requires of woman profound self-abandonment; she bathes in passive languor with closed eyes, anonymous, lost, she feels as if borne by waves, swept away in storm, shrouded in darkness, darkness of flesh, of the womb, of the grave. Annihilated, she becomes one with the whole, her ego is abolished.

In this context, we can note that Das's poetry falls back on the *Radha-Krishna* myth. Das has admitted that she has never glorified lust. Her love, she says, is, "fashioned after the love of Radha and Krishna. There is something very beautiful about love. I cannot think of it as something horrible." In fact, quite a few of her poems suggest that her quest for love is directed towards a union with Lord Krishna. She writes:

Ghanashyam

You have like a Koel built your

Nest in the arbour of my heart

My life until now a sleeping Jungle

Is at last astir with music.

["Ghanashyam"]

Therefore, we can say that Das's poetry is chiefly conditioned by the several relationships she has had. However, as Bruce King observes:

> The interest of Das' poetry is not the story of sex outside of marriage but the instability of her feelings, the way they rapidly shift and assume new postures, new attitudes of defence, attack, explanation or celebration. Her poems

> are situated neither in the act of sex nor in feelings of love; they are instead involved with the self and its varied, often conflicting emotions, ranging from the desire for securing and intimacy to the assertion of the ego, self-dramatization and feelings of shame and depression.

This complexity of love and the conflict of her passions not only make her love more intense but also infuse the theme of decay and death within it. The earnest pursuit for true love and its failure, and the agony of separation and unfulfilment lends her to the verge of break down and suicide. In her poems like "The Invitation" she all the time tries not to listen to the call of the sea. But when she realized the ultimate reality she reflects,

> Darling, forgive, how long can one resist?

So, we can say that Das's poetry is not the mere portrayal of empty feelings. Though some critics like Vimala Rao, Iqbar Kaur and Vrinda Nair, have found the poems frustratingly inconsistent, self-indulgent and equivocal. But she may be defended by saying that her poems sketch the *picture of a woman who is unpredictable, real and whose attitude to life change as she matures.* However, we cannot ignore the intense appeal of feelings and emotions in her poems which pervades such lines as:

> My love is an empty gift, a gilded empty container, good for show, nothing else. ['Captive']

Therefore, with this confidence of her persona and the belief in herself, she boldly defies the fact that her ingeniousness in expressing and her basic sexual needs shocked many and comments,

> No, they did not get shocked. They pretended to get shocked. That is to prove to others that they are innocent, that they have never stepped out of the confines of their sacred marriage. Nobody get shocked. These things have been happening for years and years.

In this context, we can refer to the comments made by one of the famous and most controversial writer of contemporary age, Taslima Nasrin, who brings about a huge reaction among the readers. She tears relentlessly the mask of the so-called hypocrite, patriarchal society as she remains in the same tone of Kamala Das, when she was asked in an interview:

> What explains the hostility in traditional societies to women's writings?

In reply to that, Nasrin says:

> In traditional societies, we have a long legacy of men controlling the body and mind of women. Such societies have valorised motherhood and fabricated concepts like chastity. Women have been the victims of those notions for thousands of years. A man can have multiple relationship and affairs and talk about them. But if a woman ever writes about her love and sexuality, she is immediately described as defiled, treacherous and abominable. In human history, whenever a woman has stood up against patriarchy and spoken of her own liberty, she has been condemned and abused in a fallen woman. Quite sometime back in my introduction to another book of mine, I wrote that I love to call myself (?) fallen (?) in the eyes of society. To me the primary condition for a woman to be pure is to be a so-called fallen-angel. Among all the awards (?) that I have hitherto collected, I consider the title (?) of Pattita (?) of fallen woman to be the highest. This is an achievement of my long struggling life as a writer and as a woman.

This comment by Taslima Nasrin implies the deep agony of not only Nasrin...but the whole womanhood. But the basic difference is that some are conscious about their rights some are not. Some pretend to be drowsy and some are forced to sleep. The personalities like Nasrin and Kamala Das, De Souza and Silgardo dares to tie the bell in the neck of the cat and as a result pass through the storm of controversy and strict exist through their writing.

So, in this context we can say that the rebellion of women for the freedom of women, which was started by the poets like Kamala Das is carried on by Nasrin through her revolutionary writings. In the light of comparing Kamala Das and Taslima Nasrin in the terms of feminism, we can notice the same background on the basis of which all these feminist writers "blackened the white sheets of paper with the stigma of [their] heart".

Since feeling from Bangladesh in 1994 Nasrin has lived in many countries and currently lives in Sweden after expulsion from India in 2008 where she was denounced by Muslim clergy and received death threats from Islamic fundamentalists. She works to build support for secular humanism, freedom of thought, equality for women and human rights. She is feminist like Kamala Das, but it will be our fault if we categorize them confining to a certain section. They are not a different species writes differently after facing the life experience in different manner. But they are we all women. In this context we can remember Andrea Dworkin referring to the official website of Taslima Nasrin,

> Feminism is hated because women are hated. Anti-feminism is a direct expression of misogyny; it is the political defence of woman hating.

If we analyse Kamala Das' *My Story* and Taslima Nasrin's *Meyebela, Utol Howa* and *Ka*, we find the same male domination on women, starting from parents to husband. From the very childhood, her life and her desires are controlled by her father and brother that is also so common about the girl child of a family. All the restrictions of a father and of a husband seemed to have been made only for women. In this context we can refer to the famous poem by Kabita Sinha,

('I am that Girl')

> ....Ami sei mayeti, je jonmo theke bibhaer jonno boliprodotto...
>
> Jar mathar baireta niye sokoler vabhana
>
> Tar vitorta niye karo kono mathabatha nai....

If we summarize it, we can understand the inhuman torture of women in the name of care and religion.

Nasrin is ruthless in her depiction of her father as an inveterate womaniser, who did not spare even the maids who worked in the house and as frequently abusive and physically violent when his wife or the children did not comply with his orders; she dispassionately show how essential it was to his sense of self to control everything; from what and how much his children were studying to how much salt Idun (Nasrin's mother) was using in cooking. The children too knew where the power centre in the family structure lay; they made their demands on their mother, but ignored even the simplest of her wishes. Nasrin herself also admitted to use her. South Asian family values, constantly celebrated in our literature and folklore are shown up for what they are based on the woman's suffering and self-sacrifice.

Nasrin also expose the hypocrisy of religion and its use by the so-called pandit or maulavi. In this context, she relates about the 'pir' called Amanullah, a Bihari Muslim fanatic whose obscurantist ideas are characteristic of the brutality and the hypocrisies of all patriarchal religions. The Pir's notion of an ideal society meant financial, emotional, sexual and intellectual abuse of women. Religion allowed men social and sexual freedom, but cut women off forcibly from the outside world without offering them a corresponding security. Young girls in the pir's own family were preyed upon by his male disciples and by their own cousins and died of failed abortions. Nasrin was sexually molested by her mother's brother and raped by her father's brother. Powerless to reveal what had happened, "observes Barat Urbashi in her article, writing the self: Taslima Nasrin's Autobiography and the silent voices of Bengali feminism".

> to her, the child felt split in two while a part of her continued to live a normal life, the other part became the silent watcher, the recorder of all that was done and said around her, the part that, finally, found its voice in autobiography.

Throughout her autobiography Nasrin shows women resisting their marginalisation and victimisation in all the ways of which they were capable. Her mother took one way out. Other women responded differently, usually having recourse to passive aggression or collusion with their oppression. Nasrin herself stole money from her brother's pocket to pay for her books and magazines and for the letters she wrote to young fellow poets. She met young men secretly in restaurants to talk about poetry, but when she discovered their interests lay in her as a sexual object she would pay her bill and walk out. Kamala Das also in a number of poems express the same experience, as how women are only treated as sex objects to the more educated or uneducated.

This kind of brutality towards women has also been shown by Nasrin, while describing about her friend Chandana Chakma's elopement with an appropriately unsuitable boy and how she entered into a conventional husband-dominated marriage and distancing from Nasrin. Chandana was dead to her family and her Buddhist father performed her funeral rites. Evidently, therefore, as Nasrin points out patriarchal oppression of women doesn't stop only one religion or ethnic group.

Nasrin's representation reads very much like Simone de Beauvoir. She is also compared with Salman. Both of them are South Asian Muslims, live in the west and have had to face death and Islamic *fatwa*. But the similarities end there. Not only did Rushdie recant, no matter how fleetingly, his apparently anti-Islamic stance, which Nasrin never did.

According to Barat Urbasi,

> I believe that the violence of the response to Nasrin's autobiography is due not so much to its perceived attacks upon Islam but, rather, to the discomfort and the fear caused by the why she asserts her right to construct her selfhood, by her refusal to accept the patriarchal norms of a society unable and unwilling to accept a woman who with scaring honesty exposes male exploitation and oppression in everyday familiar relationships in her own life.

When her opponents (almost always men) vehemently reject her views about the way the women in Bangladesh are abused, instead of answering her arguments they assault her personally as 'shameless', her three failed marriages as proof of her 'unwomanliness' and her writing as market-driven soft-pornography. Nasrin herself says she is a 'fallen' woman ( ) because she is unfeminine enough to claim her rights as a human being, to reject male protection as oppressive and exploitative and to demand social transformation: "Unless a woman becomes 'fallen' there is no way she can liberate herself from the clutch of this society."

Nasrin does not in fact blaspheme Islam, because she does not believe. Neither does she write pornography; she merely articulates what convention dictates modest women should hide. What she has done in her autobiography is to transgress the norms of expression and representation that the Bengali '*bhadrolok*' tradition—that of the educated Bengali middle class with its strongly held beliefs in 'gentility' and decorum in everyday social relationship—has always upheld by revealing what lies beneath the family values so clear to the South Asian patriarchal, patrineal, patrilocal ethos: the subterranean and ambiguous sexual experiences and feelings, mostly violent and abusive, that permeates the apparently solid edifice of the South Asian family. By naming actual, living people instead of fictionalising and distancing herself from her personal experiences, she has explicitly demanded her right to narrate herself into existence not simply as daughter, sister, wife but as person and woman.

In this respect, she is the proper descendant of Kamala Das. But, when Kamala Das started writing poetry, the Indian women hardly had any voice in the running or the management of any public services. Kamala Das thought herself to be one of the victims of the prevalent orthodox attitude towards Indian women. Having personally experienced the cruel neglect of her feminine needs, she could not help giving vent to her grievances in her poem. She strove to establish her identity as a woman through her poems and she, in fact, tried to represent the whole womanhood. She echoes that woman must gather the courage to demolish the concept of male dominance and men's egotistical superiority. In a poem entitled "The Conflagration" Kamala Das has written:

> Woman, is this happiness, thus lying buried
> Beneath a man? It's time again to come alive,
> The world extends a lot beyond his six-foot frame.

In a poem entitled "I shall Some Day" addressed to her husband, she writes in a strong tone of protest:

> The cocoon
> You built around me with morning tea
> Love words fling from doorways and of course
> Your tried lust.

Or the agonizing feelings come through such lines:

> The heart
> An empty cistern, waiting
> Through long hours, fills itself
> With coiling snakes of silence. ["The Freaks"]

The critic like Shyam Asnani, has pointed out, the frustration of her love literally boils over in poems like "The Looking Glass", "The Freaks", "Substitute". While writing this poem, she did not borrow any medium of 'modest', 'standard' language, she has shown it, as like Nasrin, in what way it should be presented.

Kamala Das as well as Nasrin has been criticized thoroughly by the critics. They address them as 'sex addicted' and 'market oriented'. In case of Nasrin, the reaction does not confine itself within criticism but also death threat and many times she has to face physical torture. The so-called attacked 'honest' and intellectuals like Syed Samsul Haq, Hasmat Jalal sued Nasrin by claiming her writing "obnoxious and false and ludicrous". Nasrin defended herself by saying,

> This is a story of my life, whatever happened in my life I tried to narrate faithfully. Some would be pleased, some would not. How can I help? Life is such. If the writers of Bangladesh think that they are saints, that they are gods, then what can I do? I tried to see them as human beings and are they not?

She is also supported by the writers like Annanda Shankar Roy, Sibnarayan Day and Amlan Dutta, Mahasweta Devi, Bibhas Chakraborty, poet Joy Goswami and Poritosh Sen. Shonkho Ghosh though a male poet, frights for women right like these poets, which is echoed from the lines of ('Yumunabati'),

> One more unfortunate weary of breath rushly importunate gone to her death.

In this way, Taslima Nasrin through her revolutionary writing, after facing so much obstructs, has been succeeded to bring a new change in thought which was started by Kamala Das as the first prominent pioneer for women liberation from the chain of male domination. Apart from Nasrin's *Autobiography* (3 parts), the Novel like *Lajja* created a huge reaction. Being a human activist, she fears not to portray the torture on Hindus by *Razakars* on the demolition on 6 December, 1992 of the 16th Century Babri Mosque in Ayodhya, U.P., India. It contained the graphic description of a rape of a Hindu woman by a Muslim man. She tears the mark of the sub-human Razakars of Khalida Zia's government, the same representative of the Hindu Taliban in India like BJP, RSS, Shiv Sena, Bajrang Dal, Vishwa Hindu Parishad, Vidyarthi Parishad. While reading *Lajja* we can quote some of the burning quotes:

> Do the protectors of Hindu interests know that there are two crore Hindus in Bangladesh? Why in only Bangladesh in every country of West Asia are Hindus resident. Have the Hindu fundamentalists pondered what their plight will be? (10)
>
> They set fire to Dhakeshwari Temple and the police remained standing inactive. It didn't stop it.... The communal terrorists numbering 2 to 3 hundred looted the homes of 25 families.

Thus Nasrin as well as Kamala Das while writing about feminism and sex, portray the picture of society in its *naked reality* to infuse the burning coal in the mind of the drowsy, insensitive spectators. Kamala Das's poem like "The Corridors", "After The Party", "The House Builders" reveals the rapacious nature of the city.

While analysing Das's poetry, Bruce King, observes:

> Alongside Das' unfilled need for love, another prominent subject of her poems is the need to assert, to conquer, to dominate. There is, for example, her obsession with an older man who 'hurt' her in her teens and whom she

> obsessively feels she must capture as her lover. In her poetry love and hate are often neighbours, just as an assertion of sexual freedom sits near feelings of self-disgust expressed through depression.... While the poems describe a longing for a man to fill her dreams with love, she is proud of her conquests and ability to make men love her. Having taken a lover she will mock him. Rather than the seduced, she often appears the seducer, the collector.... Driven by a need for an all-encompassing love to fill her days, she is also someone involved in the game of sexual triumph with its trophies.

In the same way, Taslima Nasrin for presenting "excessive" sexual exposition in raunchy phrases. The writer like Shamoresh Majumdar even called her 'a whore'. Describing the 400-page book as nothing but pornography or "autobiographical Kamsutra", leading commentator and writer Masuda Bhatti wondered why Taslima, who claims to having had bad experiences involving elderly and senior male writers, had holidayed with them in distant resorts, alone?

However, while keeping in mind these charges against these writers, we cannot deny their contribution too as they, not only of their own, but also mapped out the sufferings of all the women as a whole, and dug their pen into the root of problems.

In favour of Taslima Nasrin, Hasnan Abid recorded his reaction in www.askerkagog.com, as he says,

> Those men are pretty much upset on her and called her 'whores'. However, everybody knows that her personal and sexual life is massacred and desperate. But she does not deny that. She tells the truth. She is one faced. But the guys like you (intellectuals) are double-faced. You show their famous and good face in the day-light to the public and become pussy-suckers at night. Why is that contradiction.... She is far away from your reach. She did a great job and revolutionary job. You people like to spend the nights with women, but you people like to sue against her when she wants to tell the names in public?

Thus, we can understand the reaction of public by the writings of these feminist writers. And after this awareness, the poet like Chandrabati and others re-read the epics like *Ramayana* and *Savitri* to depict the agonizing and overshadowed picture of Sita and Savitri in the dazzling light of the great heroes like Ram and Satyauan. We only talk about ideal woman not ever about ideal man. The term like 'chastity', 'purity', 'virginity' are only associated with woman. No one ever talks about the purity or virginity of a man, but the masculinity only should (according to general conception) be presented in their inhuman strength, their heroism and their power in the domination of woman, not for the woman but for their so-called 'prestige' and social status. They are ready to worship women as idol, but when it presents itself as alive; they do not waste time to kick them at back. This is reality and if you try to present it you will be 'fallen', 'patita', and even 'whore'.

Andrea Dworkin rightly observes,

> Woman is not born: she is made. In the making, her humanity is destroyed. She becomes symbol of this, symbol of that: mother of the earth, slut of the universe, but she never becomes herself because it is forbidden for her to do so.

We can also refer to Gloria Steinem,

> We'll never solve the feminization of power until we solve the masculinity of wealth.

Therefore, we can see that the poet like Kamala Das and Taslima Nasrin are not the dropped star of the dazzling and untouchable sky, but the very product of society and they having possessed the conscience as tortured soul, they celebrate the lives of the poem of Pablo Neruda from "I come from the South":

> I was born to sing these sorrows
> to expose the destructive beasts...
> I stir up the grief of my people,
> I water their subterranean hopes,
> for to what purpose my songs,
> The natural gift of beauty and words,

If it does not serve my people
to struggle and walk with me?

Therefore, while drawing the line of conclusion we can say that Kamala Das and Taslima Nasrin are none other than the projection of our suppressed selves. They are born to sing the sorrows of not only themselves but also ours, by exposing the 'destructive Beast' like restriction of patriarchal society who try to chop off the wings of these free birds. It is not only the chauvinistic dominance that makes women weak, but it is also the unawareness of women about their rights, which make them one who have lost herself "and now beg at strangers door/ To receive love at least in small change?". So, their poetry is like messenger to create a new society where the motherhood should be honoured with the mother even if she gives birth to a girl child. At the same time, it is also an inspirational energy by infusing with the scorching light of reality to discard the feminine shyness. Therefore, it's now the time to change the role of women from a ornamented nodding doll to the incarnation of Ma Durga to destroy the Mahishasur from this suffocating rotten recycle bin of society.

While finishing this article, I cannot suppress my temptation to add my poem as a tribute to them, as it is the direct production of their influence which make me aware about my own rights and awake me from my so-called drowsy state of 'education':

'THE BROKEN NODDING DOLL'

Love me, Love me, Love me.
My dried soul is tired,
Of listening the sad song,
The amorous poem, the romantic novels.
I no more belong to the
Springs of sweet sixteen.
I can no more satisfy myself,
Listening to the story of others.
I want to jump into the,
Fathomless sea of love,

Completely purging my soul, my mind, my body,
In those passionate waves,
In the thorns of unenduring pain.
I want to act and suffer.
Not want to sit passively,
In the boredom of life,
Waiting for the day.
For my arranged partner.
Collected by my parents,
After much bargaining.
I am a social animal of 20th century.
Educated intelligent, beautiful.
And possessing all the 'feminist' instincts
But... Yet... Even...
I am chained with the,
Age-old convention, the orthodoxy,
Which is coiling the root
of the flower,
Like the poisonous serpent
To drag me to follow
The confinements of religion,
The division of class,
Rubbing forcefully all my desires,
To entertain the society, the family
The father, the husband,
Like the nodding 'ideal' doll,
In the role of a good daughter,
And a devoted wife.
"I was a good girl",
They all said.
I was modest, studious, and obedient.

They all were happy.
On my eighth birthday
I got the ink pen.
My uncle gave it to me.
To sign on the papers,
When I will be the I.A.S.
They all hoped me,
To be the ideal doll.
"My brothers, cousins—the boys
Are all bad,"
They say
Flirting, playing, and disobeying.
But living their life.

"I was a good girl",
They all said.
I was so happy.
But on that day...
When all the darkness surrounded me,
My all repressed cravings,
Demands their fulfilment.
My soul was tormented,
My mind split into two.
The storm of so-called impure desires,
For the first time,
Assailed the ideal part.
They all 'Question' to my 'self', my 'mask'.
I was struggling with myself,
In my own prison.
But it's too late...
I can't break
The image of the good nodding doll,

To play with the hungry tide,
Of the sea of annihilation.
I am far from my own land.
I became alien to myself now.
I am in a combat within myself,
Countering the attack of the egoistic thoughts.
They all shouts...
The much-repeated words
Assailed like arrows in my ears.
"You are a girl,
Do not forget that."
I followed those words,
Like a parrot,
Sacrificing all the springs of my life.
Refusing all the temptation,
Of the eternal serpent.
To lead my life forever,
In the Garden of Eden.
But on!
This good girl is
Defeated within itself.
I am not what I was.
I am loosing my image,
My fame.
I have lost my mask somewhere.
I am naked.
I wept, I wept, I wept a lot.
Know not why.
Either for loosing my fake-identity
Or after being reawakened.
From my long tortuous slumber.

Was I a hypocrite?
Have I become 'fallen' now?
I am feeling much easier.
I no longer remain,
The pussy-cat, the punching bag.
The doll of overloaded 'EXPECTATIONS'.
The Nodding doll has been broken.

## SELECTED BIBLIOGRAPHY

*I gratefully acknowledge the indebtedness of the following sources in writing of this article.*

Abdullah, Hassan Al. *Taslima Nasrin's Ka: A Cry Against a Book*. July 31, 2005.

Banerjee, Benoy Kumar. *Indian Poetry in English*, Boos Way (Kolkata), & Kaustav Bakshi, 2004.

Barat, Urbashi. *Writing the Self: Taslima Nasrin's Autobiography and the Silent Voices of Bengali Feminism*, 1 October, 2003.

Bruce, King. "Women's Voices: Kamala Das, De Souza and Svilgardo"— *Modern Indian Poetry in English*. Rev. ed. New Delhi: Oxford University Press, 2001.

Das, Kamala. *Summer in Calcutta*. New Delhi: Everest Press, 1965.

——. *My Story*. New Delhi: Sterling Publishers, 1976.

——. *The Descendants*. Calcutta: Writer's Workshop, 1967.

Dwivedi, A.N. *Kamala Das and Her Poetry*: New Delhi: Atlantic Publishers, 2000.

Habib, Haroon (in Dhaka) and Suhrid Sankar Chattopadhyay (in Kolkata): World Affairs: *A Shocker from Taslima*. In *Frontline*, Vol. 20, Issue 25, 2003.

http://taslimanasrin.com: Taslima Nasrin's Official website.

Naik, M.K. *A History of Indian English Literature*; Sahitya Akademi Publication, 1997.

Nasrin, Taslima. *Amar Meye Bela*, 2 Vols., 1999 (Kolkata: People's Book Society, 2002).

Quoted in Ali Riaz, *Voice and Silence: Contextualizing Taslima Nasrin* (Dhaka: Ankuk Prakashan, 1995).

The Rediff Interview, 9 March, 2007 (www.rediff.com)

*Tonight, Those Savage Rite: The Love Poems of Kamala Das and Pritish Nandy.* New Delhi: Arnold Heinemann (India), 1979.

# 7

# *The Dark Holds No Terrors*: Quest for Identity

*Srutimala Duara*

The meaning of the word "feminism" according to *Oxford Advanced Learner's Dictionary* is the belief and aim that women should have the same rights and opportunities as men. Feminists agree that women, like men should also have the freedom. They argue for the existence of a female as she is not considered as a human being with an individuality, honour and dignity. Those having a feminist consciousness assert the need of realization of their identity and don't hesitate to talk out the periphery of women's lives. Development of feminine virtues with female nature and carrying out the responsibilities associated with the domestic affairs are considered as the only aim for the women. Patriarchal society considers women as physically weak to venture into the world outside the four walls of their houses and inadequate to make important decisions. Hence, women are reduced in importance to the domestic sphere where they have to accept the domination of a male counterpart. Traditionally in the Hindu marriage the position of husband and wife is clearly defined. The husband is expected to be the authoritarian figure whose will should always dominate the life of the wife. The wife should regard him as the master and should serve faithfully. Thus, the traditional concept of superior husband and subordinate wife had been the guideline of Hindu marriage. In an Indian marriage it is understood that the wife will merge her name, personality, lifestyle and in fact her entire life to that of the husband. Since ages it is considered that it is a woman's duty to house, raise children and give comfort to her family. They are deprived of all those pleasures which are the prerogatives of males.

Although the institution of marriage has been long enduring, it has undergone a number of changes. The process of industrialisation and westernisation has led to the breaking up of the traditional joint families. It has also brought about politico-economic, cultural and socio-psychological changes in the life patterns and attitudes of the people of India, especially among the urban population. With the growing emphasis on education, the Indian women experienced freedom and struggled to improve her lot. Education brought economic independence of women, which in turn changed their outlook, and the traditional equation of superior husband and inferior wife. The intelligent and educated protagonist soon begins to feel restricted in the traditional claustrophobic existence. There are a lot of confident and bold women who do not yield before the male hegemony. They are aware about their honour and dignity. They know very well that they should have the same rights and opportunities as men.

Shashi Deshpande has emerged as a writer possessing deep insight into the female psyche. Her major concern is to depict the anguish and conflict of the modern educated Indian women caught between patriarchy and tradition on the one hand, and self-expression, individuality and independence for the women on the other. Women are now treated on equal terms by law as far as inheritance of property and opportunities of jobs are concerned. But on the social level, these women who have been struggling since ages to assert themselves are still being jeered by their male counterparts and forced to remain silent. The voice of this newly emerged class of women, who have the same education as the men are having and are sometimes given the opportunity of supporting themselves financially, is heard in the writings of Shashi Deshpande. Her sincere attempt to break the silence of women has been widely acclaimed in home and abroad.

For writer Shashi Deshpande, writing was a means to self-discovery. She was exasperated being known as somebody's daughter, somebody's wife, and mother. She speaks her truth gently but firmly, and her words linger on. "I don't like to call myself a feminist writer. I'm a feminist, but I don't write to propagate an ism," stresses Shashi Deshpande. It would not be correct to term her a feminist, because there is nothing doctrinaire about her fiction; she simply portrays, in depth, the meaning of being a woman in modern India. Focusing on the marital relations she seeks to expose the tradition by which a woman is trained to play her subservient role in the family. Her novels reveal the man-made patriarchal traditions and the uneasiness of the modern Indian woman in being a part of them. The women have a voice of their own, a voice that had been suppressed for centuries. These women, who have the capacity to make free choice and need not therefore depend on the choice of the male, are portrayed in her novels. A voice of protest against the marginalized condition of women as a class is also audible in her works. The bold heroines, having moral courage necessary for self-assertion replace the meek and submissive heroines who were accepted as the standard women characters.

All Shashi Deshpande's works deal with the problems and issues of contemporary middle-class women. Her heroines are sensitive, intelligent and career-oriented. She poignantly expresses the frustration and disappointments of women and describes their bitter experience in the male-dominated society. *The Dark Holds No Terrors* narrates the story of a marriage on the rocks. It is about the traumatic experience of the protagonist, Sarita. This is the story of Saru who feels like a trapped animal, trapped by her own guilty feelings. The story that unfolds is the guilt she bears for her brother Dhruva's death, along with guilt of abandoning her parents, guilt about her mother's death which she learns about accidentally, which in turn permeates her entire life, her feelings about herself, her career as a physician, her marriage, her feelings towards her husband Manu and the kids. Throughout her life she remains trapped by her need to succeed at any cost, by the prize she has paid to succeed in life, by the reason behind her ambition to succeed, by her need to find somebody who would care for her. The true substance of the novel lies in the mental processes that Saru goes through during her apparently eventless existence at her father's place. She thinks. She analyses all the dark corners of her soul. She introspects. She judges life, relationships. We find her true self while she is unweaving her mind through memories and dreams. The process demands real effort. She endeavors hard to gain what she had lost-her self-respect. She tries hard to overcome her psychological fears. "The dark holds no terrors. The terrors are inside us all the time. We carry them within us and like traitors they spring out, when we least expect them, to scratch and maul."

Saru's character can be truly understood only in the light of psychological precepts. First, she carries within her the sad effects of gender discrimination. Social psychology deals with the stereotypes about the two genders. Saru's feminism springs out as a reaction to this discriminatory psychological set up of society and her parents in particular. Secondly, Saru also has the deep-rooted mentality of an unwanted child. Psychologists have dealt in detail with the mental makeup of an unwanted child. Thirdly and most tragically, Saru suffers the bruises of a terrible physical trauma on her psyche. It tells the conflict that she has to face as a doctor and as a wife. During daytime she is popular lady doctor and in night she is a trapped animal in the hands of her husband, Manohar who is an English teacher in small college. The novel begins with Sarita returning after fifteen years to her father's house. She once proclaimed that she would never come back to her father's place. She returns being unable to bear the sexual sadism of her husband. The rest of the novel is what Sarita remembers and a brief confession to her father about her trauma. Deshpande usually has the heroine as the narrator, and employs a kind of stream-of-consciousness technique. The narrative meanders between the past and the present. Her stay in her father's house gives Sarita a chance to review her relationship with her father, husband and her dead mother. In the end she has a better understanding of herself and others. This gives her the courage to confront reality. The initial experiences in her girlhood days influenced her so heavily that she wanted to become a powerful dominant person in her life. This made her realize that she can fulfill her ambitions through education. After her school years she aspired for college education. Her neighbours become aware of her professional identity, the day she walks back in a blood stained coat, after treating victims of an accident. Instantly her profession achieves for her a position superior to Manu's. She is recognized and respected by the neighbours who came frequently to consult her. The respect that Sarita gets disturbs the traditional equilibrium of the superior husband and inferior wife. Later analyzing her marital relationship she recalls, "...but now I know it was there it began this terrible thing that has destroyed our marriage. I know this to that the human personality has an infinite capacity for growth. And so the esteem with which I was surrounded made me inches taller. But perhaps, the same thing that made me inches taller made him inches shorter. He had been the young man and I his bride. Now I was the lady doctor and he was my husband."

In a patriarchal society, it is neither accepted by the man himself, nor by the society that women should hold a better position than men. In a marriage, if the wife earns more than the husband, the separation is almost imminent. No matter how much love the man claims for his wife, when it comes to difference in earnings and status, he always expects that he has to be superior to her. Over the years, women have accepted this without question, but now that she is a little more liberated, she questions this. As even Sarita says at one point of time that had it been the time when women were chained to their husbands, and liked it that way, it would have been better for her marriage, but the idea of liberation and equality has brought turmoil in our lives because women's expectations have grown but men have not accepted it yet. Saru and Manu had been in love deeply. They married against the wishes of her parents. But later when Saru becomes more successful and respected, it creates a rift between the two, which was forever. It is really a matter of wonder that a man who claims complete love and devotion for his wife, suddenly starts to think her as his competitor. The suffering that Saru undergoes makes her consider of writing to the young students of her friend Nalu. She longs to tell them the rigid rules of tradition according to which: "A wife must always be a few feet behind her husband. If he's an M.A. you should be a B.A. If he's 5′4″ tall you shouldn't be more than 5′3″ tall. If he's earning five hundred rupees, you should never earn more than four hundred and ninety-nine rupees. That's the only rule to follow if you want a happy marriage.... No partnership can ever be equal. It will always be unequal, but take care it is unequal in the favor of the husband. If the scales tilt in your favor, God help you, both of you." Saru's long hours of introspection into her marriage makes her realize that her professional success had killed Manu's spirit. Actually her introspection helps her to free herself from the feelings of guilt that she has made Manu what he is. She decides that she would not endure any more humiliation because of Manu's failure and her success. She decides to assert herself and fight her own battle. She realizes that her life is her own which she will have to shape as well as face the events of her life. There is no refuge, other than one's own self. With this mind she confidently waits to confront her husband and decides to go back to Bombay. Actually this going back to her husband is not to endure the humiliation. Saru as a wife finds refuge in the doctor in herself. It is the doctor who is going to help the wife in her to care her husband with the power of the doctor. She is bold enough to go back her husband and cure him of his depression caused by inferiority complex and bring normal harmony in her family life. This is how she is attaining power and identity of becoming a doctor and this doctor in her has given her comfort and happiness in her personal life as well as in the life of others. This capacity to create and give happiness gives one an identity. This is the identity that Saru searched for which gave her the recognition. Thus, the novel ends with the certainty that how Saru will no longer be a victim of Manu's frustrations.

*The Dark Holds No Terrors* explores the search of a woman to fulfill herself as a human being, independent of her traditional role as daughter, wife and mother. She has examined a variety of common domestic crisis, which trigger off the search. Deshpande's concern and sympathy are primarily for the woman. While revealing the woman's struggle to secure self-respect and self-identity for herself, the author subtly bares the multiple levels of oppression, including sexual oppression experienced by women in our society. The novelist in *The Dark Holds No Terrors* clearly portrays the sexual sadism of a frustrated husband's victimization of his wife. The discord and the disillusionment of the educated woman in a tradition bound 'Indian Society' is the theme of the novel. There is the ultimate realization at the end after a prolonged mental dilemma and a long drawn introspection.

Shashi Deshpande, in her works, defines freedom for the Indian woman within the Indian socio-cultural value system and institutions. She has steadfastly resisted the temptation of creating strong, glorified female heroes, and has presented the Indian woman as facing the very dilemma of having to choose between modernity and convention. Deshpande bares the subtle processes of oppression and gender differentiation operative within the institution of the family and the male centered Indian society. Deshpande's feminism does not uproot the woman from her background but tries to expose the different ideological elements that shape her. These include religious and cultural elements such as myths, legends, rituals and ceremonies, and social and psychological factors such as woman's subordinate position in the family and her restricted sexuality. The protagonists of Shashi Deshpande's novels are modern, educated, independent women, roughly between the age of 30 or 35. Their search for freedom and self-identity within marriage is a recurring theme.

Shashi Deshpande herself has strong convictions about feminism. Apart from her belief in the equality of the gender and in the right of both the gender to live their lives the way they want, she also believes that "until women get over the handicaps imposed by society, outside and inner conditioning, the human race will not have realized its full potential". Preference of male child is inherent in our patriarchal society. Many a times it leads to sibling jealousy, as also evident in the novel, but more than that it has led to angst for her mother. The truth is that the desire for a boy is so inherent in our culture, that no matter how much people claim that girls are as desirable as boys, once in a while the fact is definitely spilled out. In a society as traditionally male dominated as the Indian society is, women have to try harder to find their identities. But the modern Indian women, as portrayed in Shashi Deshpande's novels, are definitely working towards that goal. Hindu tradition plays a big part in her fictions. Hindu values a son over a daughter.

*The Dark Holds No Terrors* focuses on woman's awareness of her predicament, her wanting to be recognised as a person than as a woman and her wanting to have an independent social image. Saru's feminist reactions date back to her childhood, when she had to contend with sexist discrimination at home. The first half of *The Dark Holds No Terrors* deals with the vicious, prejudiced and cruel attitude of a mother, a strong product of patriarchal society who considers her daughter responsible for the her son's death. "Why didn't you die? Why are you alive and he dead?"

In this way the whole novel is full of incidents showing disparity towards a woman. Sarita's mother shows inveterate hatred and enmity towards her daughter after the death of her son when she remarks: "...Daughter? I don't have any daughter. I had a son and he died. Now I am childless" (196).

Saru's mother always kept two different measuring yards, one for the son and other for the daughter. Here is one example from *The Dark Holds No Terrors* to lay emphasis on the point:

> "Don't go out in the sun. You'll get even darker."
>
> "Who cares?"
>
> "We have to care if you don't. We have to get you married."
>
> "I don't want to get married."
>
> "Will you live with us all your life?"
>
> "Why not?"
>
> "You can't."
>
> "And Dhruva?"
>
> "He's different. He's a boy."

It is the inner urge of Sarita that she wanted the equal rights like her brother, Dhruva but her mother had never given her so much value. When Saru expresses her wish to stay with her mother all her life, her mother says "You can't", "But your brother Dhruva can stay", "He is different. He is a boy." This gender difference of her mother's treatment of her son and daughter enrages Saru. She rebels against her "If you're a woman, I don't want to be one."

There were several instances, including the one when Saru's mother asks her why she did not die instead of her brother, which reflect the orientation of the society itself. "You're growing up", she would say. And there was something unpleasant in the way she looked at me, so that I longed to run away, to hide whatever part of me she was staring at. "You should be careful now about how you behave. Don't come out in your petticoat like that. Not even when it's only your father who's around." In this way a traditional Hindu woman considers it her duty to remind her daughter that she is grown up and she should behave accordingly. The first experience of menstruation is horrible for Sarita and the mother is there to frighten her with the fact that she would bleed for years and years. The mother does not let her enter the kitchen and Puja-room. She is forced to sleep on straw-mat. A separate plate is provided to her to make her exclusion complete. Still in remote villages and even among educated people a woman is considered unholy during the menstruation period. Sarita thinks about it. "Things fell, with a miraculous exact exactness, into place. I was a female. I was born that way that was the way my body had to be, those were the things that had to happen to me. And that was that."

She looks forward to the role of a wife with the hope that it will give her relief from oppression of the mother, and will give her freedom. Women, in order to achieve her freedom, seek marriage as an alternative to the bondage created by the parental family. Saru resents the role of a daughter and looks forward to the role of wife, the hope that her new role will help in winning their freedom. The novel focuses on woman's awareness of her predicament, her wanting to be recognised as a person than as a woman and her wanting to have an independent social image. Saru breaks the umbilical chord and leaves home. This is her first public defiance of the patriarchal power system. Saru's defiance is further expressed, when she becomes economically independent and marries of her own choice. Saru is disappointed with her married life. The institution of home, which is supposed to foster the growth of a child, robs the woman of her right and respectability.

The fact is that the poor daughter Sarita always bared the opposition of her mother, be it the question of choosing a husband or a profession. Sarita's married life with Manu does not run smoothly for a long time and it makes her think that even pleasure is unreal and like an illusion whereas grief seems more real having weight and substance. The fact is that there is difference of status. Saru being a lady doctor is always given more importance. People come to her, surround her, ask for her and respect her and it is something which her husband cannot digest. And this is what changes the attitude of a loving husband into a sadist. Chapter VIII of the novel informs us about Saru's sexual tortures by Manu. She cannot free herself from him and when the fit is over, he is the same smiling Manu again. This confounds her bitterly. "The hurting hands, the savage teeth, the monstrous assault of a horrible familiar body. And above me a face I could not recognise."

The strong point about Deshpande's fictions is her delineation of the woman's inner world. Her protagonists are women struggling to find their own voice and continuously in search to define herself. Her major theme is 'quest for identity'. Her main concern is the urge to find oneself, to create space for oneself, to grow on one's own.

Now Saru feels it strongly that she is responsible for her own miserable, puppet like existence. Too much dependence on institutions like marriage is also sheer foolishness. Rather one should be ready to face all the challenges and troubles of life. Saru's decision to go with Manu shows her confidence and courage in this direction. Obviously, the problem faced by Saru is the problem of hundreds of such learned and professional women who become the victim of the double stand of society. If the husband is superior to her position-wise, she has to serve him that way but unfortunately if the husband is inferior to her, she is bound to face the sadism and ego of her husband like Saru. Indian society is still tradition-bound superstitious. No one dares challenge the existing patriarchal order. Let people boast theoretically that husband and wife are two wheels of a van, two aspects of the same coin but the practical truth is that man is always considered superior to a woman. He has first right on meal, fasts are kept for his welfare and domestic walls never limit his scope. Shashi Deshpande's novel explore the problems of women in terms of illiteracy, ideological brainwashing in patriarchal societal structures, the problem of dowry, the complexity of the issue of caste and economic status. Saru is a 'New Woman', who is educated intelligent and economically independent, she could not accept her destiny as fate written on her forehead.

Many of Shashi Deshpande's women characters learn to break free of the stereotypes which surround them—the stereotype for instance of the mother and wife who remains silent and sacrifices her own needs and her own self. Although she writes about harsh and controversial topics, Deshpande does not want to be seen as someone who writes about issues and problems—she is keen to point out that she is a writer of fiction. Her characters' struggles are those of ordinary women fighting to be themselves rather than conform to stereotypes—to a fixed idea of how women should be. She states, "I always feel kind of wronged when people say I write about women's problems, because I always feel I write about human beings, many of whom happen to be women. But then when I look back at my work and I think about what issue has mattered most, it is the conflict between the idea women have of themselves and the idea that society imposes on them of what being a woman is. And there's a struggle to conform to this image, the guilt when you can't do that.... I think this image, especially in India, comes through religion, through myth, through literature, through cultural stereotypes, through movies, they're all very strong. So I've been discarding all those stereotypes and all the mythical images."

According to Shashi Deshpande, the statement of emancipation is the freedom and responsibility of choice. She is certainly a feminist writer, but this is not her feminism that sees the male as the cause of all troubles. According to her the fault lies with the woman who submits to the male's sense of superiority. The statement of emancipation is the freedom and responsibility of choice. As we see in the novel *The Dark Holds No Terrors*, Sarita emerged as a woman of determination and positive attitude, though she had seen the whole women world suffering without any cause. She undergoes similar trauma, confronts reality and, at the end, realizes that the dark no longer holds any terrors to her. She survives in a male-dominated world that offers no easy outs to women. She neither surrenders to nor does escape from the problems but with great strength accept the challenge of her own protégé. Saru also undergoes the arduous journey into herself and learns to free herself of guilt, shame, humiliation and she is also initiated into the mystery of human existence. The epigraph of the novel, "You are your own refuge. There is no other refuge. This refuge is hard to achieve," (The Dhammapada) gains its total significance when Saru realizes that the parental home cannot be a refuge. She understands that neither her father nor her husband Manohar can be her refuge. She is her own refuge. She has to overcome herself; she has to kill the ghosts that haunt her; she has to find her own way to salvation. It is to be noted that Saru, at the end of the novel, has come to realize that her profession as a doctor is her own and she will decide what to do with it. "My life is my own." She will no longer be a puppet. Her marriage is a shadow. She held on to the marriage because she did not want to prove her mother right. Only she can be her refuge. Everyone is lonely and that there is no cause for despair.

It draws attention to women's inner urge to be recognized as a human being in this male dominated society. They are highly conscious about their identity. They don't want to be happy being a mere wife or a mother.

## WORKS CITED

Beauvoir, Simone de. *The Second Sex* translated and edited by H.M. Parshily, Placadon Classics edition published 1988 by Pan Books Ltd., Cavage Place, London.

Deshpande, Shashi. *That Long Silence* (New Delhi: Penguin India, 1989).

——. *The Dark Holds No Terrors*. Vikas Publishing House Pvt. Ltd., 1980.

——. "In Conversation: Sue Dickman with Indian Writers." *The Book Review*, Vol. 19, Apr. 1995.

Joshi, Rita. "Something Felt," Rev. of *That Long Silence. Hindustan Times*, May 1990.

Mukherjee, Meenakshi. "Ghosts from the Past." Rev. of *The Dark Holds No Terrors*, *The Book Review*, Vol. 5, Mar.-Apr. 1981.

Nandakumar, Prema. "Every Woman in Bombay." Rev. of *That Long Silence.*

Ramamoorthy, P. "My Life is My Own: A Study of Shashi Deshpande's Women." *Indian Women Novelists*, ed. R.K. Dhawan. New Delhi: Prestige, 1991: Set 1, Vol. 5.

Spivak, Gayatri Chakravorty. "'Can the subaltern speak' from 'Colonial Discourse and Post Colonial Theory'". Columbia University Press, 1994.

——. *The Indian Review of World Literature in English*. Vol. 2, No. II, July 2006.

# 8

# Assaulting the Darkness: A Feminist Critique of Kiran Desai's *The Inheritance of Loss*

*Garima Gupta*

The story of *The Inheritance of Loss* focuses on the fate of a few powerless individuals, so contextualized that it explores almost every contemporary international issue, globalization, multiculturalism, economic inequality, fundamentalism and terrorist violence. With these major stories, however, are interwoven stories not overtly visible. These are the stories of the women characters whose inheritance of loss is not dictated by any major international phenomenon but by the incidence of their gender. Amidst the roar of the major stories it is the silence of these minor stories that needs to be explored as well. The novel abounds in women characters—Nimi, Sai, Noni, Lola, Mrs. Sen and the unnamed, beaten and raped wife of the falsely accused man to name a few. All are minor characters but each has her story of confrontation and conciliation with the andocentric world and each has attempted to assault the darkness of a patriarchal set up in her own way. The two characters whose stories of loss are inextricably linked with that of the judge, the main protagonist, are Nimi and Sai—the wife and the granddaughter.

Juliet Mitchell maintains that any society that is patriarchal is predicated upon the use of women as objects for exchange. Women's identity is therefore determined by "their cultural utilization as exchange objects" (408). The primary form of exchange, according to her, is that of women in marriage. This exchange though a world phenomenon is most deeply ingrained in the Indian tradition and it is only through her husband that a woman gains respectability in the Indian society. In India social security is guaranteed by a man and it is the husband that ensures the dignity of a woman.

This is what dawns on Lola when she goes to meet Pradhan to complaint against GNLF boys who are encroaching her property. Her complains, however, fall on deaf ears. Moreover, Pradhan and his boys pass obscene and lewd remarks ripping apart even the last shred of dignity she had. She comes back, locks herself in the bathroom trembling at the assault on her dignity and all her thoughts are focused only on her dead husband. "Look at what you have left me to! You and your piddling little life, and look what I have to deal with, just look. I don't even have my decency" (245). Her decency would have been guarded by her husband.

Noni, the spinster, laments having waited so long that the time and opportunity to have a husband passed away and she repeatedly advises Sai not to commit the same mistake. Not only did she fail to get married she also had to relinquish her dream of becoming an archaeologist due to the patriarchal forbiddings. As she says, "...you know my father was the old fashioned type, a man brought up and educated only to give orders..." (69).

Though in a marriage a lady gains social respectability but she has to pay for it with the sacrifice of her identity. We don't know her first name, we know her only as Mrs. Sen or Mrs. Singh. "My name is someone and anyone" occurs in the lines by Jorge Luis Borges taken by Kiran Desai as the epigraph to her novel. The character that most forcefully embodies this is the wife of the Judge Jemubhai Patel. "When she married, her name was changed into the one chose by Jemubhai's family, and in a few hours, Bela became Nimi Patel" (91). "Our names contain, our fate" (147), says Salman Rushdie. Thus the marriage changes both Nimi's identity and her fate.

When Nimi is married she is a mere fourteen-year-old girl with no concept of the bond she is being forced into. She, however, is expected to perform the duties of a wife and her fear of sex is taken as an affront by the family and the relatives of the judge. They refuse to see her beyond her gender. "'Spoiled', they said to Nimi. 'Putting on airs.' How could she not be happy with their brains Jemu, the first boy from their community to go to England?" (92). Her childhood is rendered invisible completely obliterated by her gender. The 'baubles' are not able to disguise the 'fourteen-year-old' crying in terror but the fact of her being a fourteen-year-old *girl* does. Though Jemubhai, being a very young boy himself, is gentle and sympathises with her, the patriarchal stronghold is not to be broken.

> "Force her" the uncles urged him.
>
> "Other families would not be so patient", they *warned* Nimi.
>
> "Chase her and *pin her down*", the uncles *ordered* Jemubhai.

Eventually she is branded as a "spoiled" girl who has no sense of her place in the family. As Kate Millet says, "The whole weight of responsibility, and even of guilt, is...placed upon any woman unwilling to *stay in her place*" (189) irrespective of the justness of a situation.

The Judge leaves for his studies in UK and in his struggle, the deep intense painful struggle of an immigrant, forgets he had a wife who is the first one to greet him with a garland on his return after an absence of five-years. She has waited for five years at her father's house, waited for her place beside her husband that would grant respectability to her in society. These five years there has been no communication between them. She does not know where her husband has been and what has he *evolved* into "...whatever she did know was based on a few snatches of talk that had reached them in the seclusion of women's quarter..." (166). It is her lack of knowledge and an unseen pressure to compete with English women that fuels her greed leading her to steal the powder puff with its foreign scent.

Nimi has always led a secluded life which is destined for the women in India. Even as an unmarried girl in her father's house her world was confined to the women's quarters. "Here they lived an idle existence inside the women's quarters, the strictness of this purdah enforcement increasing Bomanbhai's honor in the community..." (90). This seclusion is so ingrained in her as a person that when she moves to Bonda where the Judge tours most of the time leaving her to herself she is not able to go out. The open gate does not represent freedom, liberty or opportunity for her. It serves to further intensify her loneliness. However, this seclusion of a woman is a matter of honour for the man. Her father takes pride in it and even her husband offers it as a defense when accused of her wife siding with 'Swarajis'. As Gilman says:

> In the 'propriety family' of the patriarchate, women remain men's property in the household; they are little more than objects whose purpose is to serve his pleasure or honour. The woman 'being so kept, she cannot develop humanly, as he has, through social contact, social service, true social life'. (39)

To Jemubhai Nimi's social inadequacies are visible not realizing that they are ingrained in her by her family and society to ensure her subjugation in the patriarchal set-up.

An effective instrument in the hands of a man, guaranteed by his physical strength, in the subjugation of women has been violence, domestic and otherwise, against her. Even Freud associates sadism with masculine behaviour. "The sexuality of most men shows an admixture of aggression, of a propensity to subdue...the sexual object" (21). Jemubhai's violence is unleashed at the very first encounter with his wife after his return. In fact, it is almost deliberate. "He did not like his wife's face, searched for his hatred, found beauty, dismissed it" (168). The act of dismissal is deliberate. He is angry with her because she has stolen his powder puff and this anger gives him a perfect excuse to be violent. Nimi tries to run, escape from the room fearful of his murderous eyes. However, the room has been bolted by the family and relatives so that Jemubhai can finally subdue his wife and prove his manhood by having an intercourse with her. One is reminded of their encounter before his departure for England. His uncles order him to pin her down and though he could not do it then, now this is exactly what he does. In fact, sex is an important tool that a man uses to assert his masculinity. As Kiran Desai comments when she speaks of Bomanbhai and of his side business, "He offered soldiers unauthorized women in an authorized part of town on whom they might spend their aggrandizement of manhood..." (89).

Kate Millett establishes that within patriarchy the omnipresent system of male domination and female subjugation is achieved through socializing, perpetuated through ideological means, and maintained by institutional methods. Irrespective of her will, there is no room of escape for Nimi trapped literarily and metaphorically by the society, its ideology and the institution of marriage. Eventually despite all the struggle and attempts to free herself she is grasped by her husband whose only thoughts are of violence, hatred, anger and disgust. He does not want to make love to her or explore her feminity. He wants to break it into a million pieces and sexual violence is the most potent tool in his hand. "...he clamped down on her, tussled her to the floor...in a dense frustration of lust and fury...he stuffed his way ungracefully into her" (169). This is what communion entails for Nimi—pain, disgrace, disgust and shame. The violence does not end with just the first day and one act. In fact, it becomes a routine with the judge who finds it a convenient camouflage for his inexperience, "his inexpertness, his crudity" (169). Thus, it is for his lack that Nimi has to suffer, as to Jemubhai, "...any cruelty to her becomes irresistible" (170).

As Marilyn Frye asserts:

> The root of the word *oppression* is the element *press*. The press of the crowd; pressed into military service; to press a pair of pants; printing press; press the button. Presses are used to mold things or flatten them or reduce them in bulk,... Something pressed is something caught between or among forces and barriers which are so related to each other that jointly they restrain, restrict or prevent the thing's motion or mobility. Mold. Immobilize. Reduce. (2)

Thus, Jemubhai having reduced Nimi to his desires, now tries to mold her according to his requirements. He even hires a Miss Enid Pott to coach Nimi in English language and mannerism. It pains him that she is not polished enough to attend parties or ladies club. In fact the most successful ladies are those who actively play a part in their husbands' careers. The writer puts this across through the character of Mrs. Singh. "In playing her part in her husband's career, Mrs. Singh had attempted to mimic what she considered a typical English woman's balance between briskly pleasant & firmly no-nonsense..." (171). All the wives who accompany their husbands are ones who have allowed themselves to be immersed in the Western culture for the sake of their husbands. All these apparently modernize wives are also victims of the andocentric society where they have to mould themselves according to the social demands of their husband's vocations. And this is what the judge requires from his wife.

This moulding becomes oppressive as it becomes aggressive. During dinner he picks up different English dishes and holds them upto his wife and when she does not name them he removes it from her plate. The judge reduces her typical Indian feminity to nothingness by criticizing as regressive all that is taken as an essential element of Indian womanhood. Nimi is a typical Indian married woman with her full buttocks, oiled long hair, trinkets, bangles and bright coloured clothes as are suitable for a married Indian lady. But her Indian-ness appears so vulgar to the judge that he literally drowns her into the toilet bowl after discovering that she was squatting on the seat.

Unloved, uncared, beaten and battered Nimi is reduced to a mere shadow of a human being. For weeks she has no one to speak to, her face becomes bereft of expressions, she stops looking at herself in the mirror and finally she is entirely engulfed with one emotion—that of bitterness and dread for him. However, the hold of patriarchal set-up is such that it is not the Judge's brutality that proves to be Nimi's undoing but her release from it. As Marilyn says, "One of the most characteristic and ubiquitous features of the world as experienced by oppressed people is the double bind-situations in which options are reduced to a very few and all of them expose one to penalty, censure or deprivation" (2). An unsuspecting Nimi is forced by Mrs. Mohan to an outing which proves to be a welcoming committee for Jawaharlal Nehru. As a result Mr. Singh takes Jemubhai to task who in his turn confronts Nimi. This time the fury and the violence take a new shape that of physical assault and he beats her blue and black. As the writer says, "The anger, once released, like a genie from a bottle, could never again be curtailed" (305). Thus to sexual violence is added physical violence till he feels so consumed by it that he is scared that he might kill her.

It is at this point that he decides to send Nimi back home. She, on whom violence is done everyday in one form or the other, however, is not happy on her release. She knows she can't go back. "She could take it for herself—in fact it would be like a balm, a dark place to hide herself—but for her family—well, the thought of their shame in her behalf was too much to bear" (305). But pregnant Nimi is forced by her husband to go to her parents house. True to her fears the family feels burdened when she is not taken back by her husband even after the baby has been born and even though Jemubhai's father pleads with him. Eventually she is condemned to live with her sister and brother-in-law, who it is hinted by the writer stages an accident in which she is burned to death, to get rid of her. Thus 'gods end their sport' with Nimi who gets her release in death.

Marx maintains, "The relation of man to woman is the most natural relation of human being to human being. It indicates, therefore, how far man's natural behaviour has become human, and how far his human essence has become a natural essence for him, how far his human nature has become nature for him." If *Inheritance of Loss* is read as a tale of loss that the judge incurs in his encounter with the west, his relationship with his wife reveals that he loses more than his self. He loses his essential humanity.

The genius of Desai is such that though in the Jemubhai-Nimi relationship she gives a severe critique of the institution of marriage in a patriarchal set-up, she does not completely demolish this institution. A beautiful side to it is shown by a very minor character Kesang, the maid-servant in the house of Lola and Noni. Her love with and eventual marriage to the milkman who looks well after her and her parents as well has so much intensity and authenticity that even Lola inspite of being a social snob is touched.

Nimi's loss is loss of human dignity, human emotions in fact of human existence itself due to the "Poverty" of her gender. She, however, is not devoid of strength and her strength can be seen in her quiet resilience. As Miss Enid Pott says to the Judge as she resigns her position, "You have a swaraji right under your nose, Mr. Patel" (172). Nimi refuses to learn English, she resists adopting the English ways, to love English food. She has courage enough to fight him on their first sexual encounter and nerve enough to call him a fool when he confronts her regarding her participation in the Nehru welcome committee and most of all she does not go crawling back to him, ready to make all the adjustments demanded by him. The Judge does not enquire about her death and accepts it as an accident. He does not bother about their daughter ending his responsibility by merely financing her education and it is to their daughter that Sai is born.

Sai's inheritance of loss begins when at a tender age her parents put her into the convent and leave for Russia. Thus bereft of filial love and bonding she is brought up in a place which has only rules to offer and no emotions and feelings. When her parents die in Russia leaving her an orphan she is taken in by her grandfather, Jemubhai Patel, the retired Judge in Cho Oyu, Kalipong. Cho Oyu, however, does not prove to be a release from the emotional destitution of the convent as she is taken care of by the cook of the house.

Seemingly modern and westernized, a contrast from Nimi, her fate is nonetheless a prisoner of her gender. When she arrives at Cho Oyu, Noni is hired as her tutor and the cook tries to teach her the culinary skills indispensable for girls. But more than anything else it is in her relation with Gyan that her gender is brought to the forefront. In Jemubhai-Nimi relationship Desai had explored the man-woman relationship in a marriage; in Sai-Gyan relationship she explores the man-woman relationship (two generations later and in a supposedly more progressive society) in love.

It is her love for Gyan that makes Sai aware of her womanhood. She begins to notice herself in the mirror, notices her features and her beauty and falls headlong in love with Gyan. However, this story too is not very different from history. In a relationship the woman is so conditioned by the society that she automatically assumes a subordinate position. So in order to satisfy Gyan's ego Sai plays down her family and her westernized upbringing. She tries to hide her sophistication in order to accommodate Gyan's crudity. "Gyan asked Sai about her family, but she felt uncertain about what she should say, because she thought if she told him about the space program, he might feel inferior and ashamed" (141). When they eat together at Gompu's, Gyan uses his hands while Sai eats with a spoon. "Noticing this difference they had become embarrassed and put the observation aside" (140).

Though Gyan's lack of westernization does not bother Sai, her lack of Indianness becomes a crime in the eyes of Gyan. She continues the relationship on his terms but that is no guarantee that a man would be satisfied or happy. A woman can only hope, pray and try to win a man's favour which becomes the centre of her universe due to the patriarchal system. But it is an ever eluding *blessing*. In case of Nimi it was her Indian-ness that the Judge took as an affront; in case of Sai it is her lack of it that Gyan finds repulsive. "She who could not eat with her hands; could not squat down on the ground on her haunches to wait for a bus; ...she who thought it vulgar to put oil in your hair and used paper to clean her bottom..." (176).

So the 'falling in love' period comes soon to an end for Gyan as he gets involved in the GNLF activities. For Sai Gyan's love defined her womanhood, for Gyan it is his belonging to a cause that defines his manhood. "It was a masculine atmosphere and Gyan felt a moment of shame remembering his tea parties with Sai on Verandas..." (161). Thus, Sai begins to stand for everything which is an impediment in his attaining his manhood. In fact all his frustration with the system, his inability to manage a job and his poverty make the presence of Sai irritable to him. "He needed to be a man. He needed to stand tall and be rough... yes, he owed much to his rejection of Sai" (259-60).

Sai much perturbed by Gyan's behaviour and days of loneliness sets out to search him and maybe coax him back to her. In Cho Oyu, whose time had already passed he was the only release for her. When she finds his house, she is taken a back by the poverty of the scene and he taken her discovery as an affront. Eventually the meeting that was supposed to set things right and strike a cord of reconciliation ends up in a fight and violence. "But he threw her aside into the lantana bushes and beat about with a stick" (261), trying to intimidate her physically. He stops only when he realizes that his sister has witnessed the entire episode and may tell on him at home. One can notice a pattern here that in both the cases, Gyan's and Judge's, men resort to violence on the woman to cover up for their lack. It is his sense of shame at Sai's discovery of his poverty that leads Gyan to physically intimidate her.

Sai begins to follow him home bit then realizes that she might become the butt of ridicule. It is on the depreciation of the 'other' that self inflates and Sai realize that if Gyan would turn her into a joke he would raise his esteem amongst his peers'.... "The more he insulted her behind her back...the more the men would cheer, the more his status would grow at Thapa's Canteen, the more Sai would be remade behind her back into a lunatic female, the more Gyan would fatten with pride..." (262).

Sai, however, is not Nimi. Society might place her below Gyan but she herself does not as she feels that her dignity is worth thousand of him. She stands upto him, exposes his hypocrisy, his arrogance and his stupidity. And at the end there is an optimistic note for her when Gyan tells the cook that he would come back to her with Mutt.

Characters like Lola, Noni, Mrs Sen are shown as stereotype ladies who gossip, read a little and live for their children. They have no ambitions and no intellectual pursuits. Further, Kiran Desai has commented regarding the status of women in our society sporadically. Thus when it is realized in Jemubhai's family that he is a promising son, "The daughters were promptly deprived to make sure he got the best of everything, from love to food" (59). The artistry of Desai is such that with an offhand remark she reveals the entire social ethos. When she describes the attitude of the sisters to Mrs. Sen and when they underrate her, of how she made a living selling door to door items collected from Dum Dum Airport, Desai mentions casually that these goods were collected by "mothers collecting dowries of black market items, the better to increase their daughter's chances" (131).

A story encompassing practically every issue could not have escaped the feminist concerns. The women in Desai's novels are all pegs in the same social wheel. They may be educated, westernized or illiterate, however, their gender guarantees them only one thing and that is a second place to men in their lives.

## WORKS CITED

Desai, Kiran. *The Inheritance of Loss*. Hamish Hamilton, India, 2006.

Freud, Sigmund. *Three Contributions to The Theory of Sex*. Dover Publications, New York, 1905.

Frye, Marilyn. *The Politics of Reality: Essays in Feminist Theory*. The Crossing Press, Berkley: California, 2007.

Gilman, Charlotte Perkins. *The Man-Made World, or Our Andocentric Culture*. New York, Charton Co., 1911.

Marx, Karl. *Private Property and Communism*. 1844 (Manuscripts).

Millett, Kate. *Sexual Politics*. Granada Publishing, London, 1971.

Mitchell, Juliet. *Psychoanalysis and Feminism: A Radical Reassessment of Freudian Psychoanalysis*. Pantheon Books, New York, 1974.

Rushdie, Salman. *Midnight's Children*. Jonathan Cape, London, 1981.

# 9

# Exploring Man-Woman Relationship in the Novels of Anita Desai and Bharati Mukherjee

*Era Tyagi*

Indian Literature in English has journeyed a long way to achieve its present glory and grandeur. At present, it is enriched by a number of women writers read and acclaimed all over the world. Their works offer penetrative insight into the complex issues of life. The fictional concerns of these women writers are not limited to the world of women and their suffering as victims of male hegemony; they also express social, economic and political upheaval in Indian society.

Man-woman relationship is perhaps the most important human relationship. It is the nucleus of social life. The theme is as old as the novel itself and can be found in Richardson and Fielding on one hand, and D.H. Lawrence, Virginia Woolf, Hemingway and Faulkner on the other. Literature, of all land and people celebrates this relationship which has an important bearing on conjugal life, filial love, domestic peace, family integration and social harmony. Nowadays these themes have become more important due to rapid industrialization, growing awareness among women of their rights and individualism and the westernization of attitudes and lives of the people. D.H. Lawrence says:

> The great relationship of humanity will always be the relationship between man and woman. The relation

> between man and woman, woman and woman, parent and child will always be subsidiary.[1]

In the hands of Indo-Anglian novelists, the theme got much success. R.K. Narayan talks of the incompatible man-woman relationship in *The Guide*, Mulk Raj Anand in *Gauri*, Raja Rao in *The Serpent and The Rope*, Manohar Malgonkar in *A Bend in the Ganges* and Arun Joshi in *The Foreigner*. About the changing facts of man-woman relationship in India, one of the contemporary critic says:

> The characters of Nayantara Sahgal, Anita Desai, Bharati Mukherjee, Nargis Dalal, Kamala Das, and a crop of emerging novelists of the new decades are modern voices; utterly different from the previous characters, reflect the changing facts of this relationship in India.[2]

Among these woman writers, Anita Desai has earned a separate space for her particular interest towards psychological insights and essential concerns. Desai focuses on the personal struggles of middle-class woman in contemporary India as they attempt to overcome the social limitations imposed by tradition bound patriarchal culture. Anita Desai is a modern Indian English writer, widely acclaimed, not only in India but also in the world of fiction writing. She emerged on the literary horizon after independence focusing on the contemporary issues.

The theme of man-woman relationship in Anita Desai's novels reveals her consummate craftsmanship. She broods over the fate and future of modern woman more particularly in male-dominated society. She, however, does not challenge the futility of marriage as an institution but discloses the inner psyche of the characters through their relations.

Her portrayal of man-woman relationship has been influenced by the existing intricate social situation. Man-woman relationship seems to be of particular interest to her as in most of her early novels she writes on this theme. She concentrates on the predicament of modern woman in this male-dominated society and her destruction after the marriage. According to Desai most marriages prove to be unions of incompatibility. Men are rational and matter of fact while women are sentimental and emotional.

Their interests, their attitudes are different. Naturally, they look at things in different ways and react to the same situations differently. Mostly women have been emotionally dependent is seen not as a loss of relationship but a total loss of self, which is then seen as neuroses.

Anita Desai mostly writes about the miserable plight of women suffering under their insensitive and inconsiderate husbands, fathers, and brothers. So man-woman relationship brings characters into alienation, loneliness, withdrawal and lack of communication that frequently occurs in her novels. Most of her protagonists are alienated from the world, from society, from families, from parents and even from their own selves. When these characters have to face alienation, they become rebels.

Anita Desai looks into the reasons for marital discord and illustrates how such discord affects the family. Sometimes the inability of an individual to be responsive to the behaviour pattern of her partner leads to strain and tension in the relationship while sometimes it is an account of varied levels of sensitivity that strained relationship occurs.

All these relationships between man and woman point out the plus points and minus points of brides and bridegrooms. In the Indian society for successful or unsuccessful marriage, a woman is held responsible. It becomes successful because of her love, wisdom, sense of understanding, tolerance and sacrifice. And when it becomes unsuccessful then women alone should not be blamed for this. Joseph Addison said:

> A happy marriage has in it all the pleasures of friendship, all the enjoyment of sense and reason and indeed all the sweets of life.[3]

Marital discord recurs in the novels of Desai. Her novels, with a touch of feminist concern, portray the failed marriage relationship which often leads to the alienation and loneliness of the characters; and thus with the destruction of human relationships. Her novels like *Cry, The Peacock*, *Where Shall We Go This Summer?*, *Clear Light of Day*, *Voices in the City* and *In Custody* also deal with the theme of human relationships.

The theme of man-women relationship seems of particular interest to Anita Desai, as she writes on this theme in most of her early novels. *Cry, The Peacock* is mainly concerned with the theme of disharmony between husband and wife relationship. It is about Maya's cries for understanding and love in her marriage with Gautama. Desai looks into the reasons for marital discord and illustrates how such discord affects the family.

The Peacock's cry is symbolic of Maya's tortured cry for love and life of involvement. In this novel Maya and Gautama have strained relationship because of their incompatible nature. Maya is dreamy, sensitive, and emotional, while Gautama is realistic, insensitive and rational. Maya is poetic while Gautama detached, philosophical and remote. Maya has tenderness, softness and warmth while Gautama is hard and cold. Maya got pleasure in the world of sounds, senses, monuments, colours, tunes but Gautama was totally opposite to her.

> How useless words and opinions sounded in that palpitating night air, how petty and expendable under the gorgeous star. Poor Gautama who was so intense and had never lived and would never live.[4]

Anita Desai shows the theme of husband-wife alienation in this novel by unfolding the relationship of Maya and Gautama. Maya is married to an old man who is detached, sober, and industrious lawyer. They two are totally opposite to each other in their temperaments, nature and attitude to life. About their unhappy marriage Maya says with regret:

> It was discouraging to reflect on how much in our marriage was based upon a nobility forced upon is from outside and therefore neither true nor lasting. It was broken repeatedly, and repeatedly, the pieces were picked up and put together again, as of a sacred icon with which, out of the pettiest superstition, we could not bear the part.[5]

For Maya, an average evening is hardly more than a quiet, formal waiting. A matrimonial silence can be seen in their married life. Gautam's hardness, coldness, and incessant talks of cups of tea and philosophy disturbs Maya very much. Maya is most suffered and pained by her utter alienation in the house.

Deeply hurt and emotionally tortured, she grows alienated. The total lack of communication from the side of Gautama is not understood by her:

> How little he know of my suffering, or of how to comfort me.... Telling me to go to sleep while he looked at his papers, he did not give another thought to me, to either the soft, willing body or the lonely, wanting mind that wanted near us bed.[6]

We can understand Maya's character in a better and clear way if we go back into her past life. Her life at her father's house had little touch with reality. She was fed on fairy tales, the "Arabian nights, the glories and bravado of Indian mythology, long and astounding tales of principles and regal queens of jackals and tigers."[7] She lived as a toy princess in a toy world. Maya is an admirer of life. Thinking this she fears for her life and decided of keeping the secret for herself at any cost:

> He must not know, not even guess. Never, never, never. If he guessed new dangers would arise like sudden fires out of the cracked earth. Ah, if Gautama found out would he, might he not put me in peril of my life? Did he not love life too?[8]

Sex is not only an intensely and intrusively pleasurable experience but it can act as a revitalizing force in an otherwise sterile life. Maya's earth bound nature makes her well inclined to derive the fullest satisfaction from the intimate experience. But she is disappointed from this side even due to Gautama's age and attitude to sex. This love-making is shown as utterly devoid of passion. The tension between Maya and Gautama reaches its climax. Gautama in utter disgust says, "Really, it is impossible to talk to a woman."[8] After being frustrated by Gautama's coldness she gives herself up to a fit of pillow beating. She slept sleepless nights, as she hungered for his companionship.

> His companionship was a necessity. I required his closet understanding. How was I to gain it? We did not agree on which point on what grounds this closeness of mind was necessary.[9]

Gautama made no attempt to take interest in these things which were liked by Maya.

> Yes, yes, he said already thinking of something else, having shrugged my words off as superfluous, trivial and there was no way I could make him believe that this, the night filed with these several scents their carrying essences and associations, their effects on me, on us, were all important to the very core off the night of our moods tonight.[10]

The persistent behaviour of Maya made Gautama lose his patience and he cries out:

> Good God! He cried throwing up his hands. Are you, after all of those females who will each day, bathe and clothe their plaster gods and goddesses and feed them with sweetmeats, making yourself believe in their life, when your logic tells you they are made of mud and it is your hungry children who are real.[11]

Maya hungered and hungered. And this hunger was not satisfied. Now what was she to do? To protest but it was not taught to her by her father, he taught her to accept the life not to protest. She felt her relationship with Gautama was like a relationship with death. Under the stress of fear she lost her sense and thought thus as Gautama did not love life so it should be Gautama who should die, not she. She says, "it was I who meant to live".[12] She killed Gautama in a fit of madness and then commits suicide.

In *Clear Light of Day*, Anita Desai does not talk about husband-wife relationship rather she talks of brother-sister relationship. Bim, the protagonist of this novel does not get married because she wants to devote herself thoroughly to the care of her old Mira Masi, mentally retarted brother Baba, her younger brother and sister Raja and Tara. Bim was very fond of Raja. Bim and Raja were attached to each other, they were very close, they use to understand each other thoroughly. They used to read, play and go for walks together. Raja was fond of composing the poems and he used to read out these poems for Bim, although these poems were merely imitation of whatever he had read, yet she praised him and considered him a great poet. She took care of him, and loved like a mother and thought that one day he will take the responsibilities of the house and will fulfill the place of the father.

The colour, charm and fashion of society did not fascinate Bim, while her brother Raja was "inclined towards society, company, towards colour, song and charm".[13] It amazed and enchanted him that in the Hyder Ali household such elements were part of their lives, of their background. Raja in his illness decides to go to Hyder Ali who was in Hyderabad now. Hyder Ali fascinated and charmed Raja:

> I have to go. I have to begin my life sometime, don't I. You don't want me to spend all my life down in this hole, do you? You don't think I am to go on living just to keep my brother and sister company; do you?[14]

After reaching Hyderabad, Raja soon marries Hyder Ali's daughter Benazir. When Bim comes to know about it, she felt that her brother Raja would no more be with her, and support her. When Raja left the home, Bim sits down on the steps by Baba's side, she prepares herself to face the situation. She knows that Raja now will never come back:

> Everyone's gone.... They won't come back. We will be alone now.... We needn't worry now. You are not afraid, are you? There is no need to be afraid. It is as if we were children again—sitting on the verandah waiting for father and mother when it is growing dark. It wasn't so bad then...was it?[15]

She criticizes Raja at this moment. Their relationship goes on as think's her brother, a poet, has transformed into a businessman. She realizes that the males always neglect woman she starts hating her brother and father now. She thinks:

> Father never bothered to teach me. For all father cared. I could have grown up literate and—and cooked for my living or swept. So I had to teach myself history and teach myself to teach, but father never realized and Raja doesn't realize.[16]

Once Raja writes her a letter and tells that he has inherited the property of Hyder Ali; and assures Bim that she could stay in the house for as long she wanted, he will never ask her to vacate the house and will never increase the rent. After reading the letters she became very angry and it gave her pain, a feeling of humiliation and irritation increased in her by this letter. The relationship of Bim and Raja gets affected seriously after the letter: it weakened their relationship and it remains no love anymore here.

Now everything was changed, she found faults and mistakes in everything whatever Raja did. Bim loved everyone equally Raja, Tara, Baba, all were her life, they were parts of her, she felt perfection with them. They all could make the perfect world for her. And if anyone of them was missing, its perfection would be gone. She loved them equally and if today they're not together, it is because of her imperfect love and care.

Tears were falling down on the sides of her face and she now felt a kind of relief and peace. From her room she takes out a bundle of papers, on these papers were written the poems which Raja used to write earlier. She wants to empty her desk from all these papers, she wants to tear them. In the end she decided to tear that letter which once Raja had written to her and she had never answered it. The whole night she kept on tearing one paper after another in order to keep away of all her past memories. The next morning, when Tara was finally leaving, she asked her to give her message to Raja that she wants he should come, she wants to see him:

> Tell him how we were not used to it. Tell him we couldn't come, but he should come. Bring him back with you, Tara. Tell him I'm waiting for him—I want him to come. I want to see him.[17]

But Raja does not reciprocate towards the feelings and emotions of Bim so she gets angry. During their childhood, both Raja and Bim shared a close relationship and bonding but as Raja had grown into an adult person, became completely practical, rational and materialistic. Tara too realizes that with the passage of time human relationship, even the close relationship between a brother and a sister gets changed. Raja never thinks of his days which he passed with Bim, he does not recall the love and sacrifice of Bim.

Completely neglected Bim muses painfully and thinks now the time has changed their relationship. But after a long period of time Bim decides to patch up with Raja. She wakes up from the dreamy world of past and sees the clear light of day. The novel ends with music representing harmony. It ends with affirmation. Self-realization comes to Bim. In the end she feels repentant. She realizes:

> Although it was shadowy and dark, Bim could see is well as by the clear light of the day that she felt only love and yearning for them, and if there were hurts and wounds in her side that bleed, then it was only because her love was imperfect and did not encompass them thoroughly enough and because it had flaws and inadequacies and did not intend to all equally.[18]

In *Where Shall We Go This Summer*? Anita Desai chooses marital discord as the subject matter and highlights how the inability to lay one's should and express freely one's fear and anguish result in the snapping of communication between husband and wife. Different attitudes, individual complexes and fears add to the distances between the husband and the wife resulting in conjugal disharmony.

Raman and Sita have different temperaments and attitudes to life. Sita represents the world of emotion and feminine sensibility while Raman is a man with an active sense of the practical. Sita is a sensitive, middle-aged woman with explosive and emotional reactions to many things that happened to her, she always wants to escape the reality and does not want to grow up and face the responsibilities of adult life. On the contrary, Raman represents the reality of life. He represents sanity rationality and an acceptance of the norms and values of society.

Sita almost all the time keep on thinking about her loneliness marriage with her husband Raman. The lives which are constantly revolving in her mind throughout the novel are:

> To certain people there comes a day when they don't say the great yes or the great No. He who has the yes ready with him reveals himself at once and saying it crosses over to the path of honour and his conviction. He who refuses

> does not repent. Should he be asked again; he would say no again. And yet that No—the right No—crushes him for the rest of his life.[19]

Sita refuses to give birth to her fifth child and this shows that she does not want to continue her relation with Raman anymore as her life, her relation is tied down to duties and responsibilities. She lives with such a person who does not even understand or know her. Sita feels unloved and rejected. For Raman too it was quite impossible to believe that he used to admire and worship Sita's beauty and fire which was outstanding. But now everything has changed. Sita's beauty had turned into ugliness and fire comes out now in the form of her anger and ill-temper on him and sometimes on children even. He is unable to understand the violence and passion with which Sita reacts against every incident. His reaction to his wife's frequent outbursts is a mixture of puzzlement, weariness, fear and finally a resigned acceptance of abnormality.

There is found a huge difference between the attitude and nature of Raman and Sita. The things which seem natural and common to her husband, does not look so to Sita. There is found a wide gulf between their cultures also. Sita feels peaceful in the company of nature while Raman belongs to the city culture. She represents feelings, emotions and takes the decision from her heart whereas her husband represents logic and reason and takes the decision from his mind. So to a large extent the gap between Sita and Raman is actually due to their nature also. Sita finds that her relationship with her husband is not deep and emotional. She wishes that the day will come when Raman will understand, her emotionally. Due to Raman's attitude towards her she realizes that she is not a free spirit:

> From the way he turned, the way he disregarded her, did not see if she followed or not, she felt him release her—give her up.[20]

When in a garden, she sees a woman who was being tenderly cared and loved by her husband, after seeing this she forgets of making any compromise with her husband. She realizes suddenly, what is missed in her life with Raman so she decides to leave her husband's home. Now she recollects all the lives which she had failed to recollect until now. The entire verse was:

> The wild young beifer, glancing, distraught with a strange new branching of life at her side rims seeking a loneliness. The little grain draws down the earth to hide. Nay even the slumberous egg as it labours under the shell patiently to divide and sub-divide: Ask to be hidden and wished nothing to tell.[21]

While talking of the psyche of women and analyzing the inner conflicts in the context of husband-life isolation, Anita Desai never shows any sign of prejudiced outlook. Her women protagonists are hyper-sensitive and they are unable to cope with the harsh realities of life. Anita Desai's concern is primarily with human relationships and how in the absence of meaningful relationships, the individual suffer.[22] She probes the psychic expulsion that may affect an individual in forging long-term and significant relationships and now an individual is affected if he is unable to forge such relationships.

Bharati Mukherjee, an India born American novelist has received considerable critical attention from almost all the quarters of the globe in a relatively short span of first twenty-five years. She has been widely acknowledged as a voice of expatriate immigrant sensibility.

Bharati Mukherjee is a significant woman novelist. She was born on 27th July, 1940 in a Bengali Brahmin family of Calcutta. Mukherjee spent her first eight years with her parents and two sisters. Mukherjee and her sisters were chauffeured to the convent school, characteristic of this class of Bengalis, the family westernized in the sense that English education was valued.

In the University of Iowa Mukherjee met Clark Blaise, a Canadian fellow student at the same university. She married him, live in Canada, got Canadian citizenship, lived in Toronto and then in Montreal. She migrated to the USA with her family and become a USA citizen. She was awarded with lot of prizes. Her creative novels are: *The Tiger's Daughter, Wife, Jasmine,*

*The Holder of the World, Leave it to me, Desirable Daughters,* etc.

Bharati Mukherjee's *Desirable Daughters* is a brilliantly woven thoughtful and intelligent story of three Calcutta, India-born Brahmin upper class sisters renowned for their beauty, brains and wealth. Mukherjee follows their lives as they leave their conservative sheltered childhood home where they were inhabited and imbibed with culture tradition and valued and inculcated in them with education by catholic nuns in their convent structured school and college. The three sisters Padma, Parvati, and Tara are born exactly three years apart from each other share the same birthday. Their mother named them after the goddesses name hoping they will survive and prosper which they all do. "We are sisters three/ alike as three blossoms on one flowering tree."[23]

Bharati Mukherjee has written a remarkable novel that is both the portrait of a traditional Indian Brahmin family and contemporary American story of a woman who is in many ways broken with tradition but still remains tied to her native country.

Tara Chatterjee is the youngest of the three daughters, from the wealthy Calcutta family trapped between the old world and the new. At 19, she was married to Bish Chatterjee who was Silicon Valley billionaire. Now at 40 Tara is a divorce living in San Francisco with her teenage son and her lover Andy Karolyi—a Hungarian Buddhist.

We see the three sisters grow up in Calcutta as three peas in a pad. They have a sheltered home where they are imbibed with culture, tradition and values inspite of being inculcating with western education. Tara says:

> We didn't have adolescence and we were never teenagers. My life was one long childhood until I was thrown into marriage.[24]

But when Tara reaches America, she feels the tug between tradition and freedom as she tries to meet the expectations that are often wildly contradictory. As a modern feminine emigrant she is awakened to the notions of women's emancipation and gender rights. Hence, when surrounded by her ex-husband Bish

Chatterjee who still tries to manage her affairs for her inspite of being divorced, she compares both the men—her ex-husband and her lover and so says to Bishwapriya:

> For you love meant status symbol, honour and duty while for Andy it is nothing. More complicated than having fun.[25]

Hence we find Tara Chatterjee trying to discover herself and how she fits into her place in the universe. While she is struggling with the thought of getting back to her ex-husband and being pregnant with his child, tries to understand her relationship with Bishwapriya. In the end of the novel she tries to contemplate and rediscover herself. The Sanskrit poem in the novel itself lays out Tara's mission:

> No one behind, no one ahead. The path the ancients cleared has closed. And the other everyone's path, easy and wide, goes nowhere. I am alone and find my way.[26]

*Wife* is a story of Dimple Das Gupta, a product of Calcutta's middle class that values docility and submissions in women. From the very beginning we feel that Dimple is not like a normal girl, she thinks that marriage is a blessing in disguise. It will bring her freedom, fortune and happiness. For Dimple, the agency for freedom is after marriage is imbibed in her psyche. So she starts awaiting marriage with all her fantasies fed by magazines and films:

> Marriage would bring her freedom; cocktail parties on carpeted lawns, raising dinners for noble charities. Marriage would bring her love.[27]

As the novel opens one could see Dimple's desire to marry a man "who could give her a different kind of life". And life to her meant "an apartment in Chowrangee, her hair done by Chinese girl, trips to new market for nylon saris".[28]

Surprisingly that any Indian girl who has in her all that long tradition of love of nature, human relationships, art, music, literature, happy home with husband and children and a readiness for suffering and sacrifice, should harp so irresponsibility on freedom and love.

While there is no denying that marriage ought to be a means of liberation and not imprisonment, the freedom that this ignorant girl craves for is freedom in the modern sense. Dimple dreams of living in foreign countries. With these dreams she enters into the wedlock with Amit Basu—a guy of her father's choice, an ambitious engineer who is about to migrate to the United States. But Amit's delay in getting a job abroad frustrates her she feels uneasy at Amit's house. She doesn't like Amit's mother and sister also. She thinks that all confirmation are temporary and with the confirmation for immigration they will eventually come to an end.

Dimple Basu has always lived in a fantastic world, a world which is created by herself. But when she confronts the hard realities of life the feathers of her imagination are clipped. Amit was not the man Dimple had imagined for her. She is always taken for granted from the day they get married. She is always conscious to her physical attributes. She craves attention from Amit but find no success. The passion and fulfillment that Dimple thought "would become magically lucid on her wedding day" eludes her once she is married as Amit fails Dimple on all grounds—mental, emotional and physical. She attempts at being an ideal wife, her ideal being the archetype Sita (dutiful and docile) and also like she archetype Rambha, tries all sorts of things to entice her husband but her all attempts go unnoticed. She was just learning to compromise when the news of their going brings a ray of hope to her sullen life. She again starts having hopes of freedom from the 'other' agency that is America which defines a new concept of freedom alluring to her senses.

Bereft of Indian values, Dimple lands on the land of promise with her dreams and aspirations. Inspite of possessing an adventurous spirit, Dimple gets baffled by exposure to American culture. Nagendra Kumar explains her conditions as:

> How a boorish, an innocent Indian life can keep her news in a country where was flapping the bugs.[29]

With the partially fulfilled dreams, Dimple tries to assimilate with American culture but fails. She tries to adopt the modernity and openness of the new land but could not. She faces disillusionment as instead of interacting with the real America she takes shelter in reel America.

In America also, Amit decides her fate and put constraints upon her. Amit wants her to interact with people but becomes aggressive often the Sen's have cautioned Amit to keep Dimple away from Ina Mulick so that the former may not get corrupted by her ideas. As a result Amit forbids Dimple from even accepting Ina's drink, "she does not like alcoholic beverages. She does not even like coke."[30] She is frustrated with Amit fails to provide her not only physical comfort but also the emotional one. Her frustration increases and she begins having repulsions for Amit. Lack of job makes Amit self-centered and insensitive. He is oblivious to the emotional turmoil of his wife. She is doomed to her world of fantasies, hiding her yearnings from her husband. Lack of communication between the two couples chokes Dimple's voice and disintegrates her sensibility. She has nightmares of violence of suicide and death. The gap between them keeps on increasing. He remains indifferent to her psychoanalytical imbalances, her insomnia, her exhaustion, etc. As a result she feels attracted towards Milt Gazer, who makes her feel good, but she does not have the grit to find a foothold for her because her strings are in her husband's hands that let them loose according to his own ego.

She starts feeling lonely in multitudes. She turns to Ina, Leni and Milt Glaser for support but they fail in providing her with permanent comfort. Disillusioned, disoriented and unable to grapple with the conflict she turns into a psycho-path and states Amit seven times, thus setting her free from him from the so-called "Saat Janam" concept. Vandana Singh comments: "Her act in killing Amit is more like relinquishing of herself."[31]

The question arises: Couldn't Dimple have taken divorce or left Amit? But again does she have the strength? The decision to kill is in a frenzied state of mind which is momentous. It is not planned. The self-consciousness is an intricate part of Dimple's personality which proves to be self-destructive. As Lakshmi puts it:

> Dimple in wife symbolizes the predicament of voice without articulation and without a vision. They are visionless because they are voiceless; they are rootless because they are shootless.[32]

Mukherjee's next novel *The Tree Bride* is a sequel to *Desirable Daughter*. The protagonist Tara Chatterjee is a savy, cosmopolitan traveler, but when her home is firebombed she begins to yearn for a home. A trip back to India rekindles a desire to find her family's ancestral roots and place in the history of pre-independent India.

The novel begins on the note with the desire to trace one's ancestry. Tara Lata is one of the three daughters of Jay Krishna Ganguly—a lawyer in the Dacca High Court. Tara's fate has been decided by her father very early in her life. At the age of five she is expected to marry the 13-year-old Surendra Kumar Lahiri who belongs to a wealthy but greedy family of a nearby village. Her father has observed all the ancient Hindu practices—the giving of dowry, caste consciousness and the auspicious days. To Jai Krishna:

> His were the most obedient daughters who would make loving and obedient wives. Tara Lata, his favourite would be no exception.[33]

We see the rich man's youngest daughter dressed in her bridal sari, her little hand painted with red lac dye, her hair oiled and set. One cannot imagine the loneliness of the child about to be married. Tara Lata's wedding party is travelling through a dark jungle with the bridegroom's family, who instead of greeting throws curses at the bride calling her unlucky because the bridegroom had been beaten fatally by a snake. To save her from one life of degradation, widowhood and shame, from the fate of a ghar-jalani—a women who brings misfortune and death to her family, Tara Lata's father decides to marry her to the God of the Forest and she becomes the legendary Tree Bride. Thus, from that moment begins her life of life-long virginity.

A girl happiest night becomes her lifetime of imprisonment. It seems all one sorrow of history, all that is unjust in society and cruel in religion has settled on her. Mukherjee says that:

> There were many Tara Latas married to trees so not they could have life on earth, a place in society where they would not be considered outcast.[34]

Thus, we see that now marriage is a tool in the hands of patriarchy to subject women. She grows up playing with Sameena, the cook's daughter in the dark surroundings of trees planted around her house. Inspite of living in a remote village she teaches herself to read and write Bengali and English. She organizes protests and is an inspiration to all. She believes that no boy is too young, no sudra too poor, no woman too weak to fight for the freedom of India.

Going to the extent of donating her dowry gold for the work of freedom struggle, Tara Lata brings Mishtiganj on the map for being the biggest contributor to the freedom struggle. Tara Lata becomes a victim to a conspiracy plotted by Sameena and her husband. In order to take possession of Tara Lata's house, Sameena feeds her name to British authorities and gets her arrested. She suffers a bad death at the hands of Dominick Mackenzie—a strong defender of British India against the Japanese Empire she was hanged and her body was tossed over the prison wall into a sewage ditch where it was rubbed off by vultures and stray dogs.

*The Tree Bride* is a celebration of the strength of a woman as it traces the transformation of Tara Lata from a docile Bengali Brahmin child into an impassioned organizer of resistance against the British Raj. Both the novelists, Anita Desai and Bharati Mukherjee enjoys a well-known name in the world of literature. They both speak for the rights of women, for their liberation. Desai focuses on the condition of the real Indian woman, while Mukherjee enmeshes the impact of Western culture on ethnic Bengali society. Both the novelists trace the theme of human relationships in the most perfect order with the technique of silence and speech. Through these narratives of silence and speech Desai and Mukherjee tries to interpret women's responses to patriarchal hegemony. Silence is a symbol of oppression while speech signifies self-expression and liberation. They both depict women as a different entity. Mukherjee mixes all the aspects—

social, cultural as well as political to deal with her theme of human relationship. She suggests that our histories are all intertwined and may one day interest. Ultimately she says:

> For people like me the question of identity isn't just about I am but all the cultural, political and social influence that have shaped an Indian born American author.[35]

There is no dearth of research work on the novelists in question as they are well established ones in the realm of fiction. They have been explored from different angles in different countries yet putting them to a close scrutiny in the light of the given topic is bound to yield some interesting findings which may be of some use to scholars of Indian English in general and Indian English novel in particular.

## NOTES

1. Park, Robert E. and Ernest W. Burges, *Introduction to the Sciences of Sociology* (Chicago: University of Chicago Press, 1921), 737.
2. Surendran, K.V., *Women's Writing in India* (New Delhi: Sarup and Sons, 2002), 68.
3. Addison, Joseph, *The Spectator with Notes and A General Index* (New York: Samuel Marks, 1826), 340.
4. Desai, Anita, *Cry, The Peacock* (London: Penguin Books, 1977), 42.
5. *Ibid.*, 11.
6. *Ibid.*, 96.
7. *Ibid.*, 126.
8. *Ibid.*, 108.
9. *Ibid.*, 38.
10. *Ibid.*, 91.
11. *Ibid.*, 80.
12. *Ibid.*, 48.
13. *Ibid.*, 99.
14. *Ibid.*, *Clear Light of Day* (London: Penguin Books, 1977), 39.
15. *Ibid.*, 55.

16. *Ibid.*, 88.
17. *Ibid.*, 146.
18. *Ibid.*, 192.
19. *Ibid.*, 154.
20. *Ibid.*, *Where Shall We Go This Summer?* (London: Penguin Books, 1977), 64.
21. *Ibid.*, 198.
22. *Ibid.*, 88.
23. Mukherjee, Bharati, *Desirable Daughters* (New Delhi: Hind Pocket Books, 1989), 12.
24. *Ibid.*, 54.
25. *Ibid.*, 165.
26. *Ibid.*, 69.
27. *Ibid.*, 67.
28. *Ibid.*, 88.
29. Kumar, Amitav, *The Indian Writer as an Expatriate* (New Delhi: Penguin Books, 2003), 60.
30. Mukherjee, Bharati, *Wife* (New Delhi: Vikas Publishing House Pvt. Ltd., 1977), 77.
31. Chowdhury, Enakshi, *Images of Women in Bharati Mukherjee's Novels* (Ludhiana: Academic Association Trust, 1999), 59.
32. Lakshmi, *Literary Review: The Hindu* (Aug. 7, 2005).
33. Mukherjee, Bharati, *The Tree Bride* (Delhi: Oriental Paperback, 1985), 22.
34. Dhawan, R.K., *Fiction of Bharati Mukherjee* (New Delhi: Prestige Books, 1996), 96.
35. *Ibid.*, 102.

# 10

# Reinvesting the Self: A Gynocentric Approach to Manju Kapur's *The Immigrant*

*Madhu Shalini*

Little did Beauvoir think the impact her simple but powerful statement, "One is not born, but rather becomes a woman... it is civilization as a whole that produces this creature"[1], would make in the times to come. In fact this proposition was to act as a projectile of the Feminist thought and was to be helpful in propelling Feminist thinking. It was as early as 1869 that J.S. Mill had written about the position of women in society thus "what is called the nature of women is an eminently artificial thing—the result of forced oppression in some direction".[2] It was as early as 1869 that J.S. Mill had written about the position of women in society thus "what is called the nature of women is an eminently artificial thing—the result of forced oppression in some direction".[3] So this idea of oppression of women is something which has been acknowledged by various thinkers and is traced throughout history in various spheres of life—be it biological, psychological, historical or cultural. With the passage of time and in crossing geographical boundaries, the ideology has evolved with many facets according to its usage and interpretation. However, at its core, lies the idea of similar rights, opportunities and power for women, as enjoyed by men.

The impact of this ever-widening concept was felt in the literary circles too and thus Feminist literary theories evolved and its history shows that it has covered a long and tumultous journey from simple beginnings to present-day complex knowingness. Feminist literary theory begins by looking at women in literary texts. Earlier, in fact till the 1970's, the major body of literary creation was exclusively male-authored and exceptions were few and far between (like Jane Austen and Charlotte Bronte). As such when Feminist thinkers turned to literary criticism they came across the fact of lack of availability of texts by women writers. So their concentration was limited to examining women characters in male-authored books. For example, Beauvoir in *The Second Sex* discusses the ways of subordination of women in the texts of five male authors. She argues that all literature was subject to certain fixed social ideas about the roles of men and women in society. This move to examine texts by male authors from a feminist viewpoint came to be known as phallocentric criticism which aimed at revealing the bias against women in these texts. This idea of 'sexual politics' popularized by Kate Millett paved the way for psychoanalysis to enter the literary field. But there was certainly the need for a female-centred criticism to focus on the need of more women writers and because of its intention and purpose to focus on the female voice, it came to be known as gynocriticism.

The first aim of the gynocritics was to encourage more women writers to come forth and thereby increase their number. They also aimed at reassessing old texts which were forgotten or undervalued earlier. Gynocritics believed that the male literary tradition which was prevalent had suppressed an alternative female tradition which was in a dormant state waiting to be discovered.

Elaine Showalter was the originator of the term 'gynocriticism' who questioned and exposed the male subjectivism inherent in the value judgement of texts. It was her book *A Literature of Their Own* (1977) which gave a new direction to feminist criticism. She reassessed writers whose texts had been forgotten but her radical assertion differed from anything that had been said in the Feminist logos. She asserted that women writers wrote differently from men and so should be read differently. Because the writings by women writers had certain characteristic themes and patterns (and therefore an identity of its own), it should not be judged according to traditional critical methods. This would be doing injustice to the feminist text and important insights into it would be lost. So only a gender-specific analysis of the text would be helpful in a true understanding of its assumptions and aims.

Feminist literary critics proceed in their work on certain presumptions. Firstly, they try to explain how power imbalance caused due to gender construct is reflected in the texts. As such, secondly, gynocriticism endeavours to express structural inequalities and gynocritical theories are the tools used in discovering these inequalities or oppressions and help in transformation with the help of acts like reading, thinking, analysing, criticising and writing. Thirdly, they believe that since literature is part of reality, it does not merely present the reality, it also creates the real (by making us believe in its fictional world) and it also offers alternatives to the real (by presenting critiques of reality or providing alternative modes of being).

This paper is a humble attempt at re-reading Manju Kapur's *The Immigrant* keeping in view the aforementioned propositions of gynocriticism. Despite the fact that Feminism as a movement grew in the West, it has spearheaded into a global phenomena and even India has witnessed its sweeping wave. Although historical circumstances and values in India make women's issues different from the Western Feminist rhetoric, the basic issues pertaining to women is the same as in the West. This paper also proposes to focus on this aspect of feminism.

Indian women negotiate survival through an array of oppressive patriarchal family structures; age, ordinal status, relationship to men through family of origin as well as marriage and patriarchal attributes like dowry. Today one witnesses the writers' (specially women writers') increasing preoccupation with the problems of women. The novels of such writers assume a distinctive feminist significance by focusing on the predicament of women in the Indian society. This bourgeoning presence of women writers of fiction is too significant and exciting to miss, overlook or ignore. The reading world has finally been forced to acknowledge their presence and has sat up to notice and applaud their creative talent.

In the rigidly-formed and tradition bound societies like India, the regression that one has to put up with is usually very severe and the resultant suffering often assumes pathetic proportions for sensitive individuals. Women happen to be the worst suffers in Indian society as the social norms and moral codes have been so formed as to be particularly disadvantageous to them. This is the reason why Indian women novelists writing in English, encouraged to a certain extent by their historical and cultural contexts, have consistently presented the experiences of Indian women in their fictional works. They, thus, without any express intention, aired the secret wishes of the vast majority of Indian women whose lot it has been to suffer silently. "In view of their high intellectual accomplishments and a masterly grasp of modern sciences, including especially psychology, these novelists have ably put the suffering of their characters in sharp focus and their private worlds and the social imperatives in perspective."[4]

The Indian women novelists deal with the crises in the lives of Indian women who are subjected to physical as well as psychological oppression in a male-dominated society. The crux of the problem is that man-woman relationship has, on the whole, evolved through centuries on a set pattern—man to rule and woman to obey; man, the master and woman, the slave; man, the god, and woman the devout. This established relationship is being challenged now. These novelists have exploited their skill in projecting convincingly the agonized mind of the persecuted women. Their portrayal of the women characters invariably bears authenticity to their feminist approach, outlook and perspective. Most of the creative Indian women writers focus on women's issues and create their own world. That is why women's writings have occupied "a significant and central place in women's lives".[5]

In India, novelists of the older generation presented women as rebelling against major social issue like child marriage, denial of education to girls and the atrocities suffered by a woman in her husband's house. In the contemporary novels women react against similar social pressures and much more. Their situation adds a new dimension reflecting the complexities arising out of a modern lifestyle. This view is best authenticated by the women characters of Manju Kapur. Her women characters like Virmati, Aastha refuse to conform to the image of the effeminate, docile and long suffering woman, a picture nurtured through a male-oriented culture. Since education has opened new vistas for them, the new woman is talented, skilled and one who indulges in deep self-analysis and introspection. A meek acceptance, thus, has given way to interrogation which helps these female characters of present-day novels to seek bolder alternatives and better pastures.

Maggie Humm summarizes the basic tenets of Feminism thus:

> Feminism incorporates diverse ideas which share three major perceptions: that gender is a social construction which oppresses women more than men; that patriarchy shapes this construction; and the women's experiential knowledge is a basis for a future non-sexist society. These assumptions inform feminism's double agenda: the task of critique (attacking gender stereotypes) and the task of construction without this second task (sometimes called female praxis) feminism has no goal.[6]

These three perceptions have been reflected by Manju Kapur in her latest the immigrant where she deals with the spatial, cultural and emotional dislocations suffered by immigrants in their effort to settle in a new land, the focus being on the life of the protagonist-Nina. Kapur's assertion that she is interested in woman's problems has also been upheld in this work, for though the locale shifts from India to Canada halfway through the novel, it continues to have Nina at the centre stage.

Once quizzed about the persistent theme of women's histories in her novels, Manju Kapur e-mailed to Lindsay Pereira:

> I am interested in the lives of women, whether in the political arena or in domestic spaces. One of the main preoccupations in all my books is how women manage to negotiate both the inner and outer space in their lives—

> what sacrifices do they have to make in order to keep the home fires burning—and at what cost to their personal lives do they find some kind of fulfilment outside the home.[7]

In *The Immigrant*, as suggestive of the name, Manju Kapur is distinctly concerned with her objective approach to the expatriate experience—tracing the typical issues associated with migration like adjustment problems and culture shock, and moves beyond these to encompass the existential angst of her heroine, Nina. The heroines of her earlier novels like Virmati in *Difficult Daughters*, Aastha in *A Married Woman* and Nina in *Home* are products of the Indian social scene and face problems which confront woman in a traditional social structure. Nina's problems are aggravated because in India she faces the problems which women generally face here but in a new land, amongst new people and confronted by a different culture, her problems assume new dimensions.

> The process of cross-cultural transaction also influences the gender-based relationships. Feminists like Anna Lawenhaupt Tsung have suggested that particular forms of female marginality must be examined in relation to the condition of women's lives as migrants, minorities, wealthy, poor, Black, White, Sex-workers, maids or academics.[8]

Nina's case is similar for she has had a good education and she also has a respectable job as a lecturer in English in a college of repute in the University of Delhi. Staying in a rented house with her widowed mother, she has different problems to face. She has an identity of her own as she is financially independent in this patriarchal society. But she is unmarried and it is getting a little late by the standards of the Indian Society. Despite the freedom she enjoys, the burden of her unmarried status weighs heavily upon her. The beginning of the novel showcases Nina's predicament: "Nina was almost thirty.... Her spirit felt sixty.... Her heart felt a hundred as it surveyed the many years of hopeless longing it had known."[9]

For Nina's mother, Shanti, the marriage of her girl is a constant reminder, nagging her day and night, and this disturbs Nina. Having lost her husband, who was in the Indian Foreign Service, Shanti has only Nina to herself. Shanti represents the women of the older generation for she bears the barbs and the resentment of her in-laws, when they have to move to the house of Nina's grandparents. Nina's grandmother, nurturing conventional thoughts, wonders why Shanti is alive after the death of her son, Shankar. This is a typical Indian mindset which widows have to face despite winds of change.

The psychological trauma which women have to undergo is unfolded in the tale of Nina and Shanti. "Anger provided the energy in the house. The grandmother resented her daughter-in-law's existence, Nina resented her mother's meekness, the mother put up with everything because Nina's security depended on her patience." The psychological trauma that women have to undergo within walled spaces of the so-called homes has been captured by Manju Kapur very effectively.

We are aware that literary theories or theories in general are not an abstract activity but deeply linked with life. We have seen earlier that gynocritics believe in the relationship between the word and the world—"between texts and the reality from which they arise and in which they are subsequently read".[10] On these lines the rendering of Nina and her mother's predicament makes Manju Kapur's novel a feminist text.

As soon as Nina gets a job, Shanti and Nina shift to Delhi and this shift involves hope for Nina in her belief that in Delhi "her mother would lead a fuller life" (5) and the mother hopes that in Delhi "a husband could be found who could give her darling the home she deserved" (6). Feminists uphold the view that apart from economic subjection and psychic repression, there are other structures that tend to suppress or act as "structures of oppression because of the social and psychic inequalities of gender".[11] Which may be in the form of social deprivation, physiological, cultural or even psychological,oppressions. This is prevalent at home, the workplace, education, religious or legal system and even in women for they tend to grow on values fed to them by these external structures.

In the novel, the marriage of Nina after an eight-year-long wait was a 'means' to change her life. The way these oppressive structures work have been made clear by tracing the meanderings of Nina's psyche. The anxiety on the part of her mother filled her with rage, guilt and shame. To pacify her mother she began to pray and fast regularly. The importance of marriage in the Indian milieu is adjudged by the respectability which comes with it. The side-long glances, the whispers, the questioning looks of the neighbours and curiously wagging tongues of the relatives nagging Nina's mother are the means of social oppression. In fact even in the College Nina feels the change after her marriage with Ananda and felt a strange sense of pride.

> She never anticipated though the respect that come with marriage, Nina Sharma, an accepted member of society, married, bound for the Western big time. (101)

This shows that despite her education and economic independence, Nina still feels and seeks fulfillment in life through marriage. Beauvoir has highlighted this aspect of marriage as a great option for girls, in her treatise.

Full of apprehensions, Nina leaves for Canada but the treatment meted out to her at the airport fills her with rage and humiliation. Numerous questions are fired at her and the officials treat her as though she is less than human. Manju Kapur describes the painful process of becoming an immigrant for some Indians. Ananda and his uncle too undergo pain and humiliation but they learn to adapt easily for they have to establish themselves. Nina's case is different for she is a woman and her expectations from life are different.

Manju Kapur charts the terrain of Nina's psyche. From the beginning Nina thinks of marriage as a means to find fulfillment and give pleasure to her mother. Her idea of a complete woman is complimented by motherhood. Nina's identity is involved not merely in her agonized experiences as an immigrant to Canada, but also in her nostalgia and feminine sensibilities. The problem of Nina and her husband Ananda begins with his problem of erectile dysfunction. Moreover as she cannot conceive she thinks she is the one to blame. For her the sexual act is a means to have a child so that her life can be complete. For Ananda it is a major issue for which he has to get himself treated in order to establish himself. This difference in their approach to their personal problem furthers the discord between them. Nina observed "... that Ananda got offensive when he felt attacked" (180). She feels "They had to understand how the other felt" (168). But a lack of understanding leads Nina to a "state of permanent sexual frustration..." (181). She thinks that all her problems would be easier if she conceived. In fact when her friend Gayatri tells her she might never have a child Nina is unnerved. What Gayatri tells her and the stock-reaction of Nina envisages the traditional mindset of Indian women and echoes the Indian sensibility—"We are conditioned to think a woman's fulfillment lies in birth and motherhood, just as we are conditioned to feel failures if we don't marry" (233). Women, as Feminists believe, are subjected to artificially constructed idea of the feminine.

The rift in the relationship between Nina and Ananda is further deepened when Ananda goes for his treatment alone, lying to Nina about it. He tells Nina that he is going to California for a fortnight—one week at a dental conference in San Francisco and the other at San Diego with an old school friend. His behaviour towards Nina is quite odd before he leaves. Nina is aware of the problem and suggests that they meet doctors for it would improve their marriage. Ananda too realises this but his male ego comes in his way of acceptance—"He shuddered. The one word yes would mean acknowledging his inadequacy. And that hurt too much" (186). When Nina wants to accompany him, Ananda refuses stating financial reasons. Before he leaves she wants to go out with him for dinner alone but he takes her to his uncle's place. When Nina's professional future is being decided there, Ananda does not respond and in the role of a traditional Indian wife Nina wraps up the matter saying they would decide later. These instances are merely pointers that the relationship between man and woman is power structured and male supremacy has been established by various covert means. Beauvoir has made a pertinent comment on this form of oppression:

> The great advantage enjoyed by the boys is that his mode of existence in relation to others leads him to assert his subjective freedom. His apprenticeship for life consists in free movement...he is aware of his body as a means for dominating nature...he undertakes, he invent, he dares.... In woman, on the contrary, there is from the beginning a conflict between her autonomous existence and her objective self (her being—the other). She is not given the freedom to grasp and discover the world around her...she does not dare to affirm herself as subject.[12]

Nina feels cheated and the faults in their relationship deepen further. Nina joins a library and this opens a new chapter in her life. At the library she meets Beth and through her she joins a support group which aims at strengthening and empowering women. This phase marks the chrysalis of Nina as she opens up to a new world—that of feminism. Beth invites her to join a self-help group working on feminist principles using co-counselling to strengthen women. Nina joins the group and in the first meeting itself Beth discloses that the problems women face are tackled by therapists, professional counsellors or psychoanalysts who are usually men with biased attitudes. Consequently the "male-female power equations (are) were further replicated..." (217). These men treat the problems faced by women "as neuroses, rather than the result of stress that comes from coping in a male dominated world" (217). This group would be helpful in treating women by letting them express themselves freely and to grow without fear of criticism and thus help their individualities to grow and strengthen.

Nina comes across *The Second Sex* and becomes aware of the ideals and theories associated with it. It is a kind of personal renaissance for her as she is enlightened on matters and modes of female subversions. She is aware that in her state Ananda is her friend and her husband and also that her identity as an Indian wife is secure with him. But in this new country "She was emotionally, financially and socially heavily dependent on him" (219). The support group she joins, met to discuss the problems women faced—sexual harassment in the workplace, women coping with house work, child-care as well as a job, while the husband watched T.V. or jobless husband resenting wife's wages and other infidelities.

The constitution of the support group which Nina joins reveals this aspect of feminism—that despite the difference in historical circumstances and values between the East and the West, the basic issues pertaining to women is the same everywhere. For Nina meets others in the group who are like her. And they are not merely Indians like Gayatri and her. Out of the eight women, only two were from Asia. Nina "looked at the faces around her. Eight white, one brown, sympathetic, caring and concerned" (218). What binds these women is the uniformity in the anxieties, problems and the "stress that comes from coping in a male dominated world" (217). Gayatri is another character or member of the group who shares her trauma with the others. Both Nina and Gayatri share similar predicaments. Gayatri, as a woman feels, "Caught between her Indianness, her parent's expectations, and her own desires, which she had to admit were confused" (231).

Of course Ananda is uneasy at Nina's proposal to join the group or of her reading *The Second Sex*. He cannot understand the reason for he thinks from a masculine perspective and asks Nina "But why do you want to read such stuff? You are not deprived in any way" (220). He thinks that economic provision and the freedom which Nina enjoys is enough for a woman. He is callous to her needs as a woman, as a person. He is afraid that Nina would becomes a bra-burning feminist.

Nina too feels confused like Gayatri as she feels lost in the new world and tries to analyse why she is the way she is—

> A woman, an Indian, an immigrant.
>
> Which come first?
>
> Her female self, according to Beauvoir. From the first breath, the processes that formed that being were set in motion. (221)

Although Nina is confused, for she thinks that the views and ideas in *The Second Sex* are too Western for her, she accepts Beauvoir's central thesis that "women are defined in relation to men" (221). She sees the best exemplification of this thesis in her own case for she had given up her life and career in India for her man and marriage. Since "All her expectations of marriage and future had been bound up in motherhood" (218) she feels empty and lost in the new world. The mental construct of Nina is proof of the patriarchal forces which influence and frame the feminine psyche. Nina also confesses that her inability to conceive has added to her woes.

Nina's Indian rearing does not let her identify with much of *The Second Sex* and yet with her newly acquired freedom she enters into an extra-marital relationship with Anton. But when he rapes her on a trip, she is torn apart. Apart of her, the liberated self, needles her to seek justice for herself by exposing the man and his misdeed. She is also confident that she would get support from her self-help group for violence required counter-attack. "Now was the time to break that mindset that made woman victims" (316). Yet she cannot muster up courage to come out in the open. Suffering mentally she offers a "bowdlerized version" (316) to Ananda, concealing the actuality.

The death of her mother adds to Nina's misery but the startling discovery of a strand of hair, which reveals the presence of a third between them, shatters Nina. This puts many a thing in perspective. It is indeed ironical, for just the previous night she had thought of Ananda as her only anchor in the world. But it is a lesson learnt too late. She realizes that she has not been trained or brought up to look after herself. The typical Indian view of a woman looked upon as someone's sister, daughter, wife and mother forges the women folk to seek dependence on the male members of the family. The traditional training has taught her to look for support systems at every stage and Nina is still into that habit "Marry me, love me, above all, look after me" (328).

Without disclosing to Ananda about her awareness of his affair with Mandy, Nina applies for jobs everywhere but in Halifax. She wants to think straight about her future and "hoped independence could facilitate her thought process" (333). She also realises that life would be difficult but not unimaginable. Thus in the process of reinventing herself, Nina decides to move on. Like other immigrant women, who want to escape an unhappy past, she too thinks of pulling up her roots from Halifax and "find a new place, new friends, new family" (334). When pushed to the edge of the world she takes on a liberated view and is ready for a new life.

Keeping in mind the presumptions of Gynocritical theories that "...pursue a politics of reading, and that also presume that reading practices can make some difference to our experiences of the world,"[13] the narrative under discussion seems to have been written with a particular purpose. The outstanding perception and accuracy with which Manju Kapur captures and unveils the emotional tonality of Nina's psyche as well as her predicament makes the novel a front-ranker amongst Feminist narratives. The followers of Feminism believe that narratives are always produced out of particular reality and so they are stamped by the time, place and way of production. That literature reflects reality is an acknowledged fact. The story of Nina (or any other heroine of Manju Kapur) seems to reflect the story-line of any of the present-day leading soaps of the Indian tele-world, with their focus on women-oriented themes. Nina is thus, not a character who is a figment of the author's imagination. She is one of us. What she suffers or undergoes could happen to someone in our family or has already happened with someone we know. So the text stands as a testimonial of everyday reality. But Feminists uphold the idea that texts do not merely reflect reality but also create reality, by making the reader aware of other modes of behaviour. The way Nina reacts or the mode of behaviour she chooses at the end of the novel was unheard of until some years back. If such an alternative was offered by writers, say fifty years back, it would not be easily acceptable. But Manju Kapur is providing a bold alternative of self-assertion through the story of Nina in the present scenario.

Gynocentrics believe that since alternative ways of life or of thought can be offered through texts, texts have the power to change the world. So texts dealing with the lives of womenfolk which are also read in a specific way and about which things are written keeping that specific way (i.e. the feminist viewpoint), make a difference to the world. This proposition underlines the latest narrative of Manju Kapur as it reflects the life of Nina and also creates an alternative world, by the decision she takes at the end and walks out of the house and life of her husband Ananda.

Focusing on the spatial, cultural and emotional dislocation faced by Nina, Manju Kapur has woven a tale of a modern Indian girl, who is different from her predecessors. In not following the path oft-frequented by others like her and seeking newer pastures, Nina gives a minor jolt to the readers. In letting Nina make this decision Manju Kapur comes forth as a Feminist writer for Feminists resist the 'stereotype' response to texts as well as life that are habitual. Although the middle-class consciousness of her heroine is the sympathetic fulcrum of the text (which is common to her previous narratives too), the peculiar singularity of the immigrant lies in the dislodging of the traditional ideal of 'feminity' that teaches subservience and passivity, creating a great psychological pressure on women by the enforcement of what Betty Friedan calls 'the feminist mystique'.[14]

## NOTES

1. Beauvoir, Simone de, *The Second Sex* (rpt. Harmondsworth: Penguin, 1983), 301.
2. Mill, J.S., *The Subjection of Women* (London: M.I.T. Press, 1970), 22.
3. *Ibid.*
4. Rajeshwar, M., "The Inner World of Indian Women: Neurotic Characters of Indian Women Novelists" in *The Commonwealth Review*, Vol. IV, No. 1, 1994-95, 141.
5. Dhawan, R.K. (ed.), *Indian Women Novelists*, Set I: Vol. I (New Delhi: Prestige Books, 1991), 11.
6. Humm, Maggie, *Dictionary of Feminist Literary Theory* (New York: Harvester Wheatsheaf, 1989), 194.
7. Manju Kapur in an e-mail reply to Lindsay Pereira; June 7, 2006. http://enjoyment.independent.co.uk
8. Quoted by Aparna Rayaprol, *Negotiating Identities: Women in the Indian Diaspora* (Delhi: O.U.P., 1997), 135.

9. Kapur, Manju, *The Immigrant* (New Delhi: Random House, India, 2008), 1. Further references from the text are from this edition. Page numbers mentioned in the article itself.
10. Robbins, Ruth, "Will The Real Feminist: Theory Please Stand Up?" in Julian Wolfreys (ed.), *Introducing Literary Theories: A Guide and Glossary* (New Delhi: Atlantic Pub., 2005), 48.
11. *Ibid.*, 51.
12. Beauvoir, Simone de, *The Second Sex*, *op. cit.*, 307-08.
13. Robbins, Ruth, "Will the Real Feminist Theory Please Stand Up", *op. cit.*, 47.
14. Friedan, Betty, *The Feminist Mystique* (Harmondsworth: Penguin, 1986), 13.

# 11

# Feminist Slants in the Short Stories of Shashi Deshpande, Anita Desai and Jhumpa Lahiri

*Reena Mitra*

It is said of the short stories of Henry James that in them "he got the sound of his voice into every line he wrote"[1] and this is precisely what is expected of a writer of this genre of literature who zeroes in on a mode of depiction that best accords with his own idiosyncrasies and his way of looking at life and enables him to direct his creative faculty into channels that allow him aesthetic expression without any violence to his own disposition and propensities. He views things in a manner peculiar to himself and his vision conforms to his inherent proclivities.

Literary texts, it is thus assumed, demonstrate the author's worldview and experiences and unearth the truth about his or her universe; and, in the course of this communication these texts provide us access to the universal traits of human nature as well. Short stories in English written by Indian women writers aim tangentially at creating among people an awareness of the place of women in society and the monstrosity of the injustice meted out to them. Women's writings, an integral part of Indian writing in English, deal, explicitly or covertly, with the prevalent exploitation of women and endeavour to rid society of the dehumanizing treatment given to multitudes of them.

A study of women short story writers of Indian English fiction establishes the fact that these authors reconstruct the lives of Indian women with the specific purpose of foregrounding the latter's agony and social oppression. They proclaim a major uprising against the isolation and marginalization to which these women are subjected. Feminism is a thematic concern commonly shared by most such writers of the post-Independence era. With regard to narrative fiction, Wellek and Warren have observed that "story comes from history"[2] for literature is mostly characterized as a time-art which is linked to the unfurling of events in a particular time in life.

Anita Desai, Shashi Deshpande and Jhumpa Lahiri are eminent Indian English women writers and it would certainly be worthwhile to range over their short stories and venture to explore the feminist interpretations and inferences that may be traced in these works that are unmistakable expressions of their respective views of life. These writers, in the main, portray the world of women who are beset with circumstantial pressures and struggle hard against the antagonistic contemporary social structure that pushes them to the utmost point in the periphery and prevents them from emerging as individuals with identities of their own. Marriage and marital relationships are central to the stories of these three writers. Professionally, all the three are opposed to being marked as feminist writers, but, on exploration and scrutiny, one discovers that each of these has her own brand of feminism to offer, and in modes and nuances so ingenious that one needs real discriminatory perceptiveness to penetrate deep into the implications that emanate from their respective tales.

In the recent past a swelling number of women writers the world over have espoused the short story form, aptly labelled 'short text', and have explored with greater earnestness and fervour than ever before the latent possibilities of this genre to express the emotive and poetic imagination in themselves. The stories of these women writers simulate women's speech patterns and come alive in the different moods and situations of the women characters depicted. Their bulk of stories acquires historical significance as a milestone in the feminist movement and establishes itself as a meaningful assemblage of multilayered texts that seek to project the victimization of women all across the world. Though the complexities of a woman's experiences resist elucidation and interpretation yet these women writers aim at devising ways to present variegated human experiential encounters assimilated into their own distinctive female ordeals. It is in this context that the protean nature of the short story gains in significance and by virtue of its flexibility this genre provides to the woman writer a vehicle for her own deliverance from a hidebound, rigid and unimaginative form and language. The story becomes for her a concatenation of events upon which she strings her real and conjured up experiences. It provides her a platform for self-assertion and offers her an opportunity to explore and experiment with her hitherto muffled experiences. Initially it was the novel that seemed an apt medium for giving vent to her muted feelings but soon, the new literary medium—the short story—substituted it, depicting the female consciousness as never before:

> The novel above was young enough to be soft in her hands (i.e. the first woman who began seriously writing in the nineteenth century)...yet, who shall say that even now the novel is rightly shaped for her use. No doubt we shall find her...providing some new vehicle, not necessarily in verse, for the poetry in her.[3]

Shashi Deshpande was catapulted to fame with the publication of her shorter fiction in 1978. She is not one of those writers who have dallied with the form for relief from ennui and boredom. She is one who has taken to this form with dedication and commitment. In her novels as well as her short stories Deshpande dwells mainly on despair and embitterment, misapprehension and irreconcilability, a sense of culpability and deprivation and an inconsolable feeling of loneliness and alienation plaguing a sensitive woman hemmed in by an ill-mated marriage and adverse circumstances around her. Corroborating this view regarding the thematic preoccupations of this author, G.S. Amur remarks:

> Woman's struggle in the context of contemporary Indian society, to find and preserve her identity as wife, mother,

> and most important of all, as human being, is Shashi Deshpande's major concern as a creative writer, and this appears in all her important stories.[4]

Deshpande's target in her fiction seems to be an intimate analysis of the man-woman equation within the ambit of the family and the society. Her female protagonists stifled by the circumscribing male-dominated world struggle hard to discover their true identity. Deshpande looks closely at women's problems in a fast-changing social scenario.

It is the predicament of women, specifically the Indian middle-class women, that Shashi Deshpande focuses on in her short stories which verbalize the existential dilemmas confronted by them. But be the threats from within or without the circumstances pressing or destabilizing, the agony corporal or mental, she holds the family together, not allowing it to disintegrate. Her protagonists do not, like Ibsen's Nora in *A Doll's House*, walk out on their relationships. Efforts are made to reconstruct broken bridges not demolish them and at no cost are family ties severed.

Feminism is one of the most prominent thematic preoccupations of Shashi Deshpande as it is of the other two writers under study, namely, Anita Desai and Jhumpa Lahiri. These three writers belong to the new class of post-Independence women writers in India who began to explore dauntlessly, new sexual mores, fresh possibilities in human relationships, marital equations and motherhood. Each one of these writers has made the contemporary Indian short story a potent tool for challenging traditional pieties and ushering in a secular egalitarian way of life. Deshpande's specific focus has been on the lives of Indian women, particularly of the middle class in the social hierarchy. Her short stories are a self-probe into the existential issues that a woman in this country has to confront. She portrays the taboo-ridden Indian society that allows little space for the unhindered growth of a woman. Significantly, in many of her stories her female protagonists are not even given names and are referred to throughout in terms of pronouns. This unerringly brings forth the realization that these women have no identity of their own and need to assert themselves as self-respecting individuals. They are sensitive, self-conscious and brilliant and try to extricate themselves from the fetters of a delimiting social set-up that is asphyxiating for one who wants to live life to the full but with an unabated sense of dignity.

Elain Showalter, in *A Literature of Their Own*, traces three major phases in the historical evolution of the female literary convention and the feminist movement:

> First there is a prolonged phase of imitation of the prevailing modes of the dominant tradition, and internalization of its standards of art and its views on social roles. Second, there is a phase of protest against these standards and values, including a demand for autonomy. Finally, there is a phase of self-discovery, a turning inward, freed from some of the dependency of oppositions, a search for identity. An appropriate terminology...is to call these stages, feminine, feminist and female.[5]

Deshpande's women protagonists traverse these very three stages in their lives. They are fully conscious of the limitations of the male-dominated society and blatantly raise their voices against the prevalent "moth-eaten morality". They do not submit to desperation; they try to mould the circumstances to their advantage best as they can and what they cannot change they adapt themselves to with alacrity and a sense of self-confidence that is rare. In short, Deshpande's stories deal graphically with the problems that are posed before a middle class educated woman in the patriarchal Hindu society and with the daily slights and humiliations she suffers.

*The Legacy and Other Stories*, the first collection of Shashi Deshpande's short stories, was published in 1978 and in 1980 was published her first novel, *The Dark Holds No Terrors*. In 1990, The Feminist Press of New York brought out her novel, *A Matter of Time*, her first novel to be published in the United States of America and subsequently, there were a host of other novels that were written by her. She is a winner of the Sahitya Akademi and the Nanjangud Thirumalamba awards. Her short stories, particularly, have been greatly acclaimed and widely anthologised.

To refer to some of the relevant stories in the context of the present study in *The Legacy*, the first important story from the point of view of a feminist perspective is ‘A Liberated Woman’, which brings out the temperamental and situational contrast between partners in a marriage, that is, a successful lady doctor and a frustrated lecturer devoted to his profession. The latter, unable to bear the humiliation of being subordinated to his wife as the bread winner of the family becomes a sadist, torturing his wife in bed at night. He becomes a case for psychiatric study.

In ‘An Antidote to Boredom’, the protagonist meets a young widower at her son’s school and feels she can happily spend a lifetime with him but in this regard she soon develops a sense of guilt towards her son though not towards her indifferent husband. In another story called ‘Death of a Child’ Deshpande deals with a woman’s problem of having an unwanted pregnancy and the consequent abortion of the child. The story seems indirectly to reflect on the moral and emotional implications of a termination of pregnancy.

‘The Alien’ underscores the predicament of a young married Indian woman who experiences loneliness and lack of companionship in England where the couple has now moved and where her husband is away most of the time. In ‘A Man and A Woman’ a thirty-year-old woman whose husband has long been dead has physical relations with her husband’s younger brother, a boy of seventeen, but questions of morality and social taboos plague her all the time. Besides, she is a mere graduate and has no job prospects to support herself. This is the plight of most young widows.

In another anthology of short stories by Deshpande, *The Intrusion and Other Stories*, the title story, ‘The Intrusion’ brings out the discord between a couple on their honeymoon. The girl’s consent for marriage had not been taken and hence she thwarted every caressing advance made by husband as she did not quite appreciate the “proprietorial air” about his behaviour. In the story called ‘Ghosts’, the protagonist, lonely in an alien land because her husband, tired after work, ignores her sexual overtures, cultivates the practice of passing her hand over her own body to reassure herself that she existed and was alive.

These and many other short stories of Shashi Deshpande illustrate her preoccupation with the predicament of middle-class Indian women who are victimized by the male-dominated patriarchal society. Trapped between tradition and modernity, her women search for their identity within marriage and in most cases find it. They are realistically portrayed as wife, mother and daughter but their depiction reveals no influence of the aggressive kind that Western feminists like Simone de Beauvoir, Germaine Greer, Betty Friedan and Kate Millett propound.

Anita Desai, the second of the writers chosen for study with regard to the feminist perspectives in their short stories, started publishing her work relatively earlier than Shashi Deshpande but her career took off about the same time as the latter's did. Desai was adorned with numerous awards including the 1975 National Academy of Letters Award for *Fire on the Mountain*, the first of her novels to be published in the United States. In 1983, she was awarded the Guardian Prize for Children's Fiction for *The Village by the Sea*. She was given the Literary Lion Award in 1993 and was also named Helen Cam Visiting Fellow, Ashby Fellow and Honorary Fellow of the University of Cambridge.

Desai is known for her studies of Indian life and her acumen in observing the minutiae of human behaviour in the Indian context. She is also appreciated for her understanding of intellectual issues and her competence in portraying vividly the fusion of the Western and Eastern cultures in the fabric of Indian life. In most of her fictional works Desai focuses on the problems of contemporary life and on the struggle of individuals at the personal level. In her first anthology of short stories, *Games at Twilight and Other Stories*, Desai's primary concern is to depict the gulf between tradition and exploration, between familial harmony and individual identity. Her tales comprise intensely individual characters who do not belong to any particular class and seek to do something that remains unquestioned even if it has to be at the cost of their reputation or prosperity.

The stories of Anita Desai are not written in the style of conventional classics. They are loose structured and make characteristic use of symbolism which renders the narration poetic. She herself states that:

> even when two characters meet, they use this particular type of language—the languages of their thought, of their interior selves which has nothing to do with Geography.[6]

Her stories are pictures in words, feelings, sensations and emotions, each stroke of the brush bringing out the minutest of details. Thus metaphors, symbols and images acquire a literary brilliance when they merge together the narrative to produce a total experience of reality, reality in its external tangibility as well as in its indescribable intensities.

Anita Desai's short stories demonstrate that reality for Indian and other Third World women is formulated not by gender alone but also by other factors like the religious and cultural conventions by which they are constrained, the historical episodes that have brought about consequential reorganizations in the social order and the class and caste to which they belong. This highlighting of the delimiting circumstances calls attention to the subordinate position of women in the Indian society and exposes, the religious sanction given to the subservient position of women. It also shows that colonization on the whole, worsened the lot of women and practices oppressive towards them gained ground. The inevitable repercussions of the colonial period brought a reassertion of fundamentalist stances leading to a further curtailment of the liberty of women.

Desai is one of the few Indian novelists writing in English who have tried to grasp and review closely the predicament of the women characters in their works. She exemplifies "the welcome creative release of the feminine sensibility,"[7] which began to appear perceptibly on the literary scene after the Second World War. She was never happy with the mere recording and documentation of earlier women novelists in India for they seldom showed any interest in the psychological analysis of their characters. She herself had always been preoccupied with the existential world we inhabit and even when her focus happens to be on men, she explores the feminist perspective in her works.

It is the plight of sensitive women characters who find it difficult to adjust in the present mechanical and urbanized social world that Anita Desai seeks to portray in her stories.

She examines different aspects of the feminine psyche including the impact of man-woman relationship on it. In her stories most marriages demonstrate the incompatibility between husband and wife. As in her short story "Private Tuitions by Mr. Bose" she often depicts a highly sensitive, sterile woman married to a prosperous, middle-aged man. The husband is very often too preoccupied with his own affairs to comply with the temperamental as well as spiritual demands of his young wife. Anita Desai in her short stories aims at displaying how the spirit of the modern times has adversely affected the husband-wife relationship. Also, childhood experiences, she believes, are of great significance in the study of the mind's behaviour for they lie latent in the consciousness of the individual and often surface at unguarded moments. In *Games at Twilight* the stories like "A Devoted Son", "Surface Textures", "The Accompanist", "Pigeons at Daybreak", "The Farewell Party", "Private Tuition by Mr. Bose" and "The Pineapple Cake" are on varied themes and do not all portray women characters. However, they are witty and evocative and reveal the author's dexterity in handling this genre. Though skilfully conceived and written and aiming at remarkable imagery and distinctive characterizations, some of these stories lack emotional power or a well-evolved dramatic conflict. However, the most significant social issue that Desai focuses on is the institution of marriage in which a woman finds herself trapped. She, like Mrs. Bose, as referred to earlier, has no choice left but to languish in misery.

Anita Desai's second anthology of short stories, *Diamond Dust*, contains nine stories some of which are heavily charged with emotions and feelings. They cover a wide span of subjects and explore unobserved aspects of life. The first story, 'Royalty', explores female psychology with regard to sibling jealousy and the male psychology of turning it to his advantage. Raja had been Ravi and Sarla's friend for about thirty years, that is, from the time they were together at Oxford. Raja announced his proposed arrival in Delhi just when Ravi and Sarla were about to leave for a trip to the mountains and later said that he would like to joint them there. Instead, he went to Kashmir with the Dutta Rays. This shows the insensibility and selfishness of men like Raja. In the present context, however, we are concerned more with the way Sarla reacts to the situation.

In this volume of short stories called *Diamond Dust* a point to be noted is that there are a few stories in which the husband-wife relationship is not embittered; rather, it is one of tenderness and caring. In her relatively earlier works, *Cry the Peacock, Voices in the City, Fire on the Mountain* and *Where Shall We Go This Summer*? the marital equation is presented as one of discord and disharmony.

The second story in the collection 'Vinterscape', brings into relief the way foreigners wonder at our social and cultural values which are quite incomprehensible to them. Neither Beth nor Doris could understand how the mother was able to give away her only son to her sister out of love for the latter so that the presence of the baby could help her and compensate for the sudden death of her husband. They sincerely and genuinely accept the family of their husbands as their own.

Another story from the anthology that may be relevant here is 'Underground', which is a very touching story of an intense relationship between a husband and a wife, Bob Metaggart and Helen. An engineer by profession, Bob had to be away from his wife for long spells as his job required him to visit different countries. Anita Desai's aesthetic presentation of the tale in a language that is poetic in flavour makes the story poignant and charged with emotions.

Then, there is 'Roof Top Dwellers', a narrative with pronounced feministic perspectives. It deals with the desire of modern young women for independent living. Coming from small towns they wish to live independently in the working women's hostels of metropolitan cities, consciously leaving behind the comfort of their homes to suffer the inconveniences and restrictions imposed upon them by these hostels. When accommodation in hostels is unavailable they search for roof top dwellings which are highly priced and hard to get. Their independence is so dear to these young girls that they prefer to hold on to their jobs at any cost rather than marry the persons chosen for them by their parents, no matter how attractive the offer appears to be.

All female characters in the various short stories of Anita Desai have their own specific identity and distinctive female sensibilities. Mrs. Fernandez in 'Pineapple Cake' is less educated but aware of the realities of life and more worldly-wise than many other women. At the time of the wedding, though a gentleman has just passed away and, to her son, Victor, the cake appears like a corpse, she uninhibitedly satisfies her love for food and does not philosophise like her son. She is practical in her approach to life and the least inclined towards rumination.

Anita Desai has to her credit the depiction of a vast range of characters, particularly, women characters. The portraits of Indian wives are undoubtedly her forte for these women, in most cases are paradigms of virtue not because the author deliberately makes them so but because their quest for higher values makes them so. In stories where Desai focuses on a female protagonist the latter's struggle against the prevalent oppressive environment which takes the form of patriarchal domination is one of the many aspects manifesting the author's her feminist leanings. She cares for the individual who she feels should strive to find fulfilment. She is different from other feminists in that she believes that the individual can attain salvation through self-exploration. She does not specifically depict the problems of the Third World Feminism, though the setting is almost entirely in India.

Jhumpa Lahiri, who received the Pulitzer prize for 2000 and several other awards for her anthology of short stories, *Interpreter of Maladies* (1999) looks fixedly at the world with a sharp perceptive gaze and celebrates its expanse and variety. Her protagonists are very often immigrants who are trying to settle down in a foreign land and are caught between the past and the present, the traditional and the modern and the indigenous and the alien. Her stories are essentially tales of relationships where the prime propeller is the quest for identity. However, though essentially a chronicler of the migrant situation Lahiri does not fail to record in terms of character certain inherent feministic traits observed by her among women who are conditioned by certain instinctive aspects of life, in fact, by their very womanhood.

The complex configuration of the meaning of Lahiri's works coming through simple plots, characters and style is a testimony to the sophistication of her narrative art. In her short stories we are baffled by "The extraordinariness of experience evoked by the ordinariness of expression."[8] Her language in her short stories is simple and direct and yet the meaning comes through with impact. She does not specifically aim at conveying a crystallized idea or a message—she tries essentially to write a story, a story of relationships.

A predominant metaphor in Jhumpa Lahiri's collection of short stories, *Interpreter of Maladies*, is that of food, which becomes a persistent symbol of Indianness as all immigrants crave for their native food in a foreign land. The stories are full of details regarding Indian food, eating habits, and culture. Fiction by Indian English women writers doles out a great amount of human understanding and offers deep insights into life as lived by Indians in their own country as well as abroad. The stories have also taken up issues related to the status of women and have tried to awaken the conscience of man regarding this.

The stories in *Interpreter of Maladies* deal either with an exploration of the essential character of the respective protagonists or with the growth and development of these individuals. Sometimes, this growth is interspersed with an unexpected transformation in the basic propensities of these characters. Besides, these stories unmistakably endorse a mutually advantageous blending of the best in the East and the West and a cultivation of a balance between modernity and conventionality. Lahiri's is an art that deals more with silences than with verbal communication, more with inarticulation than with expression. Her silences themselves are pregnant with meaning and mission specific to the situation as well as universal in implication.

Jhumpa Lahiri, a distinctive story-teller with a characteristic voice and an acumen for nuance and irony, is a writer who chronicles the present times. In her short stories she had depicted the lives of Indians who have migrated to the United States of America and are negotiating daily a conflictual world in which the inherited traditional values and the norms of the baffling new world collide with catastrophic repercussions. Lahiri's anthology exemplifies how the personal diasporic experience of an author can shape his/her artistic imagination. *Interpreter of Maladies* has an intriguing sub-title, "Stories of Bengal, Boston and Beyond". Her stories have a wide range and cover three continents of people straddling tradition and modernity. Her focus is very often on women and the varying textuality of their character which is shaped by the circumstances she is enveloped in. But, her women are different in that they want to be individuals in their own right and not trailing shadows considered always in the context of men's lives. Her women protagonists are daughters, wives, mothers and mistresses and each one of these fictitious characters is subjected to the contemporary situation and their reactions and responses explored and registered. Lahiri gives clear indications of her belief that a woman must be true to her own self to be able to realize all that she aspires for. The strait-jacketed role forced on her imposes on her a life of negation and suppression and prevents her from actualizing her hopes and dreams.

Jhumpa Lahiri is not an avowed feminist and battles against being branded one but she certainly does occupy a place of pre-eminence among the contemporary women writers who express concern for women's issues. Her protagonists are modern, educated middle-class women who manacled to their typecast roles of a wife and mother, feel roofed in by the hidebound male-dominated society and on the rebound, are assuaged only by forays into the unconventional, like Mrs. Das's affair with Mr. Kapasi in the title story of the collection, *Interpreter of Maladies*. The author merely gives an account of her character's feelings and situations in life at one particular moment. She is never judgemental nor does she attempt to tell the entire story.

The story, *Interpreter of Maladies*, deals with issues like the centrality of family life and the problems of communication. If Mr. and Mrs. Das had communicated with each other they would have been a happier couple. Mr. Kapasi's response to Mrs. Das's dark secret conveyed to her that it was her own sense of guilt that was intimidating and that, in the interest of the family she must move on in life. 'Interpreter' is an open-ended story leaving the ending to the reader's imagination. Would the lady disclose the secret to the husband? How would be respond? Would they continue to stay together? The story is essentially one of marital disharmony, but the protagonist is a liberated woman and is free to make her choice according to her own perceived reality. The title of the story is suggestive of the belief that one has to interpret one's own problems and seek refuge in one's own self. The story also seems to bring home the fact that perceptions vary with the individual and each character has his or her own personal perspective.

Jhumpa Lahiri's depiction of women of different generations including the young Shobha of 'Temporary Matter' and "Boori Ma" of 'A Real Durwan' shows the world of women divided into the traditional and the modern. Her women are sensitive to the changing times and situations. They are conscious of the multiple social and cultural disabilities which is their lot in a male-dominated society.

Lahiri's women, like Mrs. Sen of the story with the same name stand at the crossroads of tradition and modernity. They can seek change but only within the cultural norms prescribed. 'Mrs. Sen' is the story of an immigrant in America whose husband is a Professor of Mathematics in a University. In this tale we see the psychological turmoil and sense of insecurity that Mrs. Sen experiences in an alien society and with a husband who does not understand her emotional needs. Lahiri's protagonists are referred to by their surnames alone to suggest the representative nature of characterization. Lahiri tells us that Mrs. Sen is modelled on her own mother—"'Mrs. Sen' is based on my mother who baby sat in our home."[9]

'The Treatment of Bibi Haldar', unlike most of the stories in the anthology, is set not in the U.S. but in Calcutta in India. With very few relations to call her own, Bibi Haldar, an epileptic woman lives in the reluctant care of her cousin and his wife while looking for a cure for her ailments and for a husband for herself. It is the community that gives identity to Bibi whose individual isolation is underscored even though she is amidst the people of her own community. She is an outcast within her own home. The male members of society are escapists and are still unable to confront a woman with problems, problems created by man himself.

In the context of the feministic perspectives in the short stories of Jhumpa Lahiri, the final story of the collection of nine, 'The Third and Final Continent', addresses the bitter realities of arranged marriages and the long process of assimilation into the American society for a bride coming from India. The continual effort at adjustment on the part of the Bengali gentleman and his wife finally bring them together in a long and loving relationship.

Despite the apparently divergent stories in Jhumpa Lahiri's collection, *Interpreter of Maladies*, there is a pattern that we may trace through all her tales. Each of the protagonists conceived by her feels that he or she alone is misunderstood or not satisfactorily understood by others and hence develops a sense of alienation and insecurity which is difficult to surmount. It is the individual's predicament in terms of loss of identity and his desperate bid to reclaim his/her culture that is explored in the stories of Jhumpa Lahiri. The women's plight under similar circumstances, whether in India or abroad, is particularly depicted with great meticulousness and sincerity for Lahiri never ignores the cause of women.

The theme of the anguish and misery of women caused by social oppression and the brewing rebellion surfacing among this marginalized segment of Indian society in the native country reverberates in the works of Indian English women writers like Shashi Deshpande. Anita Desai and Jhumpa Lahiri. These writers have unabashedly dealt with aspects of feminism that were earlier taboo for any conservative writer to address. In addition, they have also dealt with themes of life, probity and love that fortify value-based existence. Undeniably then, these writers convey their vision and philosophy of life through their stories but the mode of communication adopted is one of implication rather than of affirmation and self-assertion.

Feministic perspectives—conspicuous or quiescent—are invariably traceable in the short stories of many Indian English woman writers of the present times and the protagonists conceived by them are in most cases women, women trying to define themselves in an antagonistic and denigrating patriarchal society, to discover a space to call their own and to carve out a niche for themselves in a world that is ever ready to relegate them to the backyard. These central characters are deplorably disallowed a voice to express themselves and a yearning to realize their potential as human beings. The female protagonists at the centre of these stories are witnessed analyzing, reviewing, reminiscing sizing up or reassessing a relationship. Women are portrayed in multifarious roles and are shown fulfilling their obligations as mother, daughter, sister, wife and beloved. What is significant in these short stories is that their authors delve deep into the psyche of their characters and depict their sensibility and their sensitivities with astounding finesse and make their mark with the innovative techniques used to lay bare the minds of these characters.

## NOTES

1. G.S. Amur, Preface to Shashi Deshpande's *The Legacy and Other Stories* (Calcutta: Writers' Workshop, 1978).
2. Anita Desai, "The Indian Writer's Problems", *Perspectives on Anita Desai*, ed., Ramesh K. Srivastava (Ghaziabad, Vimal Prakashan, 1984), 3.
3. R.K. Gupta, *The Novels of Anita Desai: The Feminist Perspective* (New Delhi: Atlantic Publishers, 2002), 82.
4. W. Somerset, Maugham, "The Short Story", *Points of View* (London: Heinemann, 1958), 142.
5. Susan Ram, "Chronicle of the Cultural Interface", *Frontline*, Oct. 22, 1999, 71.
6. Gowri Ramnarayan, "Elegant Outsider", 'Literary Review', *The Hindu* (April 16, 2000), IX.
7. Elaine Showalter, *A Literature of Their Own: British Women Novelists from Bronte to Lessing* (N.J.: Princeton University Press, 1977), 13.
8. Rene Wellek and Austin Warren, *Theory of Literature* (Harmondsworth: Penguin Books Ltd., 3rd edition, 1969).
9. Virginia Woolf, *A Room of One's Own* (Harmondsworth: Penguin), 77-78.

# 12

# Goddesses and Mythological Female Figures in Mahasweta Devi's *Statue*

*Elisa Armellino*

In her short-story *Statue*[1], which is included in her collection *Old Women* (1999) with another short-story, *The Fairy Tale of Mohanpur*, the Bengali author Mahasweta Devi portrays the figure of a tenacious female character, Dulali (Duli).

It is important, for the present purposes of this paper, to give some brief details about the main events in *Statue* in order to be able, at a further stage, to understand how myth intersects with the story by revealing a deep connection between the figure of Dulali and ancient figures of female goddesses and divinities (as they are mainly described and interpreted by Barbara Walker in her study *The Crone*). This, in turn, will cast a new light on the overall meaning of the story in relation to the representation of femininity in the story.

Dulali is the daughter of the rich Bhunya family in Chhatim, a remote Indian village and, since she is a widow (her husband died when she was just six years old), she cannot marry again despite her young age. When a young man, Dyndayal Thakur (Dinu), falls in love with her, she rejects him to avoid breaking the rules of her culture and society. In order to forget her, Dinu goes away from Chhatim to study in another village, where he comes in contact with the ideals of Indian national independentism.

When he comes back, he is very much changed and refuses to become a Brahamin priest like his father. His desire is to be a teacher and to escape from the restricted views of his native place with Dulali, who is still in his heart. However, Dinu's father—in order to avoid a scandal—arranges a marriage for him.

Nevertheless, on his wedding day, Dinu sees Dulali observing him in her white widow dress from a distance and, in front of everyone, asks her to follow him and refuses to marry. Instead of fleeing with him, Dulali—for the sake of her family's reputation—decides to stay in Chhatim and awaits for her punishment. Dinu abandons the village alone, despised by his own father. In 1924, he is sentenced to death for terrorism because of his attack (in the name of Mother India and together with other rebels), of a train carrying postal money. The house of his father is levelled by elephants according to authorities' decision and total disgrace falls upon his family. Fifty-four years later, a researcher in Calcutta manages to find the letters Dinu had written to Dulali when awaiting for his hanging in prison and writes a book on him. The book is read by a minister, who decides to build a statue in honour of the freedom martyr Dyndayal Thakur. Nabin, a young member of Chhatim's Panchayat, welcomes this resolution with joy, because he believes this to be the first step towards the construction of a road that will allow his village to have contacts with the outer world. Nabin is also the nephew of Dulali, who is seventy-eight years old now.

She has spent all her life alone, with no contact with other people except Nabin. In fact, after Dyndayal's refusal to marry, Dulali's life was spared but she was secluded from the rest of the world by being sent living in a hut in extremely poor conditions. When Nabin tells her about the statue, she starts recollecting the events linked to her love for Dyndayal and, at the end of the short-story, despite all her sufferings and her old age, she finally decides to leave Chhatim with her nephew Nabin, who dreams a better future for them and also for their country.

Despite reminding of the classical stories of unhappy and constrated loves that inform so much part of literature worldwide, the story told by Mahasweta Devi is grounded on a very complex and elaborate structure, that makes several narrative threads intersect in a continuous intermingling of past and present events. In addition, there are many important references, in the text, that links this short-story and, in particular, Duli's character, to an ancient mythological tradition. As the text says about her: "She looks like the Manosha-crone of myth" (Devi 12). In addition, the title of the collection—*Old Women*—suggests very clearly that the short-stories in it present the theme of old age, which, in '*Statue*,' takes on a mythical dimension. Indeed, the "crone" is strongly in connection with the female goddess Mother Manosha who is worshipped both by Duli's and by Dinu's family. These two figures, the crone and the goddess, co-exist in the text and suggest deep symbolical interpretations of Dulali's character.

It is the Crone who embodies the goddess's destroying potential, since the Crone represents the source of life and the end of life at the same time, that is, she is the one who governs the entire cycle of nature. This cycle was, according to ancient cultures, dominated by a ceaseless process of death and rebirth and was replaced by patriarchal religions, which, as Barbara Walker points out in her study *The Crone*, "were basically antinature, viewing all flesh as sinful and all death as punishment rather than a universal recycling process" (Walker 21). The cyclical conception of time of matriarchal cultures was thus rejected in favour of the linear conception of patriarchal societies, according to which life is based on a clear beginning and ending (after which there is the *Hereafter*).

In addition, the Crone is one aspect of the first Holy Trinity (this being, at the same time, a Virgin, a Mother and a Crone). The Crone is the most terrible aspect of the three, since she stands for death and is linked also with the idea of punishment and disgrace. This is probably why her existence has been removed from men's consciousness and why only the figures of the pure Virgin and of the lovingly Mother have been preserved. In *Statue*, Dulali reminds of the figure of the Crone in several ways. First of all, like the mythical Crone, she is very old. Her old age is portrayed by Mahasweta Devi, in order also to underline the poor conditions in which Duli lives, in a very realistic and straightforward manner. As she says: "[Dulali] has white hair, torn clothes, amaciated body". The Crone (who in India is often identified with Kali Ma) is often described as a wrinkled emaciated woman, with ribs protruding from a nearly hollow stomach. Like Dulali, who is always haunted by hunger, the Crone is often represented as physically suffering.

However, despite all the negative meanings that can be attached to her, the Crone is not a negative figure per se. In fact, by being compared to her, Dulali's character is conferred dignity and respect by the author, who offers in her text quite a non conformist and challenging idea of old age, that she sees in connection with powerful mythical forces. By choosing an old woman as the protagonist of her work, Mahasweta Devi also succeeds in locating right at the centre of her story what is normally defined as a marginal unimportant character by the contemporary world. Whereas old age is often perceived as an unproductive and valueless period of human life by many societies in the contemporary world (especially when it comes to women, whose main quality is still very often considered to be their potential for having children), Dulali is portrayed, instead, as a deep spiritual character, who possesses the powerful quality of wisdom. This does not simply mean that she is wise but also that, like ancient female goddesses, she is endowed with intelligence and with logical thinking. Dulali is also explicitly linked to a female goddess and to "wisdom" by Dyndayal, who says to her: "You look like Saraswati, the goddess of learning" (Devi 30).

In addition to the characteristics Dulali has in common with the Crone, there are many others which reveal how much she is also in connection with many other interesting female figures and also how all these figures are in connection with each other. As a widow, for example, she embodies one of the categories condemned by patriarchal societies, since, as Barbara Walker notices: "[There used to be] a widespread belief that a woman who had outlived her husband had somehow used up his life force and killed him, even if unintentionally" (Walker 18). More interestingly, the female aspects of the widow and of the virgin are interrelated, since: "At Ephesus, the Virgin-Mother-Crone was often called the Widow, since she stood for the ritual death of her son-spouse, the sacred king. The Greek Mother of Gods also held the title of Widow, especially in her temple at Stymphalus" (Walker 24). The double aspect of Virgin and Widow, that is, of innocent and threatening femininity, is also embodied by the figure of Mary, who, as Barbara Walker suggests, has been revisited and transformed by Christianity losing much part of her original nature:

> Mari or Mara meant not only the Virgin, but also the Death Goddess or Huntress. Like the variant Mari, it was a word for the briny sea, which ceremonially swallowed up a number of dying savior figures including Osiris and Adonis [...]. The name of the sea-mother Mara was also taken by the biblical Naomi when she entered her Crone state of widowhood (Ruth 1: 20). In the legend of Buddha it was the name of a death spirit [...]. (Walker 25)

Thus, the figures of the Virgin, the Mother, the Old Woman and the Widow sometimes merge into one complex and multifaceted female entity. This is shown also in the description Nabin makes of her aunt Dulali, who is seen both as a decrepit and as a vital woman, in whose eyes it is sometimes possible to see unexpected light and unpredictable energy. Similarly, the female divinity appears to be young and old at the same time: "As the birth-giving Virgin and the death-dealing Crone were part of one another, death and life together were like the new seed within the withered fruit, so visions of the young Goddess invariably merged with the old one" (Walker 29).

Furthermore, we know that Nabin, when playing with other children near Duli's hut, used to believe that his Pishi (as he calls her affectionately) was a witch and, for this reason, threw stones at her. The witch is, in fact, the final form acquired, in the course of history, by the Crone. Witches, who were also called "fairies" in the Middle Ages, worshipped a Mother Goddess and for this they were often defined as "moon goddesses" (Walker 126). Like witches, who were often scapegoats for all sorts of negative events that occurred in a community, Dulali is punished by her community because she is considered to be the cause of disgrace for both Dyndayal's family and hers. She comes to be associated by all her relatives, except Nabin, with the idea of pure evil, exactly as witches were regarded at as being in contact with the devil. It is quite interesting, here, to quote the interpretation offered by Barbara Walker on the true motivations behind witches's persecutions: "The witch-hunting mania gave men an excuse for their own faults and failures. It was convenient for getting rid of unwanted, poor, solitary, or nonfertile females, contentious wives, rebellious daughters, shrewish neighbours" (Walker 132). In *Statue,* Dulali is both a "rebellious daughter" and a "nonfertile woman" (though only in the sense that, as a widow, she cannot re-marry and have children). In addition, she was a widow and widows were often identified as witches because they were women living free of male control.

Interestingly, Dulali is often described while burning pieces of wood in a corner of her hut. As the narrator says: "[S]he keeps her fire going. Burns wood and makes charcoal. She lights the charcoal and keeps the fire going" (Devi 14). Though the reason why she does this is to warm the little place where she lives, her gestures are so repetitive that she seems involved in a kind of ritual. In addition, when she recollects the image of the fire in her head, after hearing Nabin pronouncing the word "warmth", she seems to undergo a transformation: "Her eyes become the sinless stars of dawn and she looks very lovely for an escaping moment. Nabin feels an amazing empathy and attraction" (Devi 14). The adjective "sinless" somehow reminds us of the idea of purity associated with the figure of the Virgin and the fact that she looks lovely and that Nabin feels "empathy" and "attraction" for her suggests that her female aspect as a young woman is emerging and, somehow, is still alive inside her. Thus, the old and the young woman merge into one woman, who is able to make past and present meet in a single moment of ecstatic appreciation of "warmth" (which, in turn, could be a symbol of love and vital energy). Furthermore, the element of fire is reminiscent of the Great Mother and the theme of old age, since, as Carmen Concilio suggests: "The promethic fire of wisdom, learning and knowledge that was the inheritance of the Great Mother, of the Mother Goddess and of the old 'crone' is still passed by old people, before their death, to the new generations"[2] (Concilio 135). In other words, fire also stands for the gift of story-telling, that is, for the possibility of making the past survive through memories in the present. This is also what Dulali does when she speaks to her nephew Nabin and tells him about her life and what occurred to her when she was in love with Dyndayal. The effect her memories produce in Nabin is to change him and to make him a better man than the one he could have been by not inquiring about the past and accept reality as it is offered to him by his parents. In a sense, Nabin reminds of Dyndayal himself, because, like him, he cannot accept the narrow-mindedness of the place he lives in and dreams about changing it and having a better future. This also confirms the existence, in the story, of a cyclical vision of time, because the characters themselves seem to return from a distant past in the present in a constant process of renewal.

The presence of female goddesses in *Statue* is also stated explicitly and directly through the description of Manosha, who is also strongly linked to the stories of the characters. Goddess Manosha was, in fact, worshipped by the Bhunya family (that is, Dulali's family) because in ancient times she had appeared to the Bhunya king and to her queen while they were going to the river in order to drown themselves because of their impossibility of having children. Manosha helps them and, from that moment, she becomes the protector of their house and the Goddess they feel indebted to. Dulali too is seen by Nabin wandering near the shrine of Manosha, though her devotion seems largely to have been replaced by the basic needs she has by living in the utmost poverty. Therefore, she collects the votive pots that people give as offerings to the shrine and uses them as cooking utensils. Like her family, Manosha is felt somehow as belonging to a distant and forgotten world that does not belong to her anymore. However, Manosha has been part of Duli's destiny and, as we have already seen, Duli is said to resemble "the Manosha-crone of myth" (Devi 12).

Manosha stands for both a reassuring and a threatening presence. On the one hand, she offers a rebirth to the Bhunya by making possible for them to have children and by avoiding their death. She also orders them to rescue Brahamin Thakur from poverty, thus in a sense helping him too with her generosity. For these reasons, she is defined as a Mother Goddess (Ma Manosha) and, as we know, the mother is one of the aspects of the Holy Trinity, together with the Virgin and the Crone. The Mother stands for the creative power, for the energy that gives life to the entire universe.

However, on the other hand, Manosha is the vindictive goddess who punish and ruin the Bhunya family when the Brahamin Thakur, Dyndayal's father, curses them for bringing misfortune to his house through their daughter.

Therefore, she is quite an ambivalent figure. To the Bhunya king and queen, she appears as "an amazing goddess" (Devi 6): "Snake ornaments on her body, snake-crown on her head, standing in air above ground" (*ibid.*). In another passage of the text, the narrator also explains: "In the goddess-clan Mother Manosha takes ferocious form" (*ibid.*). In addition, by commenting the sad events that have drawn the Thakur and the Bhunya families to disaster, one of the characters, Sadananada Bhunya states: "By her curse the Thakur family went to rack and ruin, and our farmhand also died of snake-bite" (*ibid.*). This representation of Manosha is akin to the representation of the all-powerful Mother who personifies "the fearful potential for rejection, abandonment, death" (Walker 12). Therefore, she embodies the darkest side of female nature which co-exists with its lovingly side, exactly as, in the immense natural cycle of being, night and day, darkness and light, death and life are different aspects of the same dimensions.

This ambivalence and double or multiple nature of Manosha can be identified also in Dulali, who, as we have seen, has characteristics which remind of the Virgin, of the Mother and of the Crone at the same time. This complex intertwining of myth and reality is not in opposition at all with the realistic style adopted by Mahasweta Devi in this short-story and with her satirical and polemical intentions. On the contrary, it helps to understand both the culture in which Dulali is raised.

Another element that belongs to that culture, that is, to its deep symbolical and mythological dimension, is the snake. Manosha is adorned with snakes and introduces herself as a snake-Goddess: "The goddess says, I am the snake-Goddess Manosha" (Devi 6). In addition, in the abandoned courtyard of Dyndayal's father, there is a python to which the Brahamin has entrusted the custody of his house when he left Chhatim in disgrace. The python is defined in the text as "Mother's familiar" (Devi 10) and, therefore, is strictly linked to goddess Manosha.

However, the snake is also a symbol of the Crone and it was created by her own hands. In fact, according to Egyptian and Mesopothamic sources, it was his first spouse. There is also a very deep link between the figure of the snake and Indian culture. For example, the snake is reminiscent of "nāga", the prince-serpents that inhabit the bed of lakes, rivers and seas and that, more or less like the python in the short-story, defend and protect the place they are in and the vital energy in it. Furthermore, the characteristics of the snake as described by the Buddhist tradition are akin to those of the female goddess (Virgin, Mother, Crone), since, like her, the snake is a symbol of the force that binds births and rebirths. The serpent and the Mother Goddess are also two symbols of fertility.

Therefore, while for Christian religions and the Bible the serpent is in connection with evil, for many other cultures it is associated with life. As Barbara Walker notices, in Persian culture the Great Serpent lives in the womb of the Mother:

> Certainly the subterranean Great Serpent was long regarded everywhere as the phallic god whose great wisdom stemmed from his intimate contact with Mother Earth's uterine depths. He fertilized the Goddess Jahi, the Persian's counterpart of Eve and Lilith [...], so she might bring forth the primordial 'blood of life' and create a world population. Similarly, it was said that the serpent fertilized Eve. (Walker 154)

It is also very meaningful (though it does not correspond to any precise mythological figure) that the river Karnabati is described by Mahasweta Devi as being always dry. The absence of water suggests the lack of a salvific power in the small village of Chhatim and also in the characters' lives. Interestingly, Dulali is seen meditating near the Karnabati and the narrator states explicitly that she does not look human:

> One in a great while she leaves behind the clamour of the Manosha-fair and goes to the abandoned riverbed, on the last day of Sraban, when the sky casts a khol-blue shadow, and in the gaps of the white bonshiuli herb, on the surface of the river, one sees the clusters of yellow kadamba. She can't say why she goes. She sits on a flat stone. Then she doesn't look human. She doesn't remember the stories she heard from her father in her childhood. "Once all this was ours. Year round there was deep water in the Karnabati then". The pollen of the kadam falls upon her thin body.... She thinks and thinks.... (Devi 16)

In this description, the author succeeds in not abandoning her realistic style but, at the same time, in suggesting that Dulali is in connection with the deep spiritual dimension of her land. When she says that once there used to be water in the Karnabati, she is regretting what her family has lost but also the loss of the sacred power of the river.

Now that we have described why Dulali's character is in connection with the characteristics of female goddesses (the Virgin, the Mother, the Crone), it is also important to understand the implications of this in relation to the overall meanings of the work.

Interestingly, the mythological dimension is used by the author in a story which is very realistic in the description it offers of women's conditions and, more generally, of the society they live in. This means that the mythical element is not used to edulcorate the events in the story or simply to embellish it with a sense of the supernatural. On the contrary, the mythical elements contribute to the portrayal of Dulali as an incredibly complex and vivid character, who has several 'female identities' in her soul.

At the beginning of her story, Dulali's personality is akin to that of a passive woman who never truly reacts to what happens to her and succumbs to her own fears and sense of duty towards her family traditions. This is proved by her strong reticence to Dyndayal: she never follows him despite knowing that, as a widow, there is no future in store for her. The most significant scene, in this sense, is that of Dyndayal's marriage, when Duli finally decides to leave her house and go to the wedding to watch him, standing there in her white widow dress.

This act of courage—she knows that she is infringing rules and that she could be punished for this—is immediately thwarted by her almost unconscious decision of remaining in Chhatim instead of escaping with Dyndayal. When he calls her and asks her to leave, she loses her senses because of the terribly strong emotions she is feeling. In other words, she faints in the very moment when she should/could have taken a decision and become the true protagonist of her life.

This is reminiscent, though in a very distant cultural and literary context, of Eveline's story in James Joyce's *Dubliners*. Eveline's lover cries "Come!" to her when he sees that, instead of sailing with him for Argentina as promised, she remains at the harbour as if she were paralysed and could not move. Dinu cries: "Come, Dulali" but is obliged to leave Chhatim alone, without his beloved. Both women are unable to change their lives and to embrace love fully and confidently. Instead of flying away, they remain trapped in their usual reality, with the difference that, while for Eveline this just means to go back to her old life, for Dulali this means to be punished and to risk death (as I have already mentioned, her father would have killed her if it were not for his wife's suggestion of sparing her life but making her live alone in the nearby hut).

Therefore, Dulali is both an active and a passive character. As we have seen, her nature is quite contradictory and she is, at the same time, the protagonist and the passive spectator of her own life. As a girl, she represses her feelings and emotions for the sake of her family and seems to have no consciousness of her own right for happiness, due to the cultural and social context in which she has been raised. When she is relegated to the hut where she will spend almost her entire life, she does nothing to react against this choice (even though a reaction would have almost certainly implied a sentence to death for her). She is the victim of her fate but, as a victim, she still preserves her dignity and expresses a passive resistance to violence and hatred. In her loneliness and poverty, she acquires a spiritual strength that will gradually leads her to a better awareness.

In fact, when her nephew Nabin tells her about the statue the Panchayat wants to build in honour of Dyndayal, she starts a painful process of remembering of the past that will open new possibilities to her. The memories of her past love and, in particular, of the injustices suffered, leads her to the slow awakening of her consciousness. In order to achieve this rebirth, however, she has to cancel the old image of Dulali she has in her mind. This means that, from being the innocent passive girl she was (the Virgin), she passes to be a more self-conscious woman, who is endowed both with the power of creation (the Mother) and with the power of destruction (the Crone). Though her creative power is not linked to the function of the mother (that is, it is not in connection with fertility and children), her final decision to abandon Chhatim with her nephew Nabin is a symbolical rebirth, since by going away she succeeds in doing what she had been unable to do more than fifty years before, when Dyndayal asked her to escape with him. This brave decision is, somehow, also an act of destruction of useless social rules and, more importantly, at a symbolical level, it implies the 'killing' of her old passive self for allowing a new one to take place.

Therefore, through the character of Dulali, Mahasweta Devi succeeds in rendering the vivid portrayal of a woman who is able to rebel to unjust social rules through the power of "wisdom". Even more importantly, she does this by describing the figure of an old woman, that is, by choosing old age as the period in which the female protagonist finds her real strength and is able to express it. In addition, the characteristics that make Dulali akin to some of the main aspects of female goddesses show the existence of an enormously deep bond between her and the most ancient conceptions of femininity and female nature. This can also represent an opposition to the values imposed by patriarchal cultures, in favour of a reappropriation of the authentic meanings attached to female figures on a mythical and a symbolical level by original cultures. By suggesting the existence of a link between Dulali and female goddesses, the author somehow implies that she is very much inscribed in her culture and that what is perpetrated against her is the mere product of social injustices, even though it is done with the pretension of respecting important cultural values.

The moment that best suggests that Dulali is a wise and deeply intelligent woman is offered by her reaction at Dyndayal's statue when she sees it for the first time with her nephew, before going away from Chhatim together:

> Pishi looks her fill. Goes forward. Passes her hands over the statue's feet. A strange, unknown feeling. Why can't she not match this high, great statue with that Dinu? Has Dinu become a god? Like the open shrine of Manosha?
>
> 'Pishi, you'll get a cold.'
>
> 'Yes, let's go.'
>
> Suddenly Pishi surprised him and said in a voice of tearless dry pain, 'The flowers at his feet are already wilted, Nabin. Crows will shit on his head, dirt will cover him, haven't you seen the distress of the god at Manosha's open shrine all year round?' (Devi 72)

Interestingly, Dyndayal's statue immediately reminds Dulali of the image of the Manosha's shrine. Exactly as it happened to "the god at Manosha's open shrine", time and men's ineptitude will spoil the statue ("Crows will shit on his head, dirt will cover him"). As Nabin understands, the statue has been built only for propagandistic aims and in order to avoid coping with the real problems of the village. As he explains to Duli: "They spent 74,851 rupees for the statue—the dirt road—the function. They could have gold-plated the village with that *monei Pishi*, they would have got road, health centre, school, everything" (*ibid.*). More or less in the same way, religious symbols have been used by Chhatim's community superficially and with hypocrisy, as demonstrated by the very bad state in which the god's shrine has been kept. In contrast, Dulali's wisdom and her resemblance to the Manosha-Crone of myth belongs to a much deeper and more authentic spiritual and mythical dimension.

To conclude, the representation of female nature offered by Mahasweta Devi in *Statue*, is one of the most challenging that can be found in literature, since she portrays a female character who has mythical resonances and a realistic and critical approach to life at the same time. In addition, the author offers a description of an old woman which is deeply in contrast with common stereotypes and clichés of old age as a passive stage in human life (and especially in women's lives). In her old age, the protagonist is finally able to rebel against her isolation and finds the courage of doing what she was unable to do when she was much younger.

Through her resistance to sufferings, Dulali offers a positive female example of how to endure social injustices without surrendering to them and preserving one's dignity and critical skills despite cultural and social biases that limit the expression of free thinking and the distribution of equal rights.

When Dulali abandons Chhatim with Nabin, the text describes them as going away in the darkness, which can be a symbol of the lack of true moral values and spiritual ideals in the place they are leaving behind themselves.

## NOTES

1. The short-story *Statue* was read by me in the English translation made by Gayatri Spivak from the Bengali language (see Bibliography).
2. My translation, here, from Italian to English (see Bibliography).

## BIBLIOGRAPHY

Concilio, Carmen. "Old Woman e l'incontro con la morte in The Diary of a Good Neighbour di Doris Lessing and Fire on the Mountain di Anita Desai". *Personaggio-Donna. Lo sguardo dalla fine.* Urbino: Quattro Venti, 2001.

Coomaraswami, Ananda K. *Traditional Art and Symbolism.* Princeton: Princeton University Press, 1977.

Devi, Mahasweta. *Old Women: Statue, The Fairy Tale of Mohanpur.* Calcutta: Seagull Press, 1999.

Dhawan, R.K. *Indian Women Novelists.* New Delhi: Prestige Books, 1995.

Loomba, Ania. *Colonialism/Postcolonialism.* London: Routledge, 1998.

Walker, Barbara. *The Crone: Woman of Age, Wisdom and Power.* New York: Harper, 1995.

Zimmer, Heinrich. *Myths and Symbols in Indian Art and Civilization.* Princeton: Princeton University Press, 1946.

# 13

# Integrity or Deceit: A Critical Study of Shashi Deshpande's Novel, *In the Country of Deceit*

*Vinita Jha*

I am Sinner, I am Saint.
I am the beloved and the Betrayed.
I have no joys which are not yours,
No Aches which are not yours.
I too call myself I. (Kamala Das, *An Introduction*)

Shashi Deshpande has gained a prominent place in the Indian writing in English with her study of domesticity in her novels; she has an urge to explore and define the areas of experiences of women which have not been previously explored. In this era of Woman's awakening and empowerment, Deshpande's concern for women's emancipation is also strong. She portrays the aberrations created in the women exploitation by men, but her approach to the predicament or problems of women is different from that of all other feminist writers. She deals with the excesses committed upon the female fold for centuries leading to their deep but quiet suffering and their passive resignation. She shows how women revolt and try to search their own identity in the hostile world of male chauvinism, but she also has consideration for a home—a home of peace and love that can provide security to the women. If a home is in a position to provide her safety, a woman may never revolt against the home in that case. As Deshpande remarks,

> I am a feminist very much and I strongly react against any kind of cruelty or oppression, denial of opportunities to women because they are women...the important thing is we have the right to live ourselves. But as a writer I am not going to use my novels to carry the message of feminism. Then it becomes propaganda.[1]

Shashi Deshpande combines tradition and modernity in her characters; her protagonists show a kind of metaphysical rebellion in their thoughts and feelings.

In her first three novels, *The Dark Holds No Terrors* (1980), *If I Die Today* (1982) and *Come up and Be Dead* (1983), the most prominent theme is woman's predicament—her suffering, the struggle she undergoes to make an identity for herself, to live a life of worth. In her next three novels, *Roots and Shadows* (1983), *That Long Silence* (1988) and *The Binding Vine* (1993), we notice a gradual growth and development in writing skill and thematic style of Shashi Deshpande. These three novels are purely domestic novels. There is an inner conflict in the minds of the protagonists—Indu in *Roots and Shadows* and Jaya in *That Long Silence*. Towards the end of these novels there is a change in the behaviour of both Indu and Jaya. There is reconciliation, a self-revelation and an onward movement with confidence. In *The Binding Vine*, the author takes her protagonist a little outside the dramatic sphere. The character, pushing back her personal crisis, tries to fight for other women. Her protagonists are now glancing at society and trying to help people in crisis. Moreover, the theme of man-woman relationship is extended to other human relationship such as mother-daughter and between one woman and the other. The other themes like guilt, fear and trapped animals like women slowly fade in the middle phase. Her other three novels *A Matter of Time* (1996), *Small Remedies* (2000) and *Moving On* (2004) are appreciated as mature novels, because Deshpande takes her protagonists from the domestic field to the society at large. Women's problems in a family is set aside and the individual abilities are given more importance woman's ambitions have also become quite high compared to her earlier novels and there is also a shift from the emotional bond to the intellectual bond. Savitribai in *Small Remedies*, Sumi in *A Matter of Time* and Manju in *Moving On* are women who are able to think and live independently on their own. Shashi Deshpande's latest novel is *In the Country of Deceit* in which she has presented her protagonist, Devayani falling in love with a married IPS officer, Ashok Chinnappa, without caring for any social and ethical norms, only for enjoying special pleasure or happiness in life. As Shashi Deshpande herself justifies this kind of illicit relationship as 'adult love', by stating the fact:

> Relationships are not something one decides on. They happen naturally, especially adult relationships, and one must know what the consequences are and take responsibility for it. It is very difficult to judge if adult love is good or bad. Human beings always crave for love, even in death a dying man wants to hold someone's hands.[2]

*In the Country of Deceit* has the multilayered profound theme of love which can be explored very delicately, without any good-bad division. The present paper proposes to study the unique love story of Devayani which is as much a matter of deceit to herself as that of integrity.

*In the Country of Deceit*, the tenth novel of Shashi Deshpande was released by the famous theatre personality and playwright, Girish Karnad in Bangaluru on September 26, 2008, which presents the multifaceted human relationships in the form of adult love between two mature persons, who know very well that their relationship is without any future. Devayani, the youngest daughter of Mudhol family, chooses to live alone in the small town of Rajnur after her parents' death, especially against the advice and wishes of her elder sister, Savi and aunt, Sindhu. She seems to spend her time leisurely by teaching English, creating a garden and arranging the household things in her own artistic way. The novel successfully evokes the atmosphere of a small, non-descript town, Rajnur which is representative of round about any small town in any far flung corner in India. The sentiments and attachment of Devayani to her house is quite Indian because the reconstruction of her ancestral house shows the revival of her life after the traumatic experience of her mother's death. The house symbolizes not only her new liberated self but also her emotional bond with Savi and her aunt, Sindhu who likes to write letters to her from the USA. Keeping aside the suggestions of matrimonial bliss, Devayani enjoys the status of a self-proclaimed spinster, intellectual well-read, devoted to family, reserved and introspective, however, her solitary and quiet lifestyle changes when she is befriended by Rani, a glamorous, beautiful actress who is a new neighbour in Rajnur. In spite of their different lifestyles, they come close to each other because of their artistic temperament and aesthetic and passionate nature. Through Rani, Devayani meets Ashok, the new district Superintendent of Police, who is much older than her and already married. The love relationship between Devayani and Ashok may be explained as 'love at first sight' because the attraction between them is guided only by their basic impulse. Ashok starts courting her dramatically through regular phone calls at night. As Shashi Deshpande informs the readers: "It is very difficult to distinguish love according to the level of mental maturity. A 60-years-old man or a woman can fall in love and behave like a child. People realize the true meaning of love only when they fall in love."[3] Ashok follows Devayani and confesses before her in a clear bold voice:

> 'I'm a married man. I have a daughter, She's nine, no, she'll be ten this year. I don't know your age, but I know you are much younger....' He paused and then burst out, 'I can promise you nothing. Nothing'. He paused again. 'I know I have no right to say any of this to you, I know this is very wrong. I've tried not to. I've tried to control myself, but...let me say this just once, just this once.'[4]

Devayani tries to avoid this new intrusion of phone-calls in her self-proclaimed spinster life, but gradually she starts enjoying it. Earlier she had been suffering from a nightmare in which she tried to fly away from the trap of a stranger, but after the phone calls from Ashok, she gets frightened of her own emotional or sensual self who wants to run into his arms.

Devayani keeps herself busy in two types of diversion to drive her life steadily on the right track. The first is the land on Hattihola Road which is supposed to belong to Krishna Bhat, her maternal grandfather. The second is the glamorous actress, Rani, who is too eager to revive her show-biz career. It is during her trip to a resort on the Goa highway, in the company of Rani that finally she surrenders herself to the coils of her self-created country of deceit. Ironically, she gets easily 'convinced by the sentimental outburst of her elderly lover, Ashok Chinappa who says to her:

> I can promise you two things. I can promise you love and I can promise you honesty.[5]

After enjoying the hedonistic pleasures of love, Devayani does not feel the pangs of guilt or sin for quite sometime, and carries on her love-relationship with Ashok in a very normal and matured style, without letting the world know her immoral game of love. It is Ashok who arranges their secret meetings at small intervals, and teaches her how to receive maximum pleasure during those brief moments of their temporary relationships. Gradually, the sensual self of Devayani has been attacked by the intellectual self of her being which reminds her constantly of such hateful words like 'an adulteress,'[6] 'A mistress,'[7] 'A floozy'[8] and 'A whore.'[9] She also tries to justify her self-proclaimed honest love-affair through the beautiful, tragic affair between Anna and Vronsky in *Anna Karenina*, but finally she realizes that "adultery remains adultery, whoever the couple may be. That it is always riddled with guilt and fear, constantly swinging between euphoria and despair."[10] Devayani finds it difficult to cope with the guilt of her illicit love with a man who would never abandon his wife and daughter. Her brother-in-law, Shree's letter also helps her in reviving her real, respectable self by revealing the real meaning of love, of living together with loyalty which may yield the positive result of "an honourable marriage."[11] After a good deal of inner conflict, which has been revealed to us by the poetic prose of Deshpande, Devayani succumbs to the social norms of love, balanced with loyalty and marriage. If on the one hand, she likes to nurture the happy moments of togetherness in the country of deceit where she claims, "we could be happier than most married couples, that we could have the kind of marriage very few couples can even dream of,"[12] on the other, her social standing and reputation nags her:

This is what marriage means:

> Knowing that the years lie ahead of you, a long stretch of time waiting for you to occupy together. Taking time for granted, disjointed conversation about trifles, casual intimacies. This is what I want. I don't want clandestine meetings, drama, constant fears.[13]

Devayani's love-story turns tragic because it is not culturally-prescribed one, and therefore cannot flourish, and naturally she decides to sacrifice it at the altar of principle and duty.

*In the Country of Deceit* is basically a story of humans and human relationships which finally leads us to the strong emotion of love, which has nothing to do with the boundary of good and bad. Devayani emerges as one of Deshpande's most radical protagonists because she begins and carries on her love-affair with Ashok, with the clear-eyed knowledge that she is deceiving others, but she also argues that her lover is deceiving them even more, being a husband and a father. Moreover, he tries to maintain his love or sensual relationship with Devayani with a clear understanding that it has no future. The way Deshpande writes about the emotional and physical entanglement of Devayani and Ashok and the way she presents the dilemma or predicament of the protagonist caused by her genuine feelings of love, Deshpande wins sympathy for her protagonist despite her being in the role of the mistress, the adulteress, by keeping her protagonist very down to earth, unsparing of herself, someone who does not float in the world of fantasy but in entirely realistic; basically decent and high principled:

> It's true all mistresses crave for marriage, that, in time, their claims increase. But I don't want marriage. I have never thought of it. It has always been out of bounds for me. I never could, I never can see you and me happily married, smug in our happiness. We would always be haunted by the unhappiness of others.[14]

Devayani has the love and support of her close family members—her sister, brother-in-law, aunt and uncle, cousins who wish her to enjoy a secure and happy married life, with their sincere and natural feeling. When they discover Devayani's affair, they becamc shocked, bewildered, even distressed, but instead of denouncing her, they advise gently against it and show respect for her autonomy. Devayani is also uncharacteristically an adulteress who defies stereotypes of Indian women. Deshpande presents Devayani as an unusual and original character, who, while enjoying her romantic and experimental nature, perfectly understands the conventions and knows how to reconcile with the wider society, with grace and calm compromise:

> Why did I do it? Why did I enter the country of deceit? What took me into it? I hesitate to use the word love, but other word is there? And yet, like the word 'atonement' I kept hearing in kshama's conversation, though she never uttered it, the word love is too simple for the complicated emotions and responses that made me do what I had done.[15]

This novel is written in the first person narration, almost in a confessional mode where Devayani seems to be suffering from saint-sinner, beloved-betrayed syndrome. The title of this novel is apt, because Devayani, once embarked on this journey of love and relationship, moves beyond her normal landscape and enters the country of deceit, containing secret escapades and stolen hours.

This novel also consists the voices of Devayani's relatives, mainly in the form of letters, which chime into Devayani's life and which are women into her reality and worldview. And yet, Deshpande removes the dramatic element of the tragic end of this novel, leaving only the quiet sorrow and resilient emotional tenacity of the protagonist:

> No, I don't want to forget, I want to remember, it is not remembering, but forgetting that will be my greatest enemy.
>
> Is this what my life is going to be like from now—a constant struggle between trying to forget and wanting to remember?[16]

*In the Country of Deceit* deals not only with the theme of adult love leading to the path of deceit and adultery, but also with that of sin and redemption. Devayani seems to be a well-developed and a round character because at last she proves her integrated character by being honest to her own self. This book also discusses the good-bad facets of such a delicate emotion, love by the response of the various characters and what it makes people do. Devayani finds a very thin line dividing the act of love and that of deceit, and she comes to the conclusion that deceiving the world and also one's own self for momentary pleasures is not only wrong, but also sinful which really deserve a common condemnation. It is really an act of fidelity to her own real self that Devayani weans herself away completely from the country of deceitful love. It may be affirmed that Shashi Deshpande is not a feminist in the accepted sense of the term. She expresses her faith in the integrity of love-relationships, and is averse to the very idea of converting it into a form of deceit. It is only a perfect kind of loyalty to one's own self that can mitigate the excesses of militant feminist's ideology.

## NOTES

1. S. Prasanna Sree. "In Conversation with Shashi Deshpande". *Woman in the Novels of Shashi Deshpande: A Study*. S. Prasanna Sree (Ed.). New Delhi: Sarup & Sons, 2003, 154-55.
2. http://www.dnaindia.com/entertainment/interview, my-new-book -is-about-love-shas. 7/27/2010.
3. *Ibid.*
4. Shashi Deshpande. *In the Country of Deceit*, first published in Viking by Penguin Books India, 2008, 91.
5. *Ibid.*, 131.
6. *Ibid.*, 148.
7. *Ibid.*, 197.
8. *Ibid.*, 181.
9. *Ibid.*, 161.
10. *Ibid.*, 149.

11. *Ibid.*, 198.
12. *Ibid.*, 200.
13. *Ibid.*, 192.
14. *Ibid.*, 236-37.
15. *Ibid.*, 257.
16. *Ibid.*, 259.

# 14

# The Narrative Voices and Female History in Ashapurna Devi's *Subarnalata*

*Arpa Ghosh*

The Bengali novelist Ashapurna Devi's *Subarnalata* (1966) is a sequel to her critically acclaimed, Gyanpith and Rabindrapuroshkar winning novel *Pratham Pratisruti* (First Promise) (1964). In a television interview Ashapurna Devi once said, Satyabati, the heroine of *Pratham Pratisruti*, belongs to the generation of the author's grandmother; Subarnalata, Satyabati's daughter, to that of her mother; while Bakul, Subarna's daughter is a woman of her generation. Ashapurna confesses, she has witnessed the plight of Subarnalata's generation while she has only heard tales about the struggles of women of Satyabati's generation.

Both *Pratham Pratisruti* and *Subarnalata* are novels chronicling the struggle of Bengali middle-class wives and mothers incarcerated in claustrophobic patriarchal households. In her preface to *Pratham Pratisruti* Ashapurna Devi says:

> History of past ages is constructed out of the destruction and formation of the exterior world. This brightly lit history, full of sound and fury, is a source of inspiration, stimulation and romance for later ages. But, is the work of creation and destruction absent from the confines of dimly lit interiors? From that point the hue changes for future

> societies, ages and human mentality. The spotlight, cast on these areas reveal plenteous reserves. Yet, written history has always remained indifferent to the work carried out in the interiors of households. Interiors have always been neglected. This tale is about one of the anonymous women who first brought the glimmerings of promise into such neglected interiors.[1]

At the end of *Pratham Pratisruti*, a disillusioned Satyabati abandons her husband and leaves for Kashi, the refuge of homeless women. She says she plans to ask her father[2] a series of questions pertaining to Hindu rites and practices, family ties and bonds. Satyabati's daughter Subarnalata, in her death-bed, defiantly says, "I have lost, but I have not surrendered," implying, while breaking her physically and maiming her emotionally, patriarchy has failed to curb her indomitable spirit to question its premises.

Mother and daughter, ultimately lose their battle waged against the vulgar and mean-spirited dictates of nineteenth century patriarchy. The defeat of the mother Satyabati marked by her dramatic withdrawal from family ties is more of a disaster than an inevitable outcome. Satyabati enjoys her moments of quiet triumph in her lifelong struggle to move out of the intellectual and moral darkness that swathes the lives of women. Compared to her mother, Subarnalata, fails to score any spectacular points in her lifelong struggle against female subordination in her marital home which she enters against her will at the age of eight and where she becomes a mother for the first time at the age of fourteen. Even her death, celebrated with vulgar pomp and show by her husband and sons, is a regression in terms of everything Subarnalata has fought for in her lifetime.

Subarnalata's life is a dark study of failure in all fronts. Subarnalata's married life in terms of nineteenth century standards (the novel is set in nineteenth century Kolkata against the backdrop of India's freedom struggle) is regarded by her compeers as a huge success. Her husband is rich, prosperous and obsessed with her. She gives birth to eight healthy, good-looking children, four sons and four daughters. By nineteenth century Bengali standards Subarnalata is an exceptionally blessed woman, healthy, wealthy, her husband's beloved and proud mother of strong sons and beautiful daughters. The ugly, terrifying underbelly of her apparently ideal situation is exposed in a narrative that questions all aspects of marriage and motherhood. Subarnalata's life tottering on the shaky foundation of betrayal and treachery is an appalling failure. Compared to her mother's achievements, Subarnalata's successes are humble but significant:

> The second daughter-in-law brought the newspaper into the household, she also introduced the wearing of chemise with sari, she started the tradition of clean bedclothes in the child-birth room. It was she who gathered all the children of the household and made them sit down to study. She started quite a few things like these.
>
> She was slighted, insulted, riddled by sneers and snickerings, but she remained obstinate. She fought till the end. (49)

Subarnalata's arena of combat is the household. Her achievements are within four walls of her nineteenth century family unit comprising of a torturer, domineering mother-in-law, suspicious, malicious, violently abusive husband and his sneering brothers and their unsympathetic wives. Bringing small changes like the above in this narrow-minded family may not be a huge achievement in public terms, but it entails a lifelong uphill trudge for Subarnalata.

Most importantly, unlike as in *Pratham Pratisruti* the thrust of the novel is not in totting feminist points against a stifling patriarchy. In fact, the narrative movement of *Subarnalata* moves further and further away from the clean, chronological, linear movement of Satyabati's story into a confusing morass of desire and disappointment, longing and frustration, rational liberalism and irrational bigotry. All myths centering matrimony and motherhood are systematically crushed by the unremitting spotlight trained on Subarnalata's futile, battle-fatigued existence. At the same time, these myths are shown to dominate the ideological mindscape of Subarnalata's powerful antagonists, and in fact are replicated and strengthened in her children in spite of her valourous struggle to dismantle them. This point-counterpoint movement keeps the narrative circling in the stagnant waters of hidebound convention till the lone warrior Subarnalata is sucked into them finally and conclusively.

The reader's expectation from the sequel, nourished from Satyabati's inspiring struggle is systematically frustrated in all fronts: private and public, marriage, motherhood and female honour. All her life Subarnalata wages a heroic battle against patriarchal domination, deceit, hypocrisy and malice without a single significant victory. This detailed study of defeat and frustration is salvaged from utter morbidity by the heroism and optimism of Subarnalata's character.

Every aspect of marriage is questioned. The question posed regarding an ideal groom is:

> Educated and employed, high caste and of old, established lineage, this is the measuring rod of an 'eligible bachelor', this is what is taken into account in marriages. Who has ever gone to see the taste, thought and aim of the groom?
>
> None cares, and hence the incompatibility!
>
> So many tears beneath it all!
>
> Why only womenfolk, even men shed tears. Their souls weep.[3] (312)

Subarnalata's husband and her in-laws relentlessly oppose her dreams; whether it is the desire for a south-facing verandah in the new house built by her husband and his brothers, or her resolution to educate her younger daughters Bakul and Parul. A life devastated by blind, spiteful opposition, Subarnalata faces her final humiliation when her lifelong efforts to give literary shape to her deprived, emotionally destitute life, meets with complete failure. The publisher, her husband's elderly cousin, who is otherwise sympathetic towards women, delivers cheap, badly-bound books shamefully riddled with typing errors, and her husband and grown-up sons cruelly sneer at her earnest efforts. Shamed and disillusioned, Subarnalata burns the inferior prints and the diaries she has maintained all her life. After this final gesture she withdraws into a shell and dies shortly afterwards.

In relation to *Pratham Pratisruti*, the sequel *Subarnalata* is significantly retrogressive. The reader's expectation of female triumph and achievement is frustrated completely. The darkness of Subarnalata's life is eternal and all-encompassing. Compared to her, her mother Satyabati has a much more fulfilling life.

The career of Satyabati, heroine of *Pratham Pratisruti* moves in a trajectory that has failures, but is also one that registers important achievements. It is a linear trajectory that has a beginning, middle and a unique closure outside the calculated chess-board of marriage and death, usual closures of bourgeois novels. At the end of the novel, Satyabati abandons her husband and her responsibilities as wife and mother to leave for Kashi, which in the nineteenth century was considered to be a refuge of homeless women. Before her departure she articulates her decision to start a girls' school in Kashi and earn her living as an independent educator of unfortunate girls.

*Pratham Pratisruti* begins with a touching description of Satyabati's special relation with her father Ramkali, the wealthy ayurvedic physician of the village where the married pre-menstrual Satyabati lives with him and his family. Gradually, the narrative progresses with Satyabati departing for her marital house, her conflict with her mean-spirited in-laws, her departure to Kolkata with her husband Nabakumar, her peaceful, single household where she is the chief decision-maker, her good deeds, specially the rescue of a illiterate and penurious young girl who happens to be the illegitimate daughter of a neighbour of her father's village, from the clutches of a ruthless, exploitative zamindar family. Later, the girl grows up to be a teacher of Bethune school thanks to the positive role Satyabati plays in her life. The omniscient narrator of *Pratham Pratisruti* is reliable, mature and in sync with Satyabati's ideals and aspirations. The narration is straightforward in keeping with the chronological fidelity of the traditional master-text.

Satyabati's tale unfolds affirmatively. Satyabati gradually fortifies her position aided by providence, and earns the independence to take crucial decisions for her children. Her stress is forever on female education which she feels is the only route to female emancipation. She sends her little girl Subarnalata to school and supervises her education in a dedicated manner. Satyabati's constructive educational plans regarding her daughter receives a rude set-back when she is heartlessly betrayed by her mother-in-law and husband who clandestinely marry off the eight-year-old Subarnalata,[4] largely to get back at her, and partly due to their cynicism about female education. Coming to know about the malicious betrayal Satyabati loses all faith in family ties. Regarding her daughter she says: "If Subarna is born with the ingredients of a good human being, she will grow up to be one on her own right. She will understand her mother. Or else, like her father, she too will think her mother is completely heartless!... I have no power to stop her thoughts!"[5]

Later, in her apologetic letter to her daughter, Satyabati retraces her stance saying she should have stayed back to provide support and succour to her favourite daughter.[6] Even this retracing is a moral step forward on the part of Satyabati who dies easy with the knowledge that her daughter will forgive her desertion.

The catastrophic ending of *Pratham Pratisruti* actually runs counter to the narrative progression of the text. The act of treachery (the eight-year-old Subarna's coercive marriage) is not an inevitable act, but a mishap that could have been averted under the circumstances. Therefore, though Satyabati is an exceptionally heroic woman, deeply and fearlessly critical of patriarchal restrictions, *Pratham Pratisruti* as a text is more exemplary than representative of the female condition. Satyabati's triumphs are individual triumphs of a singular personality operating in unique circumstances. In a long introspective passage in *Subarnalata*, a comparison is drawn between Subarnalata and Satyabati:

> Behind Subarna's mother shines a brilliant solar shaft, Satyabati's father, Satyabati's polestar, the groundwork of Satyabati's life, the strength of her spine. Behind Subarna, there is only a fragment of dull cinder.... Subarna's father is the Saturn of her fate.

> And her marital fortune?
>
> Isn't the chasm huge there as well?
>
> Satyabati's husband was ineffective, incapable but not boorish and obscene. He may not have been worthy of Satyabati, but he was not a torturer.... All her life Subarna has had to live with a boorish, obscene torturer.
>
> When could she desert him?
>
> Even before she could stand erect, her shoulders and back were burdened with mammoth baggage. Was she to deny her responsibilities and see the reflection of her life in that of her children? That picture too would have been inked wirh gloom.
>
> So, Subarna can raise her face and say, 'Mother, your daughter is flawed by her inability to emulate your cruelty! She was not blessed by your small, light household.'
>
> Under which ensign will your daughter rest if she is to give vent to her righteous fury? Do not chide me mother, remember this, all lives are not the same; everyone cannot be judged by the same measuring rod! Before sitting upon judgment consider the environment of the accused! (182)

The difference between Satyabati's and Subarnalata's circumstances is highlighted. But more importantly, the textual locus of each is indicated. Satyabati is a redoubtable woman placed in unique circumstances. She has the good fortune to establish a single family unit for herself, her husband and three children (a small number compared to the early nineteenth century situation) in Kolkata away from the prying critical eyes of her superstition-ridden mother-in-law.

In contrast, Subarnalata's locus is a desubjectivized position. She is a representative of all the women incarcerated in benighted households who clamour for light and freedom. The narrative shift from *Pratham Pratisruti* to *Subarnalata* is backwards. At the same time the narrative snarls are more sensitive to the age and larger situation than to the glamour and individuality of a single life. What at first reading appears to be a regressive step —Subarnalata's morbid, stifling life issuing from Satyabati's far more promising, confirmatory life—is actually a more mature, thoughtful and responsible thematic step taken by the author. Unaided by her mother's providential good fortune, Subarnalata has only courage, determination and honest anger to fall back upon. With unalleviated clarity, the novel studies the predicament of a woman who is Satyabati's moral equal, yet who lacks her good fortune.

Incidentally, the thoughts referred to in the above quote may be Subarnalata's at the moment when after being violently insulted and abused by her husband in front of the patriotic and liberal Ambika, she is forced to return with bent head to her husband's household. At the same time, the thoughts could also be the surmise of the chatty, colloquial, parenthetical, narrative voice that keeps intruding into Subarnalata's tale to comment and judge. The voice, lively, intrusive, rude, all-knowing, irritating, creates an almost Brechtian estrangement effect, provoking and infuriating the reader, constantly interrupting, swinging and twisting the narrative flow, often lifting it out of a given time zone and moving it forwards and backwards sometimes for the purpose of superimposition, sometimes for parallelisms and sometimes for contrast.

The intrusiveness, contrariness and unpredictability of the narrative voice forces the reader to break away from the passive lull that is the habitual stance of the reader of the traditional classic realist texts. Instead of quietly and contentedly accepting certain given constants, the reader of *Subarnalata* is incessantly needled by the nagging narrative voice, that depicts the heroine sometimes from the inside (her deepest desire for the sublime and the beautiful) and from the outside (the cut-and-dried portrait of the virago and the harridan that she cuts for her in-laws, relatives and children). Rarely do these voices converge to give a holistic picture of Subarnalata. One such rare instance reads like this:

> But when has Subarnalata been afforded the leisure to be tender and affectionate? She has been engaged in lifelong battle. If Subarnalata had been soft, would she have been able to free herself from Muktakeshi's household? She

> wouldn't. Muktakeshi's son would have kept her as a subjugated woman. She would have had to kowtow to his desires, to fear his threats, and lose her soul by becoming enslaved to his furtive desires.
>
> But is her soul intact even today? 'I won't allow a sell-out!' Having vowed this, hasn't it been destroyed by relentless battle? Isn't it possible to reconstruct her destroyed soul? With effort, care, dedication? No, it cannot be. It is not possible.
>
> Subarnalata cries out, in order to battle with a demon, the goddess has to take the malevolent, demonic form of Chamunda.[7] The Beena-playing, docile Saraswati,[8] the prosperous and benevolent Laxmi[9] lack the ability to play the role. (250-55)

Apart from one or two instances like this, the voices in the text rarely coalesce. The picture that the reader receives of Subarnalata is a broken, piecemeal picture, in places riddled by ambiguity, especially in Subarnalata's relationship with her children some of whom are estranged from her and regard her as an oddball eccentric, and all of whom are distanced from her. The broken picture draws attention to the broken history of Subarnalata in particular and all women in general.

This swinging back and forth between the consciousness of the characters (especially Subarnalata) and narrative, authorial consciousness; this blurring of narrative voices, superimposition of one on another, creates a circular, repetitive, incantatory, ballad-like narrative pattern, which is very different from the more docile, dead-pan, linear narrative pattern of *Pratham Pratisruti*. The first novel is feminist in content. Its narrative form however—the classic realist text with a beginning, middle and end—subscribes to the masculinist novel-writing tradition. The sequel however subscribes to the male tradition in name only. Ostensibly, *Subarnalata* is divided into chapters and volumes. But actually, the narrative form—fragmented, oral, irreverent to unities of time, place and action, unpredictably swinging back and forth in time, and ambiguously elliptical in key portions—

confounds the predominantly male tradition of clear-cut, linear narrative in nineteenth century realist novel.

The eight-year-old Subarna's marriage marking the end of *Pratham Pratisruti*—a moment of inattention on Satyabati's part that undoes all the good she had planned for her daughter—is an avoidable accident that swings the progressive, ahead-of-its-time thematic movement of the novel back in one swift dramatic blow. Subarnalata's career, on the contrary, is not a linear movement at all. In Chapter 15, we hear the narrative voice saying:

> Subarnalata has neither ingress nor egress. Hers is a neglected existence. Around her locus, the air will scorch with heated sneering criticism, and the sky above her head and the ground beneath her feet will remind her, 'It is enough we have given you shelter, that we have given you space to be.' (128)

Chapter 10 opens with the comment:

> For how many days was Subarnalata deprived of her food and keep in Muktakeshi's household?
>
> Other chapters will have to be searched in order to know about that phase of her history. But, far from being hard-bound, the book of Subarnalata's life is hopelessly loose and untied. Unfastened pages are scattered and fly all over the place. (72)

The tragic mode of the novel is aided by its circular narrative pattern, very different from the systematic chronology of the male bildungsroman or even the female biography beginning from childhood and ending in old age. The circular pattern gives a timeless quality to the text, a cosmic connect between the past, present and future. For a short space towards the end of the novel when Subarnalata tries to write down her haphazard, chaotic thoughts in the form of a book, the technique of superimposition is repeated as a dramatic microcosmic reiteration of the narrative pattern of the entire book. The unpredictability and temporal and spatial oscillations of the first person narrative (Subarnalata's own voice) reiterates the fact that no neat linear narrative is possible while retracing suppressed female history.

In *Subarnalata*, there are multiple narrative voices. One is a rather gossipy and dramatic personage who narrates the story of the second daughter-in-law of Muktakeshi Bamni of Darjipara with a gossipmonger's verve and relish.[10] The other is a high-pitched and melodramatic voice, a significantly variant from the sophisticated omniscient narrative voice. Most chapters end with queries, for example:

> But afterwards? When Muktakeshi hiring two horse-drawn carriages and clutching her Laxmi's bundle to her breast stepped into the new house with her entire family...? (End of Chapter 1)

The queries whet reader's interest in the narrative as well as reveal gaps between event and report, fact and rumour. The voices are oral and colloquial. The narrative has the flavour of old wives' tales embellished by exaggerated, colourful details in which fiction, rumour and criticism often merge with fact.

The closure of the novel belies the reader's expectation once again. After a prolonged description of Subarnalata's illness, instead of her death closing the text, the narrative goes on to give an equally lengthy and detailed description of her last rites and how her children vie with each other to make her death a memorable event. The climax of Subarnalata's death is thus undone by the pomp and show that comes as an aftermath and makes a travesty of Subarnalata's tragic life. This is the second instance, the first being Subarnalata's shameful failure to publish her autobiography. The novel however does not end even after the double thwarting of the climax. It ends with daughter Bakul's futile hunt for remnants of Subarnalata's papers she could use in writing about her mother's failed and (for her, since Bakul is her youngest child) unknown life.

The unvarying thwarting of climax, culmination, apotheosis, is a modernist technique calculated to increase reader participation and provoke the angry and frustrated reader to think deeply about unanswered questions, if possible to come up with answers himself. *Subarnalata* is therefore a text that has a feminist theme, and uses narrative devices that have modernist and postmodernist overtones. At the same time, the vivid portrayal of the tough, determined heroine engaged in sole combat against smaller, meaner, collective social forces, gives the text a timeless, tragic dimension. As a narrative, *Subarnalata* is much more innovative, seriously feminist and modernist than *Pratham Pratisruti*. The latter remains the story of a single outstanding woman, whereas the former rises to be the representative tale of a tormented, angst-ridden tribe.

## NOTES AND REFERENCES

1. All quotations have been taken from *Pratham Pratisruti* by Ashapurna Devi. Kolkata: Mitra & Ghosh Publishers Pvt. Ltd., 1964. The translations into English are all mine.
2. Satyabati's father Ramkali is an ayurvedic physician and an enlightened man by early nineteenth century standards. His rationality has always inspired his daughter. After the demise of his wife, Ramkali had divided his property among his kin and retired to Kashi. The practice of retiring to Kashi in an advanced age was common among high-caste Hindus.
3. All quotations have been taken from *Subarnalata* by Ashapurna Devi, Kolkata: Mitra & Ghosh Publishers Pvt. Ltd., 1966. The translations into English are all mine.
4. Subarnalata had accompanied her father on a visit to her grandmother's village one summer vacation.
5. *Pratham Pratisruti* by Ashapurna Devi, Kolkata: Mitra & Ghosh Publishers Pvt. Ltd., 1964, 505.
6. The letter is part of *Subarnalata*. It is handed to Subarnalata in her middle age after Satyabati's death by her dying father.
7. Chamunda, slayer of fearsome demons, is a ferocious, war-like mother-goddess.
8. Saraswati is the Hindu goddess of learning. She plays the Beena, a stringed instrument and rides a white swan. She symbolizes grace, wisdom and contemplation.
9. Laxmi is the Hindu goddess of wealth and prosperity. Exquisitely beautiful, she is bedecked with jewels and rides a white owl. Saraswati and Laxmi, unlike Chamunda, are associated with grace, prosperity, fullness and placidity.
10. Bamni means aged Brahmin female.

# 15

# Kamala Das's Poetry: Issues of Intertextuality and Feminisms

*Purnendu Chatterjee*

The lack of formal education has been more a help than a hindrance in case of Kamala Das. Without the burden of scholarship, Das created a natural poetics of her own. Das is a poet by instinct. Writing comes to her "like a rash of prickly heat in certain seasons" and she had no control over her writings. Words came to her naturally, as she asserts, in Keatsian fashion, in the poem "Words":

> All round me words, and words and words,
> They grow on me like leaves, they never
> Seem to stop their slow growing
> From within. (*Summer in Calcutta* 9)

The spontaneity of Kamala Das as a poet is in evidence in the above lines. The simile shows that the poet never had to hunt for words, the words came to her as naturally as leaves come to a tree. Just as leaves shoot forth from the branches, words shot forth from her inside. To the poet, like Shelley's skylark, words flowed in "profuse strains of unpremeditated art".

Coupled to her unpremeditated poetry, Das showed a natural instinct for the music of words. Das never learned the intricacies of using words in her poetry to achieve a musical effect. However, she relied upon her ears for the right words. In fact, as she told in an interview to P.P. Raveendran, as Irshad Gulam Ahmed points out in his book *Kamala Das: The Poetic Pilgrimage* (2005), her ears were naturally attuned to music, because when she lived at Malabar she used to listen attentively—the attention was, of course, instinctive—the rhythmic slush and thump of the sea waves. It is obvious then that when budding poets show her their poetic creations, she does no indulge into 'school-men' like scholarly criticisms, but relies on her instinct for her comments.

Das followed the dictum that was offered by the Muse to Philip Sidney: "look into thy heart and write". In an interview to the present scholar, the poet cautioned about efforts to search for echoes of powerful "voices" in her poetry:

> I had read different European and American writers when I was young. But you must not read strong voices if you want to write poetry. Poetry erupts from within, and any strong influence destroys your originality.

Yet scholars like M.K. Naik find echoes of T.S. Eliot, Walt Whitman and Sylvia Plath in her poetry. This premise of intertextuality is a Poststructural tool. Although Saussure stressed the importance of the relationship of signs to each other, one of the weaknesses of structuralist semiotics is the tendency to treat individual texts as discrete, closed-off entities and to focus exclusively on internal structures. Even where texts are studied as a corpus, the overall generic structures tend themselves to be treated as strictly bounded. The structuralist's first analytical task is often described as being to delimit the boundaries of the system (what is to be included and what excluded), which is logistically understandable but ontologically problematic. Even remaining within the structuralist paradigm, we may note that codes transcend structures.

Julia Kristeva introduced the semiotic notion of intertextuality. Kristeva referred to texts in terms of two axes: a *horizontal axis* connecting the author and reader of a text, and a *vertical axis*, which connects the text to other texts. Uniting these two axes are shared: every text and every reading depends on prior codes. Kristeva declared that:

> every text is from the outset under the jurisdiction of other discourses which impose a universe on it.[1]

She argued that rather than confining our attention to the structure of a text we should study its 'structuration'. Thus, theorists of intertextuality problematize the status of "authorship", treating the writer of a text as the orchestrator of what Roland Barthes refers to as the "already-written" rather than as its originator:

> A text is...a multidimensional space in which a variety of writings, none of them original, blend and clash. The text is a tissue of quotations.... The writer can only imitate a gesture that is always anterior, never original. His only power is to mix writings, to counter the ones with the others, in such a way as never to rest on any one of them.[2]

Intertextuality refers to far more than the 'influences' of writers on each other. Daniel Chandler notes the following features that characterize intertextuality:

> *reflexivity*: how reflexive (or self-conscious) the use of intertextuality seems to be (if reflexivity is important to what it means to be intertextual, then presumably an indistinguishable copy goes beyond being intertextual);
>
> *alteration*: the alteration of sources (more *noticeable* alteration presumably making it more reflexively intertextual);
>
> *explicitness*: the specificity and explicitness of reference(s) to other text(s) (e.g. direct quotation, attributed quotation) (is *assuming* recognition more reflexively intertextual?);
>
> *criticality to comprehension*: how important it would be for the reader to *recognize* the intertextuality involved;
>
> *scale of adoption*: the overall scale of allusion/incorporation within the text; and
>
> *structural unboundedness*: to what extent the text is presented (or understood) as part of or tied to a larger structure (e.g. as part of a genre, of a series, of a serial, of a magazine, of an exhibition, etc.)—factors which are often not under the control of the author of the text.[3] (*italics mine*)

However, the tools of intertextuality are applicable, though partially, to Das's poetry. The concept of intertextuality may be applied to those poems where the poetic persona and the autobiographical self are different. However, in poems where Das's autobiographical self and her poetic self merge, the tools of intertextuality will throw up erroneous configurations, for in these poems the author is not dead, she is alive, pulsating and vital.

Kamala Das broke free from the metaphysical and romantic traditions and created a poetry that centered round the *self*. In *My Story* (1988), she pointed out:

> A poet's *raw material* is not stone or clay, it is her personality. (*italics mine*)

This statement implies that she does not accept Eliot's distinction between the man who suffers and the mind that creates. Her poetic creations are rooted in her personality that becomes its "raw material". It must, however, be realized that the personality of the poet is a "raw material" and in no way a finished piece of poetry. The "raw materials" undergo aesthetic transmutations before they are presented as poetic wholes. Facts and fantasy, experience and imagination are inseparably mingled in her works, thereby creating a sort of Magic Realism. But, unfortunately, often her poetry has been interpreted as a true reflection of her personality and this has resulted in unleashing a battery of trenchant criticism against herself and her writings.

In moments of creation she transcended the mundane realities and her protean creative self—spoke in million different voices. It is through her poetry that she resurrects herself and makes a bold quest for identity. The search for identity by the woman writer has been aptly explained by Linda Anderson:

> The myth of self which recent theorists have questioned may not be present for her in the same way; it is more difficult for her to believe in a self that can exist before writing, a self that is unified and continuous. Autobiography may self-consciously exist for her: an alternate place for identification. This means that there may be a greater

> formal awareness in her writing, an emphasis on the self-reflexiveness of writing, the idea of the self as written.[4]

Das's quest for identity, however, is deftly mingled with her efforts of self-realization through a search for an Ideal love in the manner of the Tamil *akam* and *kurinici* poets of classical times.

The first person personal pronoun "I", that is strewn over her poetic canvas, represent the various poetic personae and also becomes the nucleus of her poetry. The several poetic persona that stalk through the world of her love poems in her first three anthologies, *Summer in Calcutta* (1965), *The Descendants* (1967) and *Old Playhouse and Other Poems* (1973), are very different from her autobiographical self. The poetic selves and the autobiographical self—stand in multiple relations to each other, creating a mosaic in the oeuvre of Das's poetry. It is in the poems about her ancestry, the poems that express her melioriostic vision, the poems concerning self-introspection and in the poems addressed to Allah, that her poetic self and autobiographical self-merge. Sharada Iyer has shown the difference between the autobiographical self and the poetic self in Kamala Das:

> The former (autobiographical self) occupies a safe position accepted and esteemed by society..., while her counterpart (poetic self) haunts the fringes of human intercourse.[5]

The poet's fragmented self generates a kind of ambivalence that underlies the entire oeuvre of Das's poetry. Das is aware of the *double* in her poetic consciousness, as she suggests in the poem "Feline":

> There is a sea wailing beneath a sea,
> A sky behind the taut drapes of our firmament,
> A rain that rains hard and long within the summer rain,
> Another lives in me, I fear, a twin left unborn.
> (*Old Playhouse and Other Poems* 35)

In the duality of nature, Das finds an appropriate image of the duality that lies deep in her poetic consciousness. Das's poetic vision reflects dualism and this accounts for the abundance of antithesis as well as her skilful use of binaries in her poetry. Thus, any attempt to recreate her life from her love poems would not only be futile but also throw up monstrously distorted images of the poet's personality.

The fact that Kamala Das internalizes different experiences that become the domain of her poetry is made clear in the poem "Forest Fire":

> Of late I have begun to feel a hunger
> To take in with greed, like a forest fire that
> Consumes, and, with each killing gains a wilder, Brighter charm,
> all that comes my way. Bald child in
> Open pram, you think I only look, and you
> Too, slim lovers behind the tree and you, old
> Man with paper in your hand and sunlight in
> Your hair.... My eyes lick at you like flames, my nerves Consume. (*Summer in Calcutta* 53)

The "bald child", "slim lovers" and "old men" are, as T.N. Dhar aptly suggests,

> explicit references to the three prominent stages of human life, which determine the bounds of all experience.[6]

These internalizations of myriad experience create the various poetic personae that can be viewed as projections of a fluid and dynamic poetic self.

So her love poems which form a significant portion of her poetic oeuvre are neither exercises in eroticism nor reflections of a nymphomaniac psyche. The love poems record her quest for a love that goes beyond the body and touches the soul, but her attempts are doomed to failure. As Anisur Rahman points out:

> The quest for an emotional liaison and her failure to establish one is the central burden of her poetry.[7]

Her loveless marriage made her try, imaginatively in most cases, to find an ideal lover. This sets her to tap the Radha-Krishna myth. She imagines herself to be Radha waiting for her eternal lover. She also uses the Radha-Krishna myth implicitly in some of her love poems.

The love poems of Kamala Das reflect a desire for spiritual fulfillment in love through the medium of sex. The poet is honest enough not to deny the domain of the body. The body is as much a reality as is the soul. The poet desires a love that would not stop at the body, but penetrate deep into her soul. But her desires remain unfulfilled and the utter negation of the efforts to consummate soul-love make her travel through the gossamer lanes of lust till she becomes her own captive.

Kamala Das's disgust and hatred of lust is embedded in her love poems. The different poetic personae represented by the polyphonic "I" vividly project the poet's microcosm that feels revulsion to lust. Sociological factors play significant role in her candid statements on love in terms of sex. Sunanda P. Chavan rightly remarks:

> The Nayar [sic.] lineage of Kamala Das with its tradition of sexual freedom in spite of later rigidity explains the frankness of her attitude to love in terms of sex.[8]

She exposes her disgust of lust with an honesty of tone that adds a new dimension of appeal to her poetry. The disgust becomes more poignant when she ruminates upon the lost Edenic innocence of her childhood in Malabar. Her abhorrence of lust is often reflected through dreams that constitute a vital part of the feminine psyche. This adds a ring of psychoanalytical dimension to her love poems.

Though the *self*-forms the nucleus of Kamala Das's poetry and the quest for identity becomes one of her dominant themes, it would nonetheless be being rather imprecise to label her as a Confessional poet. Her poetic vision transcends the narrow confines of the self and embraces the non-personal: the poor house-builders, the hapless mothers who have lost their sons, the helpless women suffering under the patriarchal hegemony, the victimized Tamils and Sikhs and the hollow posturizations of a phallocentric society, all come under the purview of her poetry. She has also shown a concern for plant and animal life. It is obvious that her poetic vision is marked by feminist stance and show social concerns. So her poetic tone covers a wide range, from whole-hearted sympathy to deep despair, from loud protest to bitter cynicism.

Therefore, Das's feminist stances have to be located within the postcolonial Third World context. Bell Hooks in championing the cause of Black Feminism in her famous work *Ain't I a Woman* (1981) has brilliantly shown that the feminist stances of the Third World do not follow the Eurocentric models of feminism. In the Eurocentric models of feminism, sexism gets the highest priority. Kate Millett in her book *Sexual Politics* (1968) suggests that sexism is the primary mode of oppression of women and the most fundamental concept of power. However, this argument may not hold good for the Third World feminists. Jane Freedman sounds a note of warning on the point of imposing Western feminist models on the Third World feminism:

> ...white feminists are...accused of Eurocentrism in their attitudes towards women in the countries of the Third World, trying to impose Western models of feminism inappropriate to the particular conditions of women in these countries, and neglecting to analyse the ways in which colonialism and global capitalism have shaped the experiences of women in countries outside Europe and North America.[9]

In postcolonial India, feminist movements have not made the issue of sexism as it locus, but have taken diverse routes. Feminist frameworks that are anti-neo-liberalism include left-liberals, who despair that there are no alternative paradigms, and so hark back to state redress, and eco-feminists, who issue calls for a traditional past and indigenous knowledge free from domination. The problem with these feminist frameworks is that they can easily be dismissed as anachronistic. On the other side, activists and scholars who are cautiously optimistic about neo-liberalism, include those in the autonomous women's movement, who oppose anything "western" and embrace Indian "culture", which now includes women's entrepreneurial spirit; Marxist feminists, who view global integration as a necessary stage of capitalism; and agrarian feminists who work within new farmers movements and hope that global agricultural prices will become more remunerative thereby increasing the livelihoods of rural people and reigning in urban, high caste capitalists and bureaucrats. Uma Narayan has cogently argued that Indian women have specific problems, which the Indian feminist movements have sought to address:

> Issues that feminist groups in India have politically engaged with include problems of dowry-murder and dowry-related harassment of women, police rape of women in custody; issues relating to women's poverty, health and reproduction; and issues of ecology and communalism that affect women's lives.[10]

Das's feminist stances never indulge in mindless imitations of Western agendas. Her feminist politics is rooted in the postcolonial Indian sensibilities. As a radical feminist, she bitterly protested and scathingly criticized the ruthless oppression of women by the patriarchal social gods and as a left-liberal feminist, she expressed her horror of state-sponsored terrorism and, implicitly, appealed to the state for redress. However, with the passage of time and with the mellowing of her poetic vision, her feminine sensibility grew profound and her heart wailed for the marginalized and suffering humanity. So, Das's feminisms weave out patterns of evolving forms till it dissolves in her feminine sensibility that finally transforms into a grand melioristic vision. It is this melioristic vision that made her affirm:

> ...I decided that all the love within me needed an outlet, a receptacle. What better receptacle than the mass of the deprived.... I was not exactly a Mother Teresa but loving came easy to me.[11]

This statement has a ring of honesty around it. Das does not pretend that in terms of piety, she is like the Mother. In fact, Das had neither the social freedom nor the ambience to be the Mother. Born in the West, Teresa could assert her choice bravely, but Das was enmeshed—nobody asked her about her choice—with the burden of a family at the age of sixteen. However, the poet's glory lies in the fact that while she cared for the hearth and home, her heart went out to suffering humanity at large.

## NOTES

1. Julia Kristeva, *Desire in Language: A Semiotic Approach to Literature and Art*, (ed.), Leon S. Roudiez, trans. Thomas Gora et al. (New York: Columbia University Press, 1980), 69.
2. Roland Barthes, "The Death of the Author", *Image, Music, Text* (London: Fontana Press, 1977), 146.
3. Daniel Chandler, "Semiotics for Beginners" in www.aber.ac.uk/media/Documents/S4B/semiotic.html.
4. Linda Anderson, "At the Threshold of the Self: Woman and Autobiography", *Women's Writing: A Theory*, (ed.), Moira Montieth (Sussex, 1986), 59-60. Also quoted in N.V. Raveendran, *The Aesthetics of Sensuality: A Stylistic Study of the Poetry of Kamala Das* (New Delhi: Atlantic Publishers, 2000), 44.
5. Sharada Iyer, "Split-Self in the Poetry of Kamala Das", *Kamala Das: A Critical Spectrum*, (eds.), Rajeshwar Mittapalli and Pier Paolo Piciucco (New Delhi, 2001), 114.
6. T.N. Dhar, "Eros Denied: Love in the Poetry of Kamala Das", *Contemporary Indian English Poetry*, Atma Ram (Calcutta, 1989), 21.
7. Anisur Rahman, *Expressive Form in the Poetry of Kamala Das* (New Delhi: Abhinav Publications, 1981), 8.
8. Sunanda P. Chavan, *The Fair Voice: A Study of Indian Women Poets in English* (New Delhi: Sterling Publishers, 1984), 67.
9. Jane Freedman, *Feminism* (Delhi: Viva Books, 2002), 81.
10. Uma Narayan, *Dislocating Cultures: Identities, Traditions and Third World Feminism* (New York: Routledge, 1997), 13.
11. Kamala Das, *Femina*, 23 Feb.-3 Mar., 1985, 48.

# 16

# A Study of Male Chauvinism in Anita Desai's *In Custody*

*Anju Bala Agrawal*

The fiction of Anita Desai has added a new dimension to Indo-English writing. She grapples with the intangible realities of life and plunges into the innermost depths of human psyche to fathom its mysteries, the inner turmoil and the chaos inside the mind. She has introduced the psychological novel in the tradition of Virginia Woolf. Most of Desai's protagonists pass through a psychological crisis. Anita Desai's preoccupation with the individual highlighting their psychological motivations, frustrations, sense of failure and keen awareness of the futility of existence radiates from each of her novels. *In Custody* (1984) is different from her earlier novels, as the protagonist of this novel is not a female but a male. Desai's successful probing into the male psyche establishes her as a psychological novelist. She explores the psyche of male protagonist outside the circumscriptions of familial ties and obligations and successfully departs from her earlier obsessive interior landscapes of hypersensitive and neurotic women. *In Custody* portrays the problems and agonies of the wounded self. It is primarily about the functioning of human psyche.

The novel initiates with an air of gloom hung over in the atmosphere of Mirpore, the small village like town giving shelter and occupation to the novel's protagonist, Deven. Deven is a simple professor of a college in the department of Hindi, a department that carried the capacity of high literature but, presently lies, almost in a dilapidated condition, firstly, due to the lack of enthusiasm on the part of the students to master the subject—a subject that had little or no value in the job market and secondly, due to the composition of the town itself, a town of the tea wallahs and the truck drivers. In short, the town is inhabited by a class of people that form a distant part in the desire to grasp the beauties of philosophy, art and poetry. Deven, the hero of the novel, is endowed with different kinds of sensibility. He is not an alienated self. The novel focuses on Deven's awareness of the meaninglessness of existence.

Deven is married to Sarla, who is not his choice. Sarla is not like other typical heroines of Anita Desai. She is usual, ordinary, compromising and a lady of normal temperament. In the novel, we don't find obsessive preoccupation with the interior landscape of hypersensitive and neurotic women. Deven comes from a lower middle-class family and he directs his consciousness towards a wide world beyond himself and his family. His age is thirty-five. He feels that his life has been useless. He is still waiting for a break, waiting to do something worthwhile, something great. He is romantic, escapist and a weak fellow who is incapable of facing crisis. He craves for freedom. Deven's childhood was not a happy one so he develops a negative self-image and aversion. Domestic life is like a trap for him. He is reluctant to face reality. We find his fragmented psyche to view world. There is complete lack of interest and dissonance in his relationship. This results in marital disharmony. Deven plays negative role in his relation with Sarla. Both of them are frustrated in their own way. He feels himself in a cage because of marriage, family responsibilities and his job but there is no way out of it. Deven's interest in poetry has replaced the lack of domestic felicity. The life of married protagonists in Desai's novels is usually tortured. *In Custody* is not an exception to that:

> Although each understood the secret truth about the other, it did not bring about any closeness of spirit, any comradeship.[1]

Into this dismal world, comes a ray of hope in the form of his childhood friend and companion, Murad. Murad is the editor of an Urdu magazine that aims to publish long lost unpublished pieces of poems of high artistic value of the once famous, decrepit poet Nur Shahjahanabadi. Deven being an Urdu lover leaps in joy as Murad gives him the opportunity to interview the poet, something that he had wished since the time he relished the penmanship of Urdu poets and novelists. He takes it as a chance he has been waiting all these years.

The twist in the tale occurs when he finds how the life of Nur whom he considered as the epitome of reverence and regard, the God of Urdu poetry, is fraught with misery and poverty. He finds poverty not only in the sense of the lack of material goods but the poverty of the mind, the psyche. He is not only plagued by ill-health but also by his surroundings. The competition between his two wives, the noise and chaos of the fanatics, and the absence of decorum all combined create a distorted atmosphere, an unaesthetic ambience. It's Deven who gets entangled in the innumerable chains of difficulties surmounting Nur in the process of his interview. The interview turns out to be less of an oration of his lost poetry and more a revelry comprising rum, kebabs, biryani and gluttonous talks combined with an inefficient assistant and a second hand tape recorder meant to record Nur's voice. He uses it to make the work easier, as copying his words by hand would have been cumbersome. All this leads up to dismal failure, making him spend out money on food, on room rent, on bribing his first wife to fix up the appointment, followed by Nur's letter back in Mirpore about his intention to visit Mecca and to inform about his cataract operation. The whole novel portrays a descending trajectory of Deven and the rise of miseries coupled with misfortunes.

The novel questions the meaning of friendship that stands on selfishness and insensitivity as observed by Deven's relationship with Murad, the bonds of marriage mirrored in Deven's complacent behaviour towards his wife and the educational system of the nation where students with scientific backgrounds are meant for the luxuries of life whereas those with a knack for humanities are shown to rot in dingy classrooms. This fact is also revealed in the way in which Deven's Hindi students take technical classes outside in order to get employment, giving least importance to the learning of the subject within the college premises. This is a reflection of the fact that the art, culture, heritage and history of the country lies threatened in front of the emerging technological boom of the globe. Inspite of the repeated pessimisms hovering in their lives, the novel can be regarded as an optimistic tale of Deven and Nur. This is, because, Nur at the end finds himself a custodian to breathe to him his life as it actually is and Deven gets the opportunity to take the custody of the divine poet whom he almost worshiped. This is an achievement in itself. This novel of Anita Desai is a portrait of human lives as it exists in their own exclusive circumstances, of the hypocrisy and pretension lying within the human spirit, of the difference between the town and the city life, of human helplessness and oppression on the road to ones aspirations. Deven is Anita Desai's version of a character common in modern Indian novels. He reminds us Narayan's *The English Teacher* and Ruth Jhabvala's *The Householder*.

Deven is always anxious to be successful. Nur in this sense is Deven's alter ego. He had imagined he was taking Nur's poetry into safe custody, and had not realized that if he was to be the custodian of Nur's genius then Nur would become his custodian too. He realizes that their relationship will never end, even after Nur's death. The trials and tribulations which Deven faces while trying to extract something useful from Nur, who is a shadow of the man he used to be; form the crux of the book. But it is really the beautiful exploration of the layers of everyday life that Desai revels in. During the course of this slim novel, there are several passages which make us gasp with recognition, such is the power and accuracy of her vision. Even when dealing with complex and nostalgia-ridden characters like Nur, Desai displays a deftness of touch and a unique, sensitive style which fleshes out the character like few others.

Deven is a specimen of male psychology. Inspite of his weaknesses, he is a supporter of patriarchal mechanism of oppression. There is a power given by tradition even to the meekest of men like Deven that allow them to shed their unhappiness and failures by bringing it out in violence against the woman:

> To relieve it he would hurl away dishes that had not been cooked to his liking, bawl uncontrollably if meals were not ready when he wanted them or the laundry not done... it was to lay the blame upon her, remove its clinging skin upon him. (76)

It is a male psychology that shows Deven's behaviour of indirect violent manner towards his wife. Acceptable behavioural pattern is alien to him. He shows the manner when he wrecks Imtiaz Begum's aspirations by tearing up her verse. Deven's puny form of power displayed within the walls of his home does not stem from the strength of his character but rather from his deep rooted faith in the patriarchal system. Another example of Deven's male supremacy can be seen when he sees Imtiaz (second wife of Nur, the poet) on stage for it upturns the values that he clings to in order to exist. The anger that he feels is reflected in the lengthy description of the scene and the effects it has on Deven and the thoughts it triggers off. Deven's negative perception of the poet's wife finds subjective description in several pages. This shows how Deven as a male or as a member of the dominant powers feels in the face of Imtiaz's self-assertion as a marginalized female. He uses derogatory terms to describe Imtiaz. His masculine and elitist perception of Imtiaz is that she is trying to assert herself in a domain that he considers as belonging to men. Imtiaz Begum's performance as a poet even in the intimacy of her home is considered as insane by Deven who cannot conceive of a female poet aspiring to any form of recognition. "Why did Nur submit to her insane whim of performing in his house, the house of a poet?" (94). The general image of the Indian female in the male psyche is that of the silent suffering, meek and faithful. She is confined to the domestic sphere. Her voice is not heard whatever their travails. Most women conform to this image. Imtiaz Begum in this novel is a dominating figure. Actually, she is the bread winner as her performance buys Nur's alcohol and pays for the food he offers his admirers.

> Deven does not like her performance. He links her appearance and performance as related to prostitution. The question he asks about her chasteness and origins is a

> sham. "Had she been as actress once? A dancer? Where-in a brothel?" (95)

Deven is a weak and unable person, but his love for poetry and discovering a strength and reverence for poetry saves him from being a completely weak character. He visits Nur's home again and again it is like a pilgrimage for him and strengthens his reverence for the old man. Despite his initial disappointment, Deven only has to be in Nur's presence for the sake of the poet's stature and the love of his poetry to overwhelming difficulties that make the project become more and more improbable. When Murad denies paying the bill presented by Nur's wife, Deven wanders around Delhi and finally settles in front of a mosque. The dome of the mosque is likened to a bubble. He views poetry through the same image of bubble. To quote:

> If art, if poetry, could be made to submit their answers, it merely to contain them within perfect, unblemished shapes but to release them and make them available, then—he thought, then—But then the bubble would be breached and burst, and it would no longer be perfect. (224-25)

This can be called Deven's spiritual awakening. He no longer needs to get answers and accepts not to go farther beyond the outer perfection. He has started to overlook the imperfections that one notices when one comes to close or is inside the domains that one admires. He tries to root out of his mind Nur's senile demands and tries to keep an unblemished image that results only of Nur's poetry. He realizes the joy in Nur's poetry that's why he accepts the burden of being the custodian of Nur's legacy. He tries to defend Urdu language and culture to the point of endangering his career and family life. Nur and Murad do not understand his sacrifice and see in him and in his work the enemy of Urdu language. In fact, Deven is unable to decide and act upon his own decision so Murad and Nur use him as they wish. A lack of self-confidence makes him unable to publish his poetry.

Nur, inspite of being a great poet of Urdu has no sound personality. He has two wives. His elder wife stands for duty and the second one for love. His second wife is young and the controlling agent. She scolds Nur like a child. To quote:

> 'Get up!' she screamed. 'Get up! Go and have Ali clean you. How can you wallow in such filth, such muck? See what you have done to my room, in my room—see!' (65)

Nur's life is miserable. We have no details as to how Nur married Imtiaz Begum, but it has been clearly shown how inspite of his infatuation for her, he is not able to derive any happiness from her. He sees in Deven a possibility of salvation to his creativity and ignores the real reason for Deven's visit. In place of giving an interview, he asks him to come as a secretary so that he may dictate his poems. This creates a new unhappy situation. Nur becomes helpless before his wife Imtiaz Begum. His helplessness and bitterness appear through his laughter. Imtiaz Begum can go to all lengths to have her way. She takes Nur to bed in an effort to distract him from the project of recording his poetry and has Deven and the old poet spied upon and thus controlling what occurs in the house even while confined to her bed. She is like a nefarious beast. Her hair is like a "two rats' tails" (136) and her hennaed hand is like a "glove of snakeskin" (136) when she refuses to let Nur recite, her "reptilian hand swayed in the air, warningly" (136). Her own maids were afraid of her. Deven himself sees his condition as that of a trapped animal. In act, Nur is in a pitiable condition. He is under petticoat government and his wife's remark, "Do you call that a poet or even a man?" (66) shows the fall of Nur and the rhetorical question denies the basic qualification of Nur as a human being.

The whole narrative oscillates between Deven's dreams and realities, his aspiration for poetry and its illusory nature and finally into ultimate disaster. Deven's heart is filled with defeated aims, frustrated ends and thwarted wishes. The financial and social factors are also responsible for drooping spirit of Deven. In the process of visualizing Nur's death, Deven becomes conscious of the eternal nature of his relationship with Nur. He learns that even death cannot end this relationship with Nur. At the same time, during his morning walk beside canal, he thinks about death. There is an insistent longing for death as a possible exit out of this ordeal, but very soon this longing for death is sought by an all pervasive awareness and consciousness. In the end,

Deven sees a ray of hope even in his boundless suffering and humiliation. His sufferings give him a philosophical outlook. Each new calamity and misfortune fills him with the iron of resistance.

Thus, Desai has beautifully recorded the emotional turbulence and chaos of her protagonist with a remarkable fidelity and seriousness. Deven the protagonist of *In Custody* gets an insight into his authentic existence through the fear of being ruined and he finally gains the courage of his convictions. In concentrating on the inner being of human individual, she has given a new dimension to Indian English novel. She also presents an opposite side of Indian society where the male is not always dominating. Imtiaz is a strong female character who tries to defy male territory. Desai's unflattering portrayal of Nur and Deven does not turn the novel into a mere exposition of ideas or social criticism. She presents the different facets of a male psyche. To quote:

> As usual with Desai, confinement is especially a mental state and we will see that despite the movement present in this novel and that one is not accustomed to finding in Desai's works, the state of captivity of her characters is the same, stasis ruling the world of Deven whatever his endeavours may be.[2]

## NOTES

1. Anita Desai, *In Custody*, India: Random House, 2007, 76. All the references to the text are from this edition and have been indicated by page numbers in parentheses.
2. Aida Balvannanadhan, *A Study of Anita Desai's In Custody*, New Delhi: Prestige Books, 2009, 11.

# 17

# Feminist Slants in Shashi Deshpande's Fiction

*Baby Kumari*

> Thus far women have been mere echoes of men. Our laws and constitutions, our creeds and codes, and customs of social life are all of masculine origin. The true woman is yet a dream of future.

In the past three/four decades, the representations of women in Indian literature have been in the process of changing, though slowly and at times marked with ambiguities in their subjecthood. From the traditional helpless and victimised woman, suffering indignity and violence of husband/lover to a subject, she is represented as endowed with self-consciousness and agency, though thwarted at times, and with a will and dynamism to intervene in the material environment that seeks to throttle her self-actualisation.

The fictional oeuvre of Shashi Deshpande investigates the quick advancement of the New Indian Woman and the succession of her novels and character portrayals (spanning decades) reflects, traces, and captures the rapid social and cultural changes which have been taking place in urban India as a result of swift economic development and expansion. Deshpande's writings focus on social norms which may have been expected to change, but remarkably, either have not, or else have simply assumed a new guise. By smashing the mould of man-made stereotypes into which women so far have been suffocatingly cast and by bringing the reader face to face with their real nature, Shashi Deshpande tries to sculpt out the effigy of a new woman who is more palatable and real to the mind of the reader. Deshpande feminist views are evident in her novels. She rises from the narrow confines of feminist problems constantly exploring the need for human relation and interdependence. In her fiction it is never a question of man or woman but man and woman. She explores in fictional terms the psychic and moral dilemmas that a modern Indian woman encounters in her flight for freedom and a new harmony that she achieves in the end with herself and her surroundings.

In Shashi Deshpande's novels three types of suffering women characters recur with slight variations. To the first type belongs the heroine's mother or the mother figure—the traditional woman who believes that her place is with her husband and family. Whatever be her troubles, she does not leave her husband; she strives for a working relationship with him at any cost. In a sense, she represents the traditional religious ethos and confirms to the Manu code that the woman should be under the control of the father in the maidenhood, the husband in her youth and the sons during her old age. Despite being the victims of patriarchy, some of these women hold power or control over other women in the family because of their status as mothers or mothers-in-law. Jaya's mother (*That Long Silence*), Indu's (*Roots and Shadows*) and Saru's mother (*The Dark Holds No Terrors*) belong to this type. The second type of suffering women is the converse of the traditional type. Here, the woman is bolder, more self-reliant and rebellious. She cannot conform to the Sita's version of womanhood and is consciously inclined towards what could be designated as radical feminist ideology. Such Ibsenian Nora kind of women characters are very rare in Shashi Deshpande's novels. They are mostly the heroine's friends and classmates. Saru's friend Nalu holds a feminist ideology to life for the sake of which she chooses to lead an independent life as spinster. The third type of women characterizes the woman in between. Most of Deshpande's heroines belong to this category. This woman is neither traditional nor radical in her ideas and practice. She might walk out of her home in protest against her suffering, but gradually realizes that walking out does not solve her problems. Saru in *The Dark Holds No Terrors* broods over her agonies even after she escapes her marital home. Indu in *Roots and Shadows* leaves her husband to seek refuge in her ancestral home, but she is unable to accept her fate as any ordinary woman might do. These heroines suffer more because they are aware of the escape routes of two other types of women—the traditional and the radical—but hesitate to choose those options. Their initial position is one of remaining at the crossroads. It is towards the end of the novels, that Shashi Deshpande's female protagonist realizes herself and learns to live up to the challenge. Saru decides to face her husband and not run away. Indu and Jaya decide to confront their husbands and talk the matter out in order to arrive at a solution.

The female protagonists of Shashi Deshpande are not representations of traditional 'Sita' images. They are the 'new women', who could be compared to the flooding rivers that find a pathway into crevices and holes. In the three novels subjected to study here, *The Dark Holds No Terrors, That Long Silence* and *Roots and Shadows* the heroines are initially fugitives who seek refuge to escape from domestic, professional and sexual traps in which they find themselves. But each refuge, whether it is love, marriage or sex, only turns out to be another trap wherein they further lose their freedom and identity. Before their marriage, even in their parental homes, Deshpande's heroines find it difficult to adjust to the kind of family relationships that exist in the traditional middle class. They then experience uneasiness or even hatred towards their mothers, whom they view as dominating and oppressive individuals. Against their mothers' wishes, they attempt to leave their parental homes in the name of education or marriage. The fathers of the heroines on the other hand, become the source of support or even inspiration for these women. The heroines like Saru and Jaya see marriage as an escape route made in order to liberate them from the suffocation they experience in their parents' home. Their act of marrying outside their community, as in the case of Indu can also be seen as their way of rebelling against patriarchal attitudes (with the mothers themselves becoming the tools of patriarchy) towards marriage. However marriage proves to be no escape. The husbands accept their wives as working women but at the same time do not recognize or encourage the 'feminist self' in them.

In all the three novels studied here the heroines are left without any sense of fulfilment—both physical and mental—because of their husbands' lack of understanding. The heroines who have children also sense a kind of uneasiness in their relationship with their siblings. They often wonder whether history repeats itself when it comes to the misunderstanding between the parent and the child. The uncaring husband and the demanding children become obstacles to achieving individuality. Hence the feeling of being trapped comes back to them after the marriage also. Their professions or social commitments sometimes come in conflict with the expectations of the husbands and create tensions within the family. Finding it difficult to cope with the tensions arising out of their professional roles and domestic expectations, the Deshpande women initially seek relief through abandonment of their professional roles. They quit their professions and try to seek peace by confining themselves to their familial roles as homemakers. However, having moved away from the suffering traditional archetypal women long back, they find it difficult to remain as housewives. They soon find that their attempts to reconcile themselves to homemaking only add to their sufferings. When they find that giving up professional roles does not make them in anyway happy at home, the female protagonists seek to escape from their domestic roles as well. Relinquishing their roles as wives and mothers, they turn back to their parents' homes. The parental/ancestral homes become sanctuaries for their restless souls. There they begin their search for knowledge and for a solution for their private woes. To Deshpande's women, relinquishing of roles as daughters, wives, mothers, homemakers and professionals is a very painful process. When the female protagonists start living in their parental homes, they sense a relief in their new/old shelter. They go back to their elders' style of living, giving up the routines to which they got used to in their marital homes. Saru to her chagrin finds herself taking over efficiently all the chores that she administered dutifully day in and out at her marital home. Indu feels a strange sense of liberty and homecoming. She also finds herself resuming the role that her aunt played as the family head.

In assuming new roles or new attitudes towards old roles, they break the mental barriers, which they had initially built around themselves. They learn more about their mothers, and gradually overcome their feelings of alienation/hatred/resentment towards them. In fact, they tend to identify themselves with their elderly counterparts and assume the roles of their mothers or mother figures after they return home. With their contempt towards mothers deciphered, they tend to turn inward. Their stay at ancestral homes gives them the chance to recollect the past and re-evaluate their decisions and actions. Their parental homes do not provide them any permanent relief from their suffering. However, these transitory retreats help them to confront their real 'I' and understand themselves better. It is here that they explore the sexual and other causes that had led to their marital discords. Dissatisfaction in the women's sex lives is cited as one of the important factors affecting the marital relations of the Deshpande protagonists. The three novels represent three types of sexual aberration. In *The Dark Holds No Terror*, Saru explains her sexual relations with Manu, her husband, thus: "He had been the young man and I his bride. Now I was the lady doctor and he was my husband." Saru finds in him a 'protean monster' at night and a 'dutiful husband' in the day. Their sexual life is reduced to macho sadist acts inflicted on woman by man. She says: "We're on different planes. He chooses his level. And I...try to choose the one he would like to be on. It humiliates me" (1980: 90).

Neither the woman nor the man in Deshpande's novels try to do something about their marital/sexual monotony. The women specially tend to ignore the sexual roots of their marital discord. Their assumed roles do not give total sustenance, as their sexual dissatisfaction raises its ugly head at times and disrupts the harmony of their patterned living. Hence, they seek sexual gratification by resorting to extramarital relationships. Saru tries to justify her affairs with uneasiness or even hatred towards their mothers, whom they view as dominating and oppressive individuals. Against their mothers' wishes, they attempt to leave their parental homes in the name of education or marriage. The fathers of the heroines on the other hand, become the source of support or even inspiration for these women. The heroines like Saru and Jaya see marriage as an escape route made in order to liberate them from the suffocation they experience in their parents' home. Their act of marrying outside their community, as in the case of Indu can also be seen as their way of rebelling against patriarchal attitudes (with the mothers themselves becoming the tools of patriarchy) towards marriage. However marriage proves to be no escape. The husbands accept their wives as working women but at the same time do not recognize or encourage the 'feminist self' in them. In all the three novels studied here the heroines are left without any sense of fulfilment—both physical and mental—because of their husbands' lack of understanding. The heroines who have children also sense a kind of uneasiness in their relationship with their siblings. They often wonder whether history repeats itself when it comes to the misunderstanding between the parent and the child. The uncaring husband and the demanding children become obstacles to achieving individuality. Hence the feeling of being trapped comes back to them after the marriage also. Their professions or social commitments sometimes come in conflict with the expectations of the husbands and create tensions within the family. Finding it difficult to cope with the tensions arising out of their professional roles and domestic expectations, the Deshpande women initially seek relief through abandonment of their professional roles. They quit their professions and try to seek peace by confining themselves to their familial roles as homemakers. However, having moved away from the suffering traditional archetypal women long back, they find it difficult to remain as housewives. They soon find that their attempts to reconcile themselves to homemaking only add to their sufferings. When they find that giving up professional roles does not make them in anyway happy at home, the female protagonists seek to escape from their domestic roles as well.

Renouncing their roles as wives and mothers, they turn back to their parents' homes. The parental/ancestral homes become sanctuaries for their restless souls. There they begin their search for knowledge and for a solution for their private woes. In the case of Indu's affair with Naren (her cousin), we see a woman-in-guilt. Like Indu and Saru, Jaya in *That Long Silence* feels guilty of her aborted affair with Kama, her neighbour. Shashi Deshpande's protagonists might be considered as sexual profligates as they go off the track of tradition. But their extra-marital refuge fails them because their sexual freedom does not pilot them out of their predicaments. Instead of helping them to confront the problem, they only postpone the problem. When their sexual escapades bounce back, they divulge their problems to their friends or relatives. For example, Saru confesses to her father about her marital crisis to save herself from it. Her father advises her not to run away but to face the problem. The awareness of the self and the ultimate refuge in the self are inveterate experiences in the novels of Shashi Deshpande. The awareness of the self is nothing but the awakening of woman's consciousness. Elaine Showalter beautifully states how crucial this awakening is to feminism when she says, "How much easier, how less lonely it is not to awaken.... Yet we cannot will ourselves to go back to sleep" (1986: 179).

The determination to confront and accept the self is seen in all the three female protagonists of Deshpande. The act of confrontation gives them the courage to decide things for themselves and increasingly leads them to a positivistic detachment from life. Their seeking shelter in their selves guides them towards a deeper awareness of their condition. According to Deshpande, the solution cannot be 'given', because it is 'self-bound'; in other words, it depends on the individuals concerned—it depends on the fiber of their self. A deeper awareness of the self leads to the understanding of its true nature. Nevertheless, the heroines do not go to that extent. Their self-realization is psychological rather than metaphysical. Towards the end Saru refuses to call her predicament as 'fate' and would rather call it as something she 'had helped to happen' (1980: 62). For blaming only the patriarchy or only certain external causes for her predicament, takes her away from the fact that she had also to be blamed for being weak and allowing her predicament to happen. Finally, the Deshpande's women choose to be themselves, accepting themselves in whatever forms they are. When the 'way out' fails them, then the 'way in'—their delving deep into the interior resources of their selves—provides the necessary sustenance and strength to face their problems. Their determination to face the situation and their dependence only on the self-show them the way to confront the crises in their lives. Although their problems remain unresolved, their attitude towards the problem undergoes change with their understanding of the 'self'. Once they start standing on their own legs, the protagonists of 'flight' decide to stop running away from one refuge to another. They accept all that is fractured in their self and try to unify the fractions. As they decide to assert their selves against other forces that seek to enchain them, 'the dark', as Saru realizes, 'no longer holds any terror', and as Jaya and Indu visualizes, they see the hopes of happiness and peace in their family lives.

After analysing the three female protagonists, it becomes evident that it is the authentic ground of Shashi Deshpande's novels, which makes her 'feminism' typically Indian. Deshpande evolves a feminist understanding of the woman's problem out of a purely Indian climate. The most vital experience in her fiction is demonstrated by autobiographical overtones. Deshpande's feminism is not a copy of the Western feminism. It is very much rooted in the Indian soil; her reading of Western feminists has only helped to place her thoughts on feminism in order. The term 'feminism' is applied to Shashi Deshpande in the broadest sense here to refer to the writer's intense awareness of her identity as a woman, her interest in women's problems, and not in the sense that she makes an advocacy for women's rights in her fiction. In fact she does not hold the torch of women's liberation beyond making the woman realize her 'self'. If she begins with the feminist cliché of the patriarchal modes of injustice to women, she goes one step further also and brings out the injustice caused by woman on man.

She rationalizes a characteristically Indian predicament and also experiments with a classically Indian feminist solution to it. What is evolved through her intense awareness of the Indian woman's situation is a mode of narration, where the woman is at the center, speculating and working out the problem positively. Shashi Deshpande's feminism is certainly not cynical or nihilistic.

She avoids indiscriminate use of the Western feminist jargons and analyses the universal significance of the woman's problem, thereby transcending the feminist perspective. She believes that feminism is "...very much an individual working out her problem" (Mala 1989). She is quite down to earth in her feminist approach to the woman's problem. For though she is aware of the seriousness of the Indian woman's dilemma and the generation old struggles behind it, she also believes that a positive change in women's social status cannot materialize without bringing about a change in the woman's mindset first. So the novelist holds that it is the heroines' retreat in their selves rather than in any external crutches which injects a hope for the woman's redemption from her predicament. The woman's increasing involvement rather than detachment in her predicament as expressed in her novels reveals the positive, humanistic side of Deshpande's feminism. Hence Shashi Deshpande rightly considers her role as an Indian feminist as one of a 'humanist feminist' (*Ibid.* 143).

## WORKS CITED

Dasgupta, Sayantani. "Feminist Report: Reinventing the Feminist Wheel." <zena.secureforum.com/Znet/ZMag/articles/sept94 dasgupta.htm>10.03.05

Davis, Robert Con (1986). *Contemporary Literary Criticism: Modernism through Poststructuralism*. London: Longman.

Deshpande, Shashi (1980). *The Dark Holds No Terrors*. New Delhi: Vikas Pub.

——. (1983). *Roots and Shadows*. Bombay: Orient Longman.

——. (1988). *That Long Silence*. London: Virago Press.

——. (1989). Interview with R. Mala. "The Predicament of the Indian Woman: The Heroines in the Novels of Shashi Deshpande." Unpublished M.Phil. Dissertation. Pondicherry University. 1 April, 116-57.

Weedon, Chris (1997). "'Quotation from Narayan' On Dislocating, Cultures: Identities, Traditions and Third World Feminism." New York: Routledge.

——. (2005). "Key Issues in Postcolonial Feminism: A Western Perspective." <http://www.genderforum.unikoeln.de genderealisations/weedon.html>10.03.05

# 18

# Self-portrait and Self-narrative of Meerabai and Joan of Arc

*Joyashri Choudhury*

Swami Vivekananda has said that love is absolutely unselfish, that which has no thought beyond the glorification of and adoration of the object upon which our affections are bestowed. It is said of Meerabai that when she was married, she said to her husband, the King, that she was already married.

"To whom?" asked the King

"To God", was the reply.

This is so similar to the innocence and straight-forward attitude demonstrated by Joan of Arc. Volitional skills enable individuals to resist pressure to capitulate to convention, says Diana Meyers. The trial record demonstrates Joan's remarkable intellect and volitional skills. The transcripts most famous exchange is an exercise in subtlety. Asked if she knew if she was in God's grace, Joan answered, "If I'm not, may God put me there, and if I am may God so keep me." The question is a scholarly trap. Church doctrine holds that no one can be certain of being in God's grace. If the answer was in the affirmative, she would have been convicted of heresy. Her negation would have meant, confessing her guilt. Notary Boisguillaume testified that those who heard her reply were stupefied. Shaw was so fascinated that his play "Saint Joan" has parts which are in fact literal translations of the trial record.

Since people prefer the known over the unknown, Diana Meyers is of the opinion that a woman must take pains to construct her self-portrait and self-narrative in terms of unorthodox figurations of womanhood. Riding over unjust social structures, a woman must be unwavering in her commitment to the construction of the self-portrait and to the continuations of the autobiographies that they consider genuinely their own.

Joan, Meera experiencèd internalized oppression. She argues that subordination is internalized and is integral to individualized, subordinated identities. The anti-identity view of gender, conceptualized by Iris Young, refers to woman as members of a "group precursors", as against a full-fledged group. Young takes recourse to Jean Paul Sartre's idea of seriality to explain gender. A social series or group precursors is a body where the members are passively united by the objects around which their actions are oriented. A series may be defined as being formed by the 'behaviour directing meaning defining institutional and social environment. Series members get affected by the social series they find themselves allotted to. Serial existence, then becomes the norm, which leaves the individuals felling powerless, Meyers points out. Bearing their series memberships in mind people start behaving in that way. But series membership, Meyers says, "does not define the person's identity in the sense of forming his/her individual purposes, projects, and sense of self in relation to others". "Yet, individuals can choose to make none of their serial memberships important for their individual identity" (Young, 1994).

Meyers finds it difficult with this proposal of Young, because it seems to replace essentialist accounts of gendered patches and bodies with an essentialist account of gendering social structures. If social positioning is constitutive of individual identity, then all similarly positioned individuals share a common identity, or if it is taken that social positioning is external to individual identity, then it can be said that no woman's identity is gendered unless she herself lets gender come in. Since woman do not share a common identity, Meyers says, that the same can be said of members of racial, sexuality, life-stage, class and ethnic groups, it therefore can be said that Young volunteers for the voluntarist position. No one can escape one's social series. But a person becomes a member of that social group only if one elects to be so. "Series membership shapes one's identity only if one allows her to do so", says Meyers.

To come out from this vicious circle of individualist voluntarism is neither by gender essentialism nor a universal feminine identity. Meyers says that the only alternative is gendered and individualized identities. There is consensus in Young's tone also when it is being said that no woman's identity "escape the makings of gender, but how gender marks her life is her own". Identities are individualized, Meyers affirms. But no matter what warm its way into one's identity. We may not be conscious of this and we may not be able to change this. But some exceptional woman, while crafting their individualized identities have fearlessly and valiantly, struggled against all odds, to write their own life-history, basking in their own crafted norms and throwing to the winds their given social numbers by the society. It is in the light of this conception, that the present paper would like to study the life story of these women icons—who became identified as new cultural icons in their respective ages, even though these women were separated from each other in time and space. Time and space coalesces in these women's lives and their visionary zeal, illuminated the tough paths chosen by them and made them successful, some during their own life times, others after their death. One thing common to all these women was their bravery. They never once wavered from their chalked out paths. Their out of the way approaches to life, their novel and ingenious ways, makes them a class apart. Their divergence from their social serial numbers makes them exceptional. And history has been a witness to the rarified environment which they created for themselves, basked in their chosen glories and got immense pleasures in defying their codes of their serial numbers.

Lizbeth Goodman writes in 'Literature and Gender' that is one of the many forms of cultural representations (like the visual arts, photography, television, etc.) in which gender relations are routinely depicted. Literary texts can both reinforce gender stereotypes and create newer, more liberating representations of gender. It was the norm for woman to act in a lady like manner so that she may procure a husband for herself. This was depicted in the romantic novels of the 19th century. This was an era when women were discouraged from working outside her home. Aficionados of Mills and Boon and the Harlequin romances still uphold these values. There are other forms of literature which depict the New Woman as exemplified in the late 19th century theatre. Whereas, in the writings of William Faulkner, F. Scott Fitzerland and John Steinbeck, we can see some aspects and attitudes of the modernist era reflected towards woman. Weak and powerless gender roles for women and stronger and more important gender roles for men were created in the novels and stories of these writers. There is consensus in much contemporary writing about revaluation of a woman's role both in life as well as in literature.

All through the ages, unruly women have been burnt down as witches or heretics. Throughout history unruly women have not been presented in a good light. Susan Sage Heinzelman writes that whether it is historical, fictional, disruptive woman with their real or imagined excesses have long provided the material for literary and legal narratives. In her book, "Riding the Black Ram, Law Literature and Gender" she writes how in her 1820 adultery trial, Queen Caroline was depicted in a cartoon riding into the House of Lords on a Black Ram that had the face of her Italian lover. Heinzelman goes on to say that a number of women, remembered largely for her insubordinate presence have metaphorically "ridden the black ram" in the last 700 years.

Two women, one drawn from Indian history and the other from the French, exemplify self-determination which as Diana Tietjens Meyers says, connects women's voices to their lives as well as to their emancipatory potentialities. Meerabai of India and Joan of Arc of France did not allow culturally entrenched narrative templates and representational like figures of speech, mythic tales and pictorial images that penetrate the stories of women and crowd out alternative versions of their lives. Joan of Arc and Meerabai were not feminists; but the self-determination, exercising a repertoire of agentic skills that enabled them to construct their own self-portraits and self-narratives is very much akin to the feminist voice theory, whereby feminist are reconceptualizing self-determination. This ongoing 'sadhana' of self-determination made these two women and many others like them, take charge of their lives. Meerabai was a 16th century princess whose life is known more through legend than verifiable historic fact. Meera's father, Ratan Singh ruled over the fortress city of Merta, created by Rao Dudej, the Rajputani grandfather of Meera. An idol of Krishna given to her by a travelling beggar yoked her at an early age, to the love and philosophy of Lord Krishna. At the age of thirteen or fourteen, she was married to a Rajputi prince of Mewar. Her husband died very soon afterwards. Her family was shocked that she did not commit sati, burning herself alive on her husband's funeral pyre, as was the normal custom prevailing at that time.

Meera was an 'autonomous individual'. She was not a 'mere conformist' to traditional culturally entrenched narrative templates. Neither was she eccentric. No matter how scandalized her family members were at her violation of these conventions of 'sati', what is distinctive about her is that she relied on her own judgement. Her family expected her to remain secluded as a widow and to worship the family deity, the goddess, Durga or Kali. Instead of following the traditional norms of a widowed princess, Meera began worshipping Lord Krishna. Ignoring gender, class, caste and religious boundaries, she spent her time caring for the poor.

Meera's father and father-in-law were both killed while fighting against the invading Muslims. Her in-laws were horrified at this Bhakti worship. The legends tell of many attempts on her life by her husband's family. A poisonous snake, a poisoned drink, drowning but each time she miraculously escaped.

Meera knew who she was and what really mattered to her was how deeply she cared about Lord Krishna. She joined a religious community in Vrindavan, a place holy to Krishna. She wrote hundreds of songs and started an innovative way of singing these songs, a 'raga'. About 200-300 songs are accepted by scholars as being written by Meera—another 800-1000 is uncertain. She wrote in Rajasthani and Braj Bhasa languages and these songs were translated into Hindi and Gujarati. According to Usha S. Nilsson, the 'padas' of Meera provide a miscellany of Meera's spiritual experiences at different stages in her spiritual life.

Meera, though a delicate young lady, entered the perilous journey on the spiritual amidst great difficulties. She was adamant in her resolve. Meera enacted the introspective understanding of her 'true' self in her everyday life. Gandhiji saw Meera as a symbol of a woman who has the right to choose her own path, forsake a life of luxury and in a non-violent resistance find liberations.

A brief study of Modernism at this point of our study would show and throw some interesting light. Modernism is in one sense a literature of the city, whether that city be the London of Eliot or Woolf, the Paris of Lewis or Barnes or the Dublin of Joyce. As Katherine Mullin says, "Urban experience is characterized by isolation within the crowd; by a concomitant sense of anonymity and alienation, and by both the dangers of crime and the exhilaration of urban diversity and adventure." The art historian, Grieselda Pollock, points out how the stroller "symbolizes the priviledge-class or freedom to move about the public arenas of the city observing but never interacting, consuming the sights through a controlling but rarely acknowledged gaze". Yet, as Katherine Mullin tells us, while men might stroll anonymously and unmolested through urban spaces, women often occupied a more conspicious and therefore, unstable position.

For respected middle class women, some public spaces like the bars, cafes, clubs and even public laboratories were out of bounds at the turn of the 20th century. Woolf's genteel Pargiter sisters find that 'for any of them to walk to the West End even by day was out of the question. Bond Street was as impassable, save with their mother, as any swamp alive with crocodiles. The Burlington Arcade was, nothing but a fever-stricken den as far as they were concerned. To be seen alone in Piccadilly was equivalent to walking up Abercorn Terrace in a dressing gown carrying a bath sponge.'

Woolf here eloquently outlines how women's access to the city was heavily circumscribed. Women of her class, Katherine

Mullen points out who wished to explore the metropolis were forced to devise reasons or pretexts for doing so, ranging from shopping, as Rachel Bowlby and Erica Rappaport have recently shown, to urban philanthropy, as Judith Walkowitz has explored. As rightly pointed out by Katherine Mullen, mere strolling in the paradigmatic urban space of modernist writing was, for many women, a compromised and compromising pleasure.

The unstable position of Meerabai as a stroller makes an interesting study Meera as a stroller least perturbed her Meera did not have to devise pretexts to get access to her part of the city. The Modernist stroller is so much akin to her counterpart from the past. She was involuntarily pulled to the city, towards the streets through her sheer love for Krishna. She danced in the streets. She had a spontaneous love for Krishna. She never cared for public criticism and the injunctions of the Shastras. Meera had Raganuga or Ragatmika Bhakti. She was fearless in nature. In her divine intoxication, she danced in public places. She had no sex idea. She crossed caste-boundaries. She was sunk in the ocean of Prem.

The cultural space was denied to Meerabai during her own lifetime. Unheeding of this denial, Meera went on composing songs expressing her love and devotion to Krishna. For Anathnath Basu, Meera is a poetess of rare gifts, who has left her songs as a spiritual heritage. According to Krishna P. Bandahur, most critics are of the opinion that Meera did not deliberately choose her words to create an effect but considered her poetry to be the spontaneous outpouring of her heart. David Halpern claims that although Meera was not seeking literary acclaim, some of her lyrics have been called among the greatest of Indian Literature. Nancy Martin Karshaw praises Meera's padas as exceptionally beautiful songs of love and longing for God. For Usha S. Nilsson Meerabai's poems hold a very special place in medieval Hindi poetry. Few poets have surpassed the lyrical quality of Meerabai's verses Andrew Schelling says that Meera walks with those who had composed the world's durable poetry.

When a society discourages self-explorations and self-expressions, it discourages attention to symptoms of discontent and shields social ideologies and institutions from probing examinations and oppositional activism, says Diana Meyers. Meerabai encountered a society that suppressed autonomy and thereby perpetuate unjust social structure. Meera resisted this pressure and as John Stratton Hawley summarizes the power and the story of her life as a saint, "Whoever she was...she fired the imagination with her fearless, defiance...the only one of her gender to have earned a place on the honour roll of north India Bhakti saints, she exerts a fascination that none of her male counterparts can match."

How rightly has Diana Tietjens Meyers pointed out that people do not choose their genders (or for that matter race, ethnicity, sexuality, stage of life or class). These are thrust upon us and nor is it within one's power as an individual to escape gender from one's life, she continues. But nevertheless real life heroines have succeeded in constructing their autobiographies by their fearless natures, notwithstanding the gender to which they were born.

Joan of Arc was not a feminist. Yet, because of her cross dressing and of her insistence on her divine voices, made her be burnt at the stake as a heretic, Joan's life has created a literature of its own. Mary Gordon writes, "Savior of France and the national heroine of that country, Joan lives in the imagination of the world as a symbol of that integrity of purpose that makes one die for what one believes. Jeanne la Pucelle, the Maid is the shining example of what a brave spirit can accomplish in the world of men and events." Joan first heard the unearthly voices, which she knew to be the messages of God, when she was a mere fourteen-year-old girl. Just as Meerabai had the beautiful cosmic vision of seeing Krishna in the tree, in the stone, in all beings, in fact in everything, so also, Joan heard her voices. The voices are dear to her. She speaks of her joy in their presence. There is a sense of sadness when the voices leave her. Both Meera and Joan had cosmic and mythic experiences. Joan's language may not have been as florid as her female mystics, but she uses the synthetic image of light—a combination of sound and vision—this is commonplace in descriptions of the mystical experience. Mary Gordon says that, "The experience of her voices happen to her in the deepest level of a creation of flesh, blood, mind and spirit, the whole of herself is absorbed in the vision that emanates from what she knows to be the source of love and truth and salvation." John J. Crawley in the "Lives of Saints" says that Joan's voices revealed to her the purpose of their visits. An ignorant peasant girl was given the high mission of saving her country. She was asked to take Charles' to Rheims to be crowned and then drive out the English. Meera was fortunate in that way not to be molested in the streets of the cities and towns that she roamed about singing in praise of her lord. But Joan of Arc was not so fortunate. Joan after her trial agreed to wear feminine clothing when she was abjured. A tribunal member was later told that a great English lord had entered her prison and tried to take her by force. As given in the testimony of Jean Massieu, Joan resumed male attire either as a defense against molestation or because her dress had been stolen and she was left with nothing to wear. In terms of doctrine she had been safe in disguise herself as a page during her journey through enemy territory and she was safe to wear armour during the battle. The Chronique de la Pucelle states that it deterred molestation while she was camped in the field. The clergy who testified at the posthumous rehabilitation trial affirmed that Joan wore male clothing in prison to deter molestation and rape. Preservation of chastity was another justifiable reason for cross-dressing. Her clothing would have shown an assailant and men would think of her less likely as a sex object. So whether a woman is a stroller, during the ancient times or in the present era, or whether the public spaces that a woman occupy, bars, cafes, clubs, and even public laboratories, whether one is Virginia Woolf's gentle Pargiter, or whether one is Meerabai or Joan of Arc, woman's access to the city (or town, village, hamlet) is heavily circumscribed. Women have to devise reasons for being a stroller and find means of protecting herself from her predators, even though the only space she is eligible to occupy may be the four walls of a prison cell.

Joan referred to the Pottiers inquiry when questioned on the matter of her dress. The Pottiers record no longer survives but circumstances indicate the Pottiers clerics had approved of her practice. She had a mission to do a man's work and it was most befitting that she dress the part. Joan kept her hair cut short throughout her military campaign and while she was in prison. The theologian, Jean Gerson, her supporter during the Rehabilitation trial also did the same.

Although condemned to death by the Inquisition of the Catholic Church for her cross-dressing, almost five hundred years later, Joan was canonized by the Church as a saint. Joan was condemned for witchcraft and cross-dressing by the Inquisitorial tribunal. The former charges were later dropped because they were difficult to prove and the judges instead focused on the assertions that her visions, which she believed were of a higher authority than the Church, had actually instructed her to adopt men's clothing. Joan was burned alive at the stake in Rouen when she was only nineteen. The authorities, twenty years after her death, believed that Joan had actually been a holy person. They started investigating the legality of her trial. An inquisitor Jean Brehal subsequently announced that Joan had been unjustly convicted and that she was a martyr. Joan was beautified in 1909 and canonized as a saint in 1920.

Throughout history, a narrow and constricted space has been grudgingly allotted, if at all it is allotted to women. The tiny space that the women have occupied has always been envied and fraught with suspicion. The historical figures of Meerabai and Joan of Arc show that their self-determination connects their voices to their lives as well as their emancipatory potentialities.

It is not significant to note that the help that Joan received during her short, eventful life came from women. King Charles VII's mother-in-law, Yolande of Aragon, confirmed Joan's virginity and financed her departure to Orleans. Anne of Burgundy, the Duchess of Bedford, and wife to the regent of England; declared Joan a virgin during pretrial inquires. For technical reasons, this prevented the court from charging her with witchcraft. This ultimately provided part of the basis for her vindication and sainthood. From Christine de Pizan to the present, women have looked to her as a positive example of a brave and active female. Both Joan and Meerabai were exceptional. They succeeded in creating their self-portraits self-narratives.

## WORKS CITED

Ingham, Patricia. *The Language of Çender and Class*. Routledge, London, 1996.

Meyers, Diana Tietjens. *Gender in the Mirror*, Oxford University Press, 2002.

Rooney, Ellen (Ed.). *Feminist Literary Theory*, Cambridge University Press, Cambridge, 2006.

# 19

# The Act of Defiance in Shashi Deshpande's *The Dark Holds No Terrors* and *Roots and Shadows*

*Deepali Sharma*

The winner of the Sahitya Akademi Award for the best Indian novel of 1982-83 and the Nanjangud Thirumalamba Award in 1991, Shashi Deshpande is one of India's foremost novelists writing in English. She is a major novelist both in terms of the number of novels and their literary quality and has gained reputation as a serious writer with tremendous potential. She initiated writing in earnest only from 1970. She has in the thirty plus years of her writing career, authored more than twenty books, ten novels, several collections of short stories, writing for children and has through them addressed several social issues of contemporary India. Short stories were her debut writings which were printed in several magazines. She attempts to portray woman as an individual who breaks loose from the traditional constraints and refines her identity in tune with the changed social atmosphere of the modern times. Nirmala Prakash observes: "Shashi Deshpande's novels despite all the suffering, tension and agony that her protagonists undergo, end on an optimistic note."[1]

Through the centuries, Indian woman has tried to create her own space within a patriarchal society which regards her as primarily as adjunct to a man. Women have ruled vast households. Women have found voices in music, art and literature and yet, by and large, they have unquestioningly accepted their subaltern position in society. The Indian woman of the twentieth century is placed in a rather different and more complex situation. The Indian social environment has felt the impact of modernization, education and the mass media. Economic compulsions have led to a significant widening of the horizons of a woman's life without a corresponding re-definition of social values, placing her proverbially speaking, in the horns of a dilemma. According to Anuradha Roy: "Educated, enlightened, demanding more from herself and life than her predecessors, conscious of an identity apart from that which links her to a male, she is yet faced by numerous age old assumptions about the temperament she is expected to possess, the attitudes to be displayed, and the role to be played."[2] Woman's experiences, her dilemmas are an epitome of an uneasy transitional phase through which Indian society is re-defining itself in keeping with the changing times. Her outlook broadened through education and a greater exposure to the outside world, she has to confront many demons, both external and internal which still demand from her an unswerving allegiance to an ideal of womanhood forged through centuries of patriarchal impositions. But she has perforce to examine and re-evaluate what her predecessors had accepted as unchangeable and incontrovertibly right. In an article on the need to decode gender consciousness in texts, Sukrita Paul Kumar makes an interesting and pertinent point. She refers to Elaine Showalter's well-known differentiation of feminist consciousness into three separate phases—"the feminine phase of internalization, the feminist phase of revolt and the female phase of self-discovery."[3] She points out that in the Indian context: "there is no such historical linearity; what is witnessed here is the simultaneous existence of all three. A long cultural history diverse live mythology combined with a fairly long exposure to western education lends a strange complexity to the modes of existence here" (*AR* 71).

Shashi Deshpande's aim has also been to depict and analyze the Indian woman, her conflicts against the background of coeval Indian. She has made use of her life experiences, and her works continue to make significant contribution to Indian writing in English. The issues and themes in her novels arise from the situation of woman at the cross roads of a transitional society, changing from traditional to modern. This paper explores the complexity of contemporary existence where woman is precariously poised between two worlds, one which she cannot totally reject and the other which she cannot easily accept. This is a vital phase in the evolution of a feminist consciousness in the protagonist. An increasing awareness that patriarchal forces are defacing her identity is now combined with a growing refusal to surrender to such forces. Revealing a remarkable insight into the nature of a woman's mind, she depicts woman in myriad roles—wife, mother, daughter and an individual in her own right. She always concerns herself with a woman's search for her identity. The woman in the novels of Shashi Deshpande, in order to achieve her freedom seeks marriage as an alternative to the bondage created by the parental family. The simple need to be independent eventually becomes a demand of the inflated ego and takes shape as the love for power over others. She resents the role of a daughter and looks forward to the role of a wife with the hope that her new role will help her in winning her freedom. As Prasanna Sree Sathupati observes: "The parental home symbol of tradition and old world values has no room for Shashi Deshpande's women, for they breathe the air of rituals that obstruct the growth of a woman as a being."[4]

Indu and Saru seek freedom through marriage, a room of their own and autonomy. Saru's situation is explicitly described in the novel: "I had come away from my parents in a fever of excitement after the last battle. The die was cast, the decisions taken, my boats burnt. There could be no turning back. Then, this ridiculous anticlimax."[5] Saru in *The Dark Holds No Terror*, hails from a tradition bound family which leaves scars on her psyche. Sharing the similar backdrop as that of Indu, Saru has no love lost for her family, especially her mother. Treated as a second rate citizen in her own home, owing to gender discrimination, she develops a deep and severe hatred towards her mother. The sibling rivalry between herself and her brother Dhruv verges almost on the unnatural. "He is different. He's a boy," these words establish the tradition bound Indian mother against whom Saru has to rebel all through her life. Her impotent anger makes her rage against her mother: "If you are a woman, I don't want to be one" (*DHNT*). Saru goes against her family and joins medical profession. It is once again against the wishes of her mother that she marries Manohar, a man of her choice. The departure of the protagonist from the mother is the first step towards autonomy.

Defiance seems to be the second nature to Saru. She defies her mother to become a doctor, defies her caste to marry outside, and defies social conventions by using Boozie to advance her career. To her chagrin, Saru realizes that her marriage to Manu, instead of promised freedom, led her once again into unwanted bondage. Saru's success as a doctor leads to the discord in her marriage and disintegration in her relationship with Manu. Saru's success breeds insecurity in Manu and Saru recognizes the fact: "Now I know that it was there it began…this terrible thing that has destroyed our marriage" (*DHNT* 37). Intolerable as he is of Saru's importance in the role of a doctor, yet he cannot ask her to give it up. The material comforts he hesitates to do without. Instead he tries to soothe his male ego by physically asserting himself over her. His transformation from a doting husband into a sadist invokes terror in the heart of Saru and she comes to detest the very word love: "Love…how I scorned the word" (*DHNT* 65).

Despite her hatred of Manu's physical sadism Saru refuses to take any action and loathes to admit failure. Saru refrains herself from announcing it to the world that her marriage has been a failure. She admits: "I have been clinging to the tenuous shadow of a marriage whose substance has long since disintegrated, because I have been afraid of proving my mother right" (*DHNT* 179). It is in order to get away from the mother who accused her of having murdered her brother that Saru marries defiantly. But even this supposition turns out to be nothing but a mirage. Undecided about her stance as a woman, Saru returns to her family house. Even the parental home does not provided the required refuge. Instead of feeling overjoyed of being home, she feels enclosed. She even fails to relate to her father: "As she drinks her tea…too sweet and strong…. He (father) sat gingerly on the edge of his chair like an unwilling host entertaining an unwelcome guest. And that I suppose is what I really am. What gave me the idea that I could come back?" (*DHNT* 14). Saru's feeling of homelessness is an affirmation of her sense of seclusion. Saru leaves home twice in the novel to seek release, once to establish her independence from mother's suppression and the second time to establish her indispensability to her husband and children. The home-hunt is in essence a peace-hunt. Home is what one makes of any house. Saru could once make a happy home of just a room with Manu. It was a time when the external world did not matter at all to them and it is not healthy to live in seclusion. How they can relate to the external world and yet be an organic unit is what home is all about. One has to be at peace with oneself, to be at peace with others. Despite her driving need for a stretching hand, a comforting touch, Saru refuses to be let down by the feeling of aloneness. She takes stock of herself: "All right, so I'm alone. But so's every one else. Human beings... they're going to fail you. But because there's just us, because there's no one else, we have to go on trying. If we can't believe in ourselves, we're sunk" (*DHNT* 200). The perfect partnership between Madhav and the father is a demonstration of the meaningful interdependence. It is a perfect pattern where they make no demand to each other.

Suddenly it comes to her that neither Manu nor her father can be her refuge. She has to seek her own refuge and find her true self. This journey into herself, this self-exploration (search for identity) reveals her that she has to be at peace with herself before achieving anything. She decides not to pretend and struggle anymore as it only brings solace and loneliness. Integrity is the key to wholeness and this she realizes: "The guilty sister, the undutiful wife...all persons spiked with guilt. Yes, she was all of them, she would not deny that now. She had to accept these selves to become whole again. But if she was all of them, they were not all of her. She was all that and so much more" (*DHNT* 207). Learning truth by oneself is the first step towards autonomy and Saru is able to achieve this. Her earlier doubts as to retaining her professional integrity as a doctor evaporate in thin air as she tends, confidently, to Sunita's illness. She tells her father: "And oh yes, Baba, if Manu comes, tell him to wait. I'll be back as soon as I can" (*DHNT* 202). With this self-realization occurs the tacit understanding that any meaningful relationship is interdependent. Integration alone would make her whole again and confrontation of the disintegrating elements alone would make that possible. Escapism is no permanent solution nor should one look to anything outside of oneself to provide the solution but seek it within.

The title of the novel effectively presents the need for confrontation in terms of light and darkness. Saru's caution to Dhruv—"the dark holds no terrors. That the terrors are inside us all the time. We carry them within us, and like traitors, they spring out when we least expect them, to scratch and maul" (*DHNT* 76-77) is what she needs to apply to herself. In a world slowly opening out doors of opportunity to women, the urge to extend themselves beyond the confines of domesticity is very real for many educated women. Saru in *The Dark Holds No Terrors*, and Indu in *Roots and Shadows*, are on the surface, successful emancipated women with fulfilling careers; Shashi Deshpande shows that in reality, they have not yet emotionally extricated themselves from patriarchal impositions, both direct and indirect.

Shashi Deshpande's heroines reject rituals that are vestiges of the past. Indu in *Roots and Shadows*, wanted to explore the inner struggle of her. She represents a set of the modern women who are educated and are very much in contact with the society, dealing with the critical problems like love, sex marriage, settlement and individuality. Indu reviews everything with reason. She analyzes the ideals of detachment and freedom and tries to achieve them. She tries to listen to the voice of her conscience and revolts. Indu is projected against the women belonging to the older generation. To an old generation, a woman's life is nothing but to get married, to bear children, to have sons and then grandchildren and the ideal woman is the one who does not have her own independent identity. Indu wanted to protest against these conventional laws which are moulding the female character as only symbols of lust. In *Roots and Shadows*, Indu too searches for release from the constraints of the tradition-bound institution of marriage in search of an autonomous self. The realization of the need to conform for survival and the awareness that conformity is the great destroyer of selfhood, and the only self that can be achieved is the self born in interpersonal relationship make Indu cry: "This is my real sorrow that I can never be complete in myself, there was somewhere outside me a part of me without which I remained complete, then I met Jayant, and lost the ability to be alone."[6]

Highly sensitive, intelligent and educated Indu could be said to be a representative of modern young woman. Indu, a middle class young girl, brought up in an orthodox Brahmin family, headed by Akka, the mother surrogate in the novel, left home full of hatred for the family, for Akka specially and she had sworn never to go back. Indu, who had lost her mother at birth, identifies throughout the novel, Akka as the mother figure. She revolts against Akka, her world, her values and marries Jayant against the wishes of Akka. In marrying Jayant, Indu had thought that she had found her alter ego—had found in him a spiritual and psychological level of closeness. But marriage with Jayant had forced her to realize that self is an elusive centre that one could never exchange roots with another that this was an illusion and she felt cheated. Losing her own identity and living in the wake of her husband troubles her enormously. She does not find herself modern young woman any different from her mother. There is no doubt that she loves Jayant and wants him by her side at all times. But the selfsame love seems to be shackling her to his side and is preventing her from taking stock of her as a separate entity: "What I feel for Jayant.... Can I compress all of it within this world. It is much more, so overwhelming a response of the whole of me to him. Sometimes I wonder if I will love him one day and live by myself. The only way in which I can be myself, my whole self again" (*RS* 97).

Unable to come to terms with either her love for Jayant or her true self, Indu finds herself stifled and suppressed. Her marriage, she finds, is robbing her of her identity as a person apart and separating from her husband. Feeling entrapped yet she hesitates to come out of her entanglements. Her realization that she too is being moulded into the very image of woman she tried to break away from, worries her. In the first place, she has broken from her family because she wanted to prove herself to be as different and as unlike as possible from women like Akka. It is her sole reason for her rebelling against the family norms and marrying Jayant. But marriage to Jayant does not prove to be the heaven she hopes for and dreams of. Her return to her parental home comes as a revelation to Indu. The feeling of homelessness is indicative of inner disintegration. Tension between the different parts with in one's self takes away the harmony within and without. The novel gains its feminist stance in Indu's exploration into herself but it also moves beyond the boundaries of feminism into a perception of the very predicament of the human existence. Shashi Deshpande suggests that Indu has learnt to see not only her life full of possibilities for growth and grace, but the very meeting of life itself. At the end of the novel Indu realizes that Akka is not as sadist as thought earlier, Indu has confronted her real self and she knows her roots.

The women in *Roots and Shadows*, and *The Dark Holds No Terrors*, do not present themselves as the women who want to go in self-quest, and are free from the restrictions imposed by society, culture, nature and are also free from their own fear and guilt. Commenting on *Roots and Shadows*, O.P. Bhatnagar remarks: "The novel deals with a woman's attempt to assert her individuality and realize her freedom. It depicts how it brings her into confrontation with family, with male-dominated society."[7] Indu's struggle for selfhood, her struggle towards liberation of the mind, her struggle for an emotional and intellectual definition of herself as a self-actualizing person, is in a sense to fight against her womanhood. Indu refuses to be the mother of a child that is not wholly welcome in a marriage that has become non-real because love is non-real in a marriage and that, therefore, makes her feel trapped in a negative situation since it threatens her positive struggle for independence, for selfhood, and her effort at intellectual liberation.

Indu's dilemma expresses Shashi Deshpande's feminist policies against gender roles imposed upon women in a patriarchal culture. Ever ready to please Jayant, Indu acquiesces to his desires. Indu gradually realizes that she does not exist for her but for Jayant, the archetypal male, imperialistic and subjugating. She feels in her a sense of existential insecurity, but she ultimately realizes that she has been chasing shadows, leaving her roots far behind in the family and in Jayant too. Naren, with whom she develops an adulterous relationship, is nothing more than a mere shadow to her. He has no permanent place in her memory. She realizes that marriage had stunted and hampered her individuality because she had regarded it as a trap and not as a bond. She realizes that each time, she had cut off some part of her real self to please Jayant, but this had turned their marriage into a farce. Thus, Indu's uncompromising and paradoxical feminine self that frantically longed for self-expression, finally finds its roots in the home and with her husband. Shadows disappear from her vision and she sees the clear light of day with the realization and discovery of her identity. The meek, docile and humble Indu of the early days finally emerges as a bold, challenging, conscious and rebellious woman. She resigns her job, thus defying the male authority, hierarchy and the irony of a woman's masked existence. Her self-discovery is the frightening visions of the feminine self's struggle for harmony and sanity. She comes out of her emotional upheaval, and decides to lead a meaningful life with her husband. The home she had discarded becomes the place of refuge, of solace and consolation. It is Akka's house which offers her ample opportunities to know herself. It is here that she is able to discover her roots as an independent woman, as a daughter, as a mother and as a commercial writer. The end of the novel sees a new Indu-determined, free and always in search to make her marriage work, but on new terms. She decides to spend the money; Akka has left her the way she wants and not according to other people's wishes. She finds personal freedom and completeness. Indu now takes matters into her own hands; she faces the fact of her own fault in her problems with Jayant. She will now try to save her marriage, but without compromising her principles or her individuality. Through the character of Indu, Shashi Deshpande has represented the new woman who is aware of her situation, her quest, her identity, her place and her role in the family and in society.

Shashi Deshpande's protagonists often end up discovering good traits in people whom they had earlier dismissed as selfish or cruel. Similarly, they also discover the seamy side of those whom they had all along taken as angels of love or fair play. Shashi Deshpande does not believe in portraying her characters in black and white. After their circuitous journey through life and marriage, her protagonists, who have started their journey from their parental homes in search of the freedom of the self, come to realize. They struggle to transcend the restrictive roles. They rebel, reject and seek freedom from the traditional norms and way of life. If the bonds that bind human life help individuals in continuing their lives despite the betrayals and cruelties associated with human survival, everybody has a life of one's own to live.

The struggle of women in Shashi Deshpande's novels is to give shape and content to their individual existence in society, culminates in a crisis and ends in compromise. New bonds replace the old; that's all. In the end comes the realization that freedom lies in having the courage to do what one believes is the right thing to do and the determination and the tenacity to it. That alone can bring harmony in life. Thus, perhaps the writer has tried to convey to the society that the need of the time, in this transitional phase, is not a total revolt but a gradual change in the society for which everyone has to put some effort to bridge the gap between the old and the new generation.

## NOTES

1. Nirmala Prakash, "From Margin to the Centre: Shashi Deshpande and Arundhati Roy", ed. T.M.J. Indra Mohan, *Shashi Deshpande: A Critical Spectrum* (New Delhi: Atlantic Publishers & Distributors, 2004), 204.
2. Anuradha Roy, Patterns of Feminist Consciousness In Indian Women Writers: A Study of Anita Desai's *Cry, The Peacock*, Nayantara Sahgal's *Storm in Chandigarh*, Attia Hosain's *Sunlight On a Broken Column*, Rama Mehta's *Inside the Haveli* and Shashi Deshpande's *That Long Silence* (New Delhi: Prestige Books, 1999), 70, hereafter cited in the chapter.

3. Sukrita Paul Kumar, "Decoding Gender in Literary Texts", *Indian Literature*, 1993, 157.
4. Prasanna Sree Sathupati, "Conflict and Identity in Shashi Deshpande's Novels", *Indian Women Novelists*: Set III: Vol. 4, ed. R.K. Dhawan (New Delhi: Prestige Books, 1995), 17.
5. Shashi Deshpande, *The Dark Holds No Terrors* (New Delhi: Penguin Books, 1990), 37, hereafter cited in the chapter.
6. Shashi Deshpande, *Roots and Shadows* (Hyderabad: Disha Books, 1992), 34, hereafter cited in the chapter.
7. O.P. Bhatnagar, "Indian Womanhood: Fight for Freedom in Shashi Deshpande's *Roots and Shadows*", 45.

# Index